Leadership Matters

American Association for State and Local History

Series Editor: Russell Lewis, Chicago History Museum

ABOUT THE SERIES

The American Association for State and Local History Book Series publishes technical and professional information for those who practice and support history, and addresses issues critical to the field of state and local history. To submit a proposal or manuscript to the series, please request proposal guidelines from AASLH headquarters: AASLH Editorial Board, 1717 Church St., Nashville, Tennessee 37203. Telephone: (615) 320-3203. Website: www.aaslh.org.

ABOUT THE ORGANIZATION

The American Association for State and Local History (AASLH), a national history organization headquartered in Nashville, TN, provides leadership, service, and support for its members, who preserve and interpret state and local history in order to make the past more meaningful in American society. AASLH is a membership association representing history organizations and the professionals who work in them. AASLH members are leaders in preserving, researching, and interpreting traces of the American past to connect the people, thoughts, and events of yesterday with the creative memories and abiding concerns of people, communities, and our nation today. In addition to sponsorship of this book series, the Association publishes History News, a newsletter, technical leaflets and reports, and other materials; confers prizes and awards in recognition of outstanding achievement in the field; and supports a broad education program and other activities designed to help members work more effectively. To join the organization, go to www.aaslh.org or contact Membership Services, AASLH, 1717 Church St., Nashville, TN 37203.

Leadership Matters

Anne W. Ackerson and Joan H. Baldwin

A division of
ROWMAN & LITTLEFIELD
Lanham • Boulder • New York • Toronto • Plymouth, UK

Published by AltaMira Press
A division of Rowman & Littlefield
4501 Forbes Boulevard, Suite 200, Lanham, Maryland 20706
www.rowman.com

10 Thornbury Road, Plymouth PL6 7PP, United Kingdom

British Library Cataloguing in Publication Information Available

Library of Congress Cataloging-in-Publication Data
Ackerson, Anne W., 1953-
Leadership matters / Anne W. Ackerson and Joan H. Baldwin.
p. cm.
Includes bibliographical references and index.
ISBN 978-0-7591-2183-6 (cloth : alk. paper) -- ISBN 978-0-7591-2184-3 (pbk. : alk. paper) -- ISBN
978-0-7591-2185-0 (electronic)
1. Historical museums--United States--Administration--Handbooks, manuals, etc. 2. Museum direc-
tors--Training of--United States--Handbooks, manuals, etc. 3. Leadership--United States--Hand-
books, manuals, etc. I. Baldwin, Joan H., 1953- II. Title.
E172.A23 2013
303.3'4--dc23

2013041541

Printed in the United States of America

For Geoffrey, who always believes in me.

To my friends and colleagues of the Gang of Five for their encouragement and camaraderie.

And to Museum Leaders everywhere: Put leadership first and guide your institutions safely into the future.

Contents

Acknowledgments

We heartily thank our interviewees for their candid, thoughtful, enthusiastic, often poignant and sometimes funny reflections on their personal career journeys, museum leadership today, and what the heck it all means.

Hope Alswang, Executive Director/CEO, Norton Museum of Art (Florida); Dina Bailey, Director of Exhibitions and Visitor Experiences, National Underground Railroad Freedom Center (Ohio); Trevor Beemon, Manager of Digital Communications, Atlanta History Center (Georgia); Jamie Bosket, Vice President, Interpretation and Events Division, George Washington's Mount Vernon (Virginia); Edward R. Bosley, James N. Gamble Director, The Gamble House (California); Robert Burns, Director, Mattatuck Museum (Connecticut); Colin G. Campbell, President, Colonial Williamsburg Foundation (Virginia); Janet Carding, Director and CEO, Royal Ontario Museum, Toronto, Canada; Gonzalo Casals, Deputy Executive Director, El Museo del Barrio (New York); Anne Cathcart, Curatorial Assistant, Chesterwood (Massachusetts); Catherine Charlebois, Curator of Exhibitions, Collections and Oral History Programs, Centre d'histoire de Montreal, Canada; Melissa Chiu, Museum Director and Senior Vice President, Global Arts and Cultural Programs, Asia Society Museum (New York); Christy S. Coleman, President and CEO, American Civil War Center at Historic Tredegar (Virginia); Kippen de Alba Chu, Executive Director, Iolani Palace (Hawaii); James Enote, Executive Director, A:shiwi A:wan Museum and Heritage Center (New Mexico); Ilene J. Frank, Executive Director, Rensselaer County Historical Society (New York); Pamela E. Green, Executive Director, Weeksville Heritage Center (New York); Beth Grindell, Director, Arizona State Museum, The University of Arizona (Arizona); Timothy Grove, Education Chief, Smithsonian National Air and Space Museum (Washington, D.C.); Lynne M. Ireland, Deputy Director, Nebraska State Historical Society (Nebraska); Jennifer S. Kilmer, Director, Washington State Historical Society (Washington); Robert A. Kret, Director, Georgia O'Keeffe Museum (New Mexico); Burt Logan, Executive Director and CEO, Ohio Historical Society (Ohio); Andrew E. Masich, President and CEO, Senator John Heinz History Center (Pennsylvania); Tonya M. Matthews, PhD, Vice President of Museums, Cincinnati Museum Center (Ohio); Anne Grimes Rand, President, USS *Constitution* Museum (Maine); Nathan Richie, Director, Golden History Museum (Colorado); Van A. Romans, President, Fort Worth Museum of Science and History (Texas); Ellen M. Rosenthal, President and CEO, Conner Prairie Interactive History Park (Indianapolis); Nina Simon, Executive Director, Santa Cruz Museum of Art & History (California); Rebecca M. Slaughter, Director, Branigan Cultural Center (New Mexico); Ryan Joshua Spencer, Manager, Firestone Farm and Equine Operations, The Henry Ford (Michigan); Chris Taylor, Diversity Outreach Program Manager, Minnesota Historical Society (Minnesota); Sally Roesch Wagner, Executive Director, Matilda Joslyn Gage Foundation (New York); Kent Whitworth, Executive Director, Kentucky Historical Society (Kentucky); and David W. Young, Executive Director, Cliveden (Pennsylvania).

Julie I. Johnson's 2012 doctoral dissertation on museum leadership learning coupled with her subsequent conversation with us helped us greatly in framing the issues of training and development that we discuss in chapters 3 and 4.

Our colleagues, Robert J. Janes, Editor-in-Chief of the journal *Museum Management and Curatorship*; Nancy Villa Bryk, Professor in the Historic Preservation Program at Eastern Michigan University; Kristin Herron, a funder-friend and terrific writer; and Christine Miles, Director Emeritus of the Albany Institute of History and Art, read the manuscript in various stages, challenging us to strengthen and hone each chapter. Their input has been exceedingly valuable and humbling; in turn, we tried mightily to incorporate as many of their suggestions and admonitions as possible.

Marsha L. Semmel graciously agreed to write the Foreword in the midst of moving to an exciting new career with the Noyce Foundation's Leadership Institute. By her own admission she is a glutton for punishment, and we are happy to take advantage of her willingness to multitask.

Gretchen Sullivan Sorin, Director of the Cooperstown Graduate Program (SUNY Oneonta) and Martha Morris, Associate Professor and Assistant Director of the Museums Studies Program at George Washington University, provided us with important information about the field and the status of leadership education in museum studies graduate programs. Victoria Herow of the Edsel Ford Memorial Library at The Hotchkiss School worked tirelessly to locate books and articles on our topic and to whip the bibliography into shape.

We thank the Museum Association of New York, where we were able to explore and write collaboratively about next-generation leadership, succession planning, and the state of the New York State museum community. These projects helped to clarify our thinking about the need for greater emphasis on museum leadership at both the staff and board levels.

We are indebted to our friend and colleague, Bob Beatty, Vice President for Programs at the American Association for State and Local History, for his unbridled enthusiasm about this topic and for being a terrific cheerleader of our work. It was Bob's excitement that helped move us from talking to writing. The next pitcher of beer is on us, Bob.

To Charles Harmon and Marissa Parks, our current and former editors at AltaMira Press and Rowman & Littlefield Publishing Group, our thanks for giving us this opportunity to capture on the page what has been a long-running conversation between the two of us.

Anne W. Ackerson
Joan H. Baldwin
August 2013

Foreword

Marsha L. Semmel

Stories. History museums bring stories to life through collections, programs, and experiences. Stories connect us to our heritage and to our culture and identity. They help us make sense of our world and ourselves. We recognize the importance and centrality of stories to our work, yet how often do we capture the stories of our museum leaders?

Although Michael Spock, formerly of the Boston Children's Museum and the Field Museum, has pioneered two significant museum storytelling projects, *Philadelphia Stories, A Collection of Pivotal Museum Memories* (2000) and *Boston Stories: The Children's Museum as a Model for Non-Profit Leadership (2013)*, *Leadership Matters: Conversations with History Museum Leaders* distinguishes itself through its fieldwide focus in the context of broader leadership literature and practice.

In this volume, authors Anne W. Ackerson and Joan H. Baldwin hope to "spark a leadership revolution among our history museum colleagues." Hypothesizing that "if history and cultural heritage museums were to invest as much in leadership training and development for boards and staff as they do in collections management and care, programming, and management techniques, they might weather the boom-bust-glut-scarcity scenario more resiliently and creatively," Ackerson and Baldwin take us on a highly readable and personalized journey to make their case.

Framed by "ten simple myths" and "ten simple truths" about leadership in history museums—and concluding with a proposed leadership agenda—the core of this absorbing book comprises compelling interviews with thirty-six diverse museum leaders.

These leaders have taken multiple paths to their current positions; they play leadership roles in a variety of small and large, urban and rural, and multidisciplinary institutions. They range in age from their midtwenties

xviForeword

through their midseventies. Not all are CEOs. Indeed, Ackerson and Baldwin stress the importance of recognizing and rewarding leadership at many levels of the organization.

From each leader, we learn about education, professional (and personal) trajectory, mentors, challenges, lessons learned, and values. The interviewees further comment on their leadership approach and provide advice to "next generation" leaders.

Ackerson and Baldwin nest these conversations in a synthesis of current leadership literature that emphasizes "intentional" leadership and identifies eight fundamentals and qualities necessary for leadership in today's dynamic, diverse, and global knowledge society. The four interpersonal "fundamentals" include convergence, multidimensionality, agility, and something the authors dub "in tune and in touch" (making place and space for people). The four personal traits are self-awareness, authenticity, courage, and vision. They form the organizing structure for the thirty-six interviews.

As someone who has served in a variety of leadership roles—and is currently devoting the lion's share of my time to supporting global museum leaders in their personal and professional growth—these qualities ring true.

Thankfully, rather than offer a "how-to" manual for CEOs or a catalogue of best practice and institutional case studies (although, as we read the book, we learn much about a variety of museums, historic sites, and cultural organizations), *Leadership Matters* focuses on the personal (and interpersonal), nuanced, and environmentally sensitive dimensions of leadership. There *is* no single, all-purpose "cookbook" for success.

Most of these thirty-six leaders (like myself) took serendipitous paths to their positions. Reading about their journeys, I was reminded of a memorable conversation I had with one of our board members when I served as president and CEO of Conner Prairie. This trustee, a high-ranking executive in a locally headquartered, multinational corporation, counseled that "there is no path" to leadership. Indeed, he rarely hired aspiring young executives who had charted their future long-term career course with unwavering certainty.

Instead of providing a one-size-fits-all prescription, Ackerson and Baldwin unpack the eight leadership fundamentals and qualities to probe their many dimensions, which include self-direction, passion and compassion, integrity, commitment, vision, humor, flexibility, creativity, honesty, trust, listening, and collaboration. As universal and essential as these qualities have always been to effective leaders, the authors argue persuasively that they are absolutely critical to meet the challenges of today and tomorrow.

They are right. The world is changing faster than ever. The context and circumstances of how and where people learn, how learners define authenticity and trust, and the nature of "institutionalized" learning (whether it is in a school or a museum) is in the midst of a sea change. Research on the brain and the neuroscientific and behavioral research on learning, massive demographic shifts, the worldwide predominance of mobile devices, and the power of social media are some factors fueling this change. How will our museums redefine their roles to respond to the needs and demands of today's learners? What will be our contributions to community well-being and solving pressing community problems and challenges? Leadership will play a key role in determining how and in what ways our museums remain vital to the lives of individuals and their communities.

Therefore, the issue of demonstrating our "public value" hovers over this entire volume as a core to leadership. As Ackerson and Baldwin caution: "Failing to be clear about value creates a climate where history and cultural heritage museums cease to have a place at the table in any discussion about national history education, social studies, civic education . . . we are a field benched during community planning; nor are we seen as ready collaborators for tourism or economic development."

In today's era of bounded resources, tremendous competition for government and private funds, and increasing demands for accountability and impact—as well as massive challenges in learning and civic literacy, huge gaps in the public trust, and widespread yearning for meaningful community gathering places—how will our museums make their case and make a difference?

Through its analysis of relevant leadership literature, parsing valid versus questionable assumptions about museum practice, and capturing the authentic voices of so many museum leaders, *Leadership Matters* serves as a welcomed resource. Spurred by their conviction that leadership development has been a neglected and undervalued aspect of museum practice, Ackerson and Baldwin gather, synthesize, personalize, and contextualize history museum leadership today. They make the case for the urgency of shifting priorities now. And, in the process, we readers have the opportunity to meet many interesting people who have generously shared their leadership stories, exposing their vulnerabilities as well as strengths, and acknowledging that they, too, are still on a path of learning and discovery.

Marsha L. Semmel
Senior Advisor, Noyce Leadership Institute and Independent Consultant
on Leadership, Partnerships, and Policy for Cultural Institutions

Introduction

At the core of every museum is leadership. No matter an institution's age, size, location, or discipline, its focus, tenor, and tone come from its leadership. Leadership frames intangible values and underpins its tangible assets. Leadership comes in many guises—proactive, reactive, or benign, it can drive an institution forward or bind it to the past; it can be a lightning rod for change or preserve stasis. It can move mountains or set a museum back a decade. Good, bad, or indifferent, leadership drives everything, yet in theory and practice it receives little direct attention or support for its development. Largely an untapped resource, it is a potent antidote to the malaise afflicting the museum field as a whole and history museums in particular.

Leadership is about individuals *and* institutions. As you read this book, remember each of us has the power to make choices about personal leadership that affect our boards and staffs. We've written this snapshot of museum leadership, focusing in particular on history and cultural heritage organizations, to help you understand the power of individual leadership and its relationship to organizational strength. While you have a choice about the type of leader you want to be and the type of leadership your institution needs, it is the intentional practice of leadership that will change the field.

Today's history and cultural heritage museum leaders are part visionary and part foot soldier. But what makes them tick? Are there attitudes, philosophies, and skills that set some people apart from the thousands charged with moving institutions forward? What lessons can we draw from their stories? Now more than ever, success as a museum leader doesn't necessarily come with longevity, scholarship, or curatorial achievement. In fact, today's successful leaders often bring myriad skills to the table, creating a style that works both personally and professionally. The most successful combine leadership's amalgam of tasks and hoop jumping with imagination, courage, and innovation.

As two former history museum directors, we understand the demands a cultural institution point person faces. We know firsthand the satisfaction and frustration of the leadership journey. As longtime friends, our mutual curiosity about how museum leaders approach their work—how they succeed, flop, soar, crash, maintain, deliver, and sometimes all of the above—is a constant topic of conversation. We dissect the reasons people we admire leave the field. And we agree that certain individuals are magnetic enough to make us want to pack our bags, close our bank accounts, and show up at their door to say, "hire me." Like many of you, we're drawn to the imaginative, courageous, and innovative leaders, perhaps hoping to see a glimmer of ourselves in them.

With that as our backdrop, we set out to profile a range of people considered by their colleagues to be effective museum leaders. We were interested in their career journeys in the hope that along the way we might discover what leadership looks like after the first decade of the twenty-first century. We believe their stories offer a unique window into how successful museum leadership manifests itself at a variety of levels, fostering healthy museums in a distracted, diffuse twenty-first-century world. All in all, we tapped into a mother lode of insights, interviewing thirty-six engaging, innovative, and entrepreneurial history and cultural heritage museum leaders in the United States and Canada, leaders from every institutional level and department, from veterans to emergent professionals.

As we contemplate the leadership landscape at a particularly precarious moment for the history and cultural heritage museum field, we are increasingly convinced that organizational challenges experienced by so many institutions are rarely attributable to financial issues alone. In other words, *it's not always about the money*. Once the excuses and spreadsheets are pulled away it is clear that a board's and a director's ability to govern and lead intelligently, and motivate an institution, are as important—if not more so—as the quantity of its programming or the quality of its collections or the size of its bank account.

In too many cases good governance and great leadership simply do not flourish. Is the absence of leadership more noticeable in the face of cuts in federal or state programs, graying audiences, and dwindling school visitation? How do changing audience and donor demographics coupled with too much or too little regulation affect leadership? Does leadership play a role in the field's failure to market itself better or speak with a unified voice? No one can dispute the devastating effects of the 2008 crash that gutted more than a few endowments, but how did some organizations ride out the storm?

When the public wants history, when it wants it at all, it thirsts for entertaining, high-drama history or perhaps a cleaned-up theme-park version of it.

Foundation, government, and corporate grants once fueled groundbreaking programs and encouraged best practices; now with funding shrinking while the number of institutions chasing it grows, there's been far less risk taking by funders to push history museums forward. Visitors want to see collections in comfortable, accessible, and well-lit spaces, so if organizations build new galleries and multimedia rooms visitors will surely come—and return again and again. Pundits and bloggers point out that many historic houses and outdoor history museums are on the respirator, victims of their pursuit to encase the past in amber. Somewhere, in the tangle of excuse and explanation, smart, thoughtful leadership quickly takes a backseat to the day-to-day maintenance of a museum's intricacies, which are almost always overshadowed by huge numbers of needy objects from the tiniest thimble to hulking, aged buildings.

Tell us if this sounds familiar: You are a history museum director. Your Monday morning schedule includes: a strategic planning huddle with staff to recast the museum's programmatic mission, a meeting with a major donor who just might want to fund a reenvisioned program, and preparation for a board meeting later in the week that will focus on two major topics: repositioning the museum in the community and shoring up a battered spreadsheet.

You're ten minutes into catching up on the weekend's email, when the phone rings. It's the board president asking to review the board meeting agenda. By the time you have sorted out whether to include a walk through a refurbished exhibit gallery before or after the repositioning discussion, you discover you are late to a curatorial staff meeting about the exhibit scheduled for that refurbished gallery. Back at your desk, you find a message from the accountant, who has finished the audit. There are some issues in the management letter that need attention, not to mention the endowment's anemic performance during the last quarter.

Get the picture? Is this a leader's life, endless whiplashing between macro and micro, forcing quick decision making or no decision making at all? Peel away the tasks, however, and underneath is a stew of collaboration and interaction, requiring strategic thinking and long-term vision. Peppering this stew is the organization's energy coupled with a leader's own strengths and flaws. This is the real world of the twenty-first-century history museum leader as we see it. What we wanted to know was why some succeed where others tread water. What we learned is that leadership is a skill, albeit a highly individual one. We also learned, as this book proves, that leadership isn't a skill that waits solely for an executive position. It works anywhere in the building. But that doesn't mean everyone has the tools to be a leader.

We knew museum colleagues were doing imaginative and interesting things with cross-industry ideas, raw talent, no safety nets, and a bit of luck. In a field hamstrung by myopic administrators, it is time to hear about effective leaders and the passion and personal commitment behind their stories.

This book tries to capture the collective knowledge of a group of museum leaders in the United States and Canada at one moment in time— this moment. We were not really interested in where they work as much as how they got there, and more importantly, how they think.

In selecting our interviewees, we sought recommendations from colleagues at national, regional, and state museum associations, graduate programs, and in independent practice. We also used the museum community itself through listservs and social media. Each recommendation included a brief justification as to why the individual met the criteria of being an engaging, innovative, and entrepreneurial leader, and why the field needed to hear about them.

In the end we had a roster of one-hundred-plus individuals who presented a rich complement of stories and lessons. Being mindful that good leadership occurs throughout the workplace, we made an effort to balance the group in terms of age, gender, ethnicity, position, institutional size, and geography. Not everyone interviewed calls the corner office home. Some are team leaders or department leaders; a few are singular influencers in small shops. We expanded our parameters to include what we call cultural heritage museums, institutions that use artifacts, art, traditions, language, and knowledge of racial or ethnic groups or societies. These museums almost always incorporate history in some form into their exhibitions and programs. We also reached out to leaders who began or spent substantial time in history museums before migrating to other types of museums. And we spoke with some who came to museums from other fields.

What qualities led to selection? In leadership as in many other things, there is no one-size-fits-all. To begin with, we used Wharton professor Stewart Friedman's book *Total Leadership Model*. We liked Friedman's holistic approach to defining leadership success. He believes in leadership that is real; leaders who act authentically by clarifying what is important; leaders who are whole, who act with integrity, respecting the whole person; and leaders who are innovative, who act with creativity and courage, experimenting to find new solutions and answers. He writes,

> There's always some risk when you try new things. Effective leaders, though, at all levels in organizations and in different stages of life, muster the courage to persist by working to identify and minimize resistance, from inside and out, and by realizing how their initiatives serve purposes beyond what they can sniff with their own noses. They never stop searching for new ways to contribute their talent and energy to causes they believe in. They inspire others to focus energy on the collective good; by doing so, they inspire others to experiment.[1]

As these interviews show, today's history and cultural heritage museum leaders come from a variety of career paths. Sometimes bypassing the traditional graduate degree in museum studies or history for an MBA, today's leaders bring a complex collection of sophisticated skills to the table. It was these individuals we wanted to meet. During the course of our telephone interviews (most of which lasted sixty minutes or more), we asked every individual the same two questions: Did you enter the field knowing you wanted to lead? What prepared you for your current leadership position? Mindful of both individual and organizational privacy, our questions were about the act and attainment of leadership. We wanted to map individual journeys to see where the similarities lie. We asked about the preparation for leadership: Was it something rooted in childhood, in a parent who placed a premium on independence? Can leadership be learned, or is it stamped in DNA from conception?

Based on our interviews, a number of conclusions began to emerge, beginning with the fact that good leadership is an intricate construct. It is about relationships. It is nuanced. It is courageous, and even in small, underfunded places, it can be sophisticated.

As with many things in life, you can head in one direction only to end up in a completely unexpected place. Our goal was to explore museum leadership, but along the way our understanding and appreciation for the talents, passions, and philosophies today's leaders bring to work each and every day grew. From them we discovered leadership fundamentals and qualities that set the bar for effective leadership, not just in twenty-first-century history and cultural heritage museums, but in organizations across the nonprofit spectrum.

NOTE

1. Stewart Friedman, *Total Leadership: Be a Better Leader, Have a Richer Life* (Watertown: Harvard Business School Press, 2008), 186.

Chapter One

Ten Simple Myths *(and Why You Shouldn't Believe Them)*

When it comes to museum leadership, whether we talk about boards or staff, there are a handful of myths that are part of the lore and language of our industry. Frequently found in history and cultural heritage museums, they unintentionally define leadership in today's museums. So go ahead and admit that you might have bought into a few of these old chestnuts. Acknowledging myths like these and finding their meaning helps us understand our sometimes fallible and evolving profession.

While many museum professionals give these myths short shrift, too often board members and the public cling stubbornly and foolishly to them. Unchecked, they stall growth, complicating life for history organizations and a profession addressing real, urgent, and complex twenty-first-century challenges. It's time to wrestle them to the ground and move on.

Myths like these are part of the reason our field needs revision or reinvention, particularly as it confronts leadership for the twenty-first century. In a sense, these myths were the catalysts for this book. Their pervasiveness makes leadership's challenges more difficult. They shape perceptions, and they have stunted the growth of a profession. You may have a few of your own workplace myths to add, but here is our short list.

- *Anyone can run a museum.*

  The myth-logic goes something like this: Since most museums don't face the demands of the for-profit rat race, performance expectations are relaxed, and the pace is slow and gentle. As a result, history museum jobs are relatively stress free and are the envy of those toiling in the fields of commerce. Sometimes expressed (with envy) as, "You must have such a fun job. I'd love to do that!"

Most of us know by personal experience that this is categorically not true.

- *If you've led one museum, you can lead any museum.*

There are many broad similarities among museums: collections, oversight provided by a board of trustees or a committee of a parent entity, programming for constituencies, and often a physical plant to house it all. That's where the similarities end; all the rest is variable, wildly or weirdly idiosyncratic, and in many cases, vulnerable.

- *Academic expertise, administration, and management's hard skills trump the soft skills of communication, creative problem solving, and interpersonal relationship and trust building.*

Most boards of trustees seem to think so. Perhaps that's because corporate-think dominates the boardroom. Sure, a good leader must master a body of information; otherwise, she won't be treated with respect. But if leaders aren't able to humanize their knowledge and themselves—in other words, be able to relate to others in truly authentic and open ways—no amount of hard skills mastery will inspire enthusiasm and confidence. When you conjure up your most favorite board presidents, directors, co-workers and teachers, what kept you wanting to work hard for them? Was it only because they had a photographic memory for profit-and-loss statements? It's good to remember this: "The soft stuff is the hard stuff."[1]

- *Building collections takes precedent over building talent.*

Museums *are* about collections, and great collections are amassed and interpreted with skill and care, ideas and vision. Leaders play important roles developing, shaping, and presenting collections. Value is in the eye of the beholder, and a good collection without good leadership sends a variety of value-laden messages to its community, including "we're too good for you." In the final analysis, collections are just one piece of the museum puzzle. If they were the only piece, we could lock the place up and throw away the key.

- *We don't have to make money, because we're a nonprofit.*

Contributing to the public benefit is the primary motivator of nonprofits (and certainly one that is of great ongoing interest to incorporators and regulators), and it's impossible to do that with no cash in the bank. Nonprofits must be responsible to their bottom lines in order to feed society's soul and sustain their good work. However, there is great risk in losing sight of the mission when the attention of board and staff leadership is *all* about money.

- *We are the source of our own best ideas.*

Also translated to "no one knows us better than we know ourselves," and more specifically, "museum culture is its own place." So very many history and cultural heritage museums are far behind the leadership innovation curve due to invisibility or isolation in their communities. Their implacable deference to hierarchical decision making insulates them from ideas and solutions flowing between and among sectors. More times than we care to count, we have heard our colleagues balk at the notion that they could learn something from another museum discipline, much less another industry. The museum field as a whole tends to segregate itself by discipline. And frankly, this is probably true of many other professions—for example, do brain surgeons hang out with general practitioners? Probably not. But over the long haul, segregation discourages creativity, innovation, and (dare we say it?) the ability to make positive, healthy, and sustainable organizational change. For educational institutions, such as museums, that stake their professional worth on the creation and exchange of information and ideas, this is especially dangerous.

- *Compensation is secondary, because the work is its own reward.*

This goes for the entire nonprofit sector, and while the work *is* tremendously rewarding, the last time we checked we still pay the same amount for a gallon of gas as Donald Trump.

- *If you build it, they will come.*

This phrase, most notably from the 1989 film *Field of Dreams*, is an oftheard mantra among new, would-be, and struggling old museums looking for the Fountain of Youth. Now that we've mixed up all sorts of metaphors, the fact still remains that acquiring old buildings or building new buildings for the express purpose of generating public support, boosting sagging visitation, or plumping up a leader's resume is an expensive response to what is more likely a lack of clarity about mission, leadership, and audience engagement. The phrase needs to be replaced with "Could be a field of dreams . . . or could be just a cornfield."

- *We could get a grant for that!*

No, no you can't. Grants are almost always highly competitive, meaning an organization must make a solid case for support that ties activities to mission and audience. Grants almost always come with requirements that for some organizations make them practically impossible to administer. Grant funding is often not reliable, most especially for general operations, so take seriously the creation of an overall game plan for fund development. Our bottom line: grants are not the staff of life. Grants and their attendant consultants alone won't fill your organization's leadership needs. Organizational leaders will.

- *Money solves all problems.*

Of course, money really helps. If the roof leaks or a painting needs to be conserved, well, money will fix it. But if your institution's big idea or product is poorly conceived and delivered, if it's not meeting the real needs of real people, money won't buy you the passion, imagination, and attention your organization needs.

NOTE

1.   Frances Hesselbein, Marshall Goldsmith, and Richard Beckhard, eds., *The Leader of the Future* (San Francisco: Jossey-Bass, 1996), 189.

Chapter Two

What Brings Us Here?

Museums have inadvertently arrived at a metaphorical watershed where it is now imperative to ask broader questions about why people do what they do, to confront a variety of admittedly unruly issues, and to propose some new choices.

—Robert R. Janes, "The Mindful Museum," 2010

Like it or not, each of us enters this field on someone's shoulders. Or as some of our interviewees put it, we all owe a debt to the museum leaders who shaped our profession. Just as our institutions are stamped for better or worse by the personalities of founders, directors, trustees, and important donors, museum leaders are also influenced by the field's path breakers of the past. Institutions that thrive do so because their leaders—both board members and executives—reinvent themselves and their institutions to cope with changing times. For that, they can thank their versions of Gene Autry, Ann Pamela Cunningham, Henry Ford, Joan Maynard, or Ruth Abram, founders who made their visions a reality—leaders who overcame the challenges of founding or being a first director or curator. Individuals who asked, "Why not?"

We, too, stand on the shoulders of a long line of writers who have documented and critiqued the museum field. Our work carries on, and hopefully carries forward, three-plus decades of evolving, focused discussion about museum leadership as the all-critical means to an end, not an end in itself.

In the course of writing his seminal work, *Museum Masters*, published in 1983, Edward P. Alexander described his reaction to the twelve early museum leaders he chose to profile:

The present study has been an eye-opener to its author. He has marveled at the ingenious ways these museum masters have devised to meet the problems encountered in carrying out their aims. He has come to see that the modern museum movement in its history of a century or two has experimented with many approaches and arrangements, and has built a strong body of experience, the successes and failures of which modern museum workers can consult in meeting present-day opportunities. . . . Museums are indeed learning centers, with a long and vital tradition that has produced important cultural leaders. And these museum masters may well convince modern museum workers that they constitute a stronger and better defined profession than they hitherto had realized.[1]

Alexander's book was a path breaker in that it focused on leaders, not managers, but the field waited eight years for another writer to weigh in on the leadership question. Published in 1991, *Leadership for the Future* is a series of fifteen essays collected and edited by Bryant Tolles, then director of the Museum Studies Program at the University of Delaware, with a prologue recounting the rise of America's history museums by none other than Alexander. With topics as varied as the director as fund-raiser and the director as energizer, the essays acknowledged for the first time the shifting nature of leadership within the profession.

In the two decades leading up to Tolles's book, the museum field's emphasis was on the mastery of *management*, even though some authors used *management* and *leadership* interchangeably and others considered leadership as one of several criteria of good management. Identifying and strengthening management practices—the hard skills of running institutions—was aimed at bringing the business functions of museums in line with, or at least parallel to, those of for-profits. As Stephen Weil would note, this was a time when the American Association of Museums initiated the Accreditation Program, museum associations first published financial management and human resource guidelines and handbooks, and the first museum management training programs were established. He mused that this growing management focus was most likely driven by funders and donors wanting reassurance that their support was being well spent, as well as by the perception that "professional managers from other sectors" were invading the ranks of museum staff. Weil writes, "By way of defense, museum workers themselves needed to learn new management skills."[2]

Reviewing the eagerly awaited American Association of Museums's 1984 report, *Museums for a New Century*, Vincent Moses, the curator of history for the City of Riverside (California) Historic Resources Department, wrote in the *Journal of San Diego History*, "To accomplish all of these goals (of the twenty-first-century museum as outlined in the report), however, we must find new and differently trained professionals and museum managers who are not afraid of innovation and change."[3]

The 1990s was a time when the field widely acknowledged and coalesced around the educational and public roles of museums—and their implications for museum staff—beginning with the publication in 1990 of Stephen Weil's and Earl F. Cheit's book *Rethinking the Museum and Other Meditations*, which pondered the social and cultural significance of museums. Weil and Cheit's book, along with *Excellence and Equity: Education and the Public Dimension of Museums* (1992), published by the American Association (now Alliance) of Museums, demanded, in part, that museum leadership amp up an outward-facing focus, differing from the management-oriented literature of the 1970s and 1980s. The AAM's self-proclaimed landmark document outlined three key ideas, the third of which was aimed at the need for "dynamic, forceful leadership from individuals, institutions, and organizations within and outside the museum community [as] the key to fulfilling museums' potential for public service in the coming century."[4] It addressed leadership in a variety of ways, calling for everything from cultural diversity among trustees, staff, and volunteers; to professional development and training; to the commitment of "leadership and financial resources—in individual museums, professional organizations, and training organizations and universities—to strengthen the public dimension of museums."[5] In its action plan, the report envisioned a museum's organizational structure based on internal dialogue and transcendence of hierarchy, combined with external input to pave the way for cross-fertilization of ideas. Aimed primarily at education departments, it posits the leadership model works institutionally. "Leadership is the foundation. Museum leaders set the tone for the institution and establish the values that guide decision making. . . . Sensitive, strong leadership will also guide museums as they seek to include a broader spectrum of their communities."[6]

Little known, but important because of their emphasis on leadership versus management, are two theses: Barbara Bonner's "Museum Directorship—A Changing Profession: Perspectives of 28 Current and Former Museum Directors in New York City," written in 1988, and Andrée Hymel's "Museum Directorship: A Digest of Contemporary Opinion," written in 2000. Both were completed for graduate programs at Columbia University, and Hymel's builds neatly on Bonner's, addressing changes in the decade from 1990 to 2000, where Bonner's spans the twenty-plus years from 1960 to the late 1980s. Both, like this book, relied on interviews with directors as a window into what happened in the field. Bonner identified a crisis in museum management resulting from a field that requires a diverse set of skills; a polarity between director/curators with directors pulled into the field from outside; and perhaps most critically a dearth of qualified leaders.[7] Writing more than a decade later, Hymel concludes that Bonner's crisis had abated. "Although the expectations of directors have multiplied in the past decade, the more recent participants demonstrated a greater understanding of the extended obligations of the position and readiness to accept its complex challenges."[8]

By the time Sherene Suchy published *Leading with Passion* and Gail Anderson published the first edition of *Reinventing the Museum: Historical and Contemporary Perspectives on the Paradigm Shift*, both in 2004, the ground had shifted yet again. With a PhD in organizational management, Suchy provides a look at the field from the outside. She sees the decade of the 1990s as one of huge internal change, and leadership in the museum field as neglected territory. Acknowledging the huge variety of museums, Suchy focused instead on "the leadership characteristics that are applicable across a broad range of organizations and domains of expertise."9

Counterpointing Suchy's work, Anderson's collection of essays examines a field in transformation written largely, but not exclusively, from the inside. Crediting leaders for challenging the role of museums in society, Anderson underscores the fact that organizational change implies and requires enlightened leadership on the part of boards and staff. "Strong leadership is critical for leading a museum through any degree of institutional change, and visionary leadership is essential for leading a museum through fundamental change."10

The second edition of Anderson's collection, published in 2012, continues the conversation, stressing, "In the end, the collective vision and leadership capacity of a museum is a significant indicator of how successful and effective the institution will be [in] an ever-changing world and marketplace."11

The Center for the Future of Museums captured a series of video commentaries in 2009. Called "Voices of the Future," they are now available on YouTube. Philip Nowlen, then head of the Getty Leadership Institute, muses in his video about the possibilities that could develop if more museums used their many resources to engage with communities about a range of current social issues, among them the future of the humanities in public education. Citing institutional complacency and fear of the unknown as two factors preventing many institutions from leading outward, he called upon museum leaders to be responsible, demanding the most from themselves and their institutions.12

For more than a generation, these voices and others at conferences, keynotes, seminars, and in publications reminded the field about the importance of leadership and admonished us all that good leadership is as critical to a museum's success as a diverse, relevant, community-based educational institution. There are many museum leaders who've embraced the message that responsible, substantive, and transparent change requires leadership that is also responsible, substantive, and transparent. Far less discussed, however, has been *how* leadership—as a state that one could consciously learn, practice, and hone—can be internalized to meet the contemporary challenges Anderson, Janes, Nowlen, Weil, and so many others describe for us.

For the most part, the interviews for this book bear out the narrative arc laid out by the authors we've cited. Our leaders' stories are generally not stories of crisis but journeys of commitment to the potential of museums, of self-discovery, of passion, and, ultimately, of leading outward. Complexity is relative, and Alexander assures us that this is the case from the moment Charles Willson Peale pulled back the red velvet drape on his cabinets of curiosity in late eighteenth-century Philadelphia. But as our world becomes diverse and ever smaller, not to mention increasingly fast paced, multifaceted, multitasking, attention deprived, and schizophrenic in its desires, all types of museums find themselves at a crossroads of reinvention. If not, they risk being left literally or figuratively in the dust.

AT THE METAPHORICAL WATERSHED

With few exceptions, the annals of history museum founding and building are a history of patrician traditions, dominated by white male boards and staff driven by the desire to preserve their understanding of the noble past. As interviewee Nina Simon writes,

> The vast majority of American museums are institutions of white privilege. They tell histories of white male conquest. They present masterpieces by white male artists and innovations by white male scientists. The popular reference point for what a museum is—a temple for contemplation—is based on a Eurocentric set of myths and implies a white set of behaviors. Other reference points for museums—as community centers, as place-based narrative vehicles, as social or performance spaces—are suspect and often branded as "unprofessional."[13]

In fact, not so long ago there was a time when a connoisseur's knowledge and keen eye, coupled with a patron's deep pockets, were enough to create a museum and keep it spinning happily on its axis. Today, the number of museums founded in the connoisseur/patron tradition is increasingly rare. Since the 1976 American bicentennial, the shift from individual patrician founder to community-based preservation has become more pronounced. Smaller history and cultural heritage museums are a rapidly growing segment, more likely developing from a community groundswell rather than an individual longing to preserve history and culture, secure imperiled buildings or landscapes, or collect and protect dying traditions. This shift from the wealthy to the common man/communal founder, egalitarian though it may be, has created an awkward patchwork quilt of institutions (many unworthy of the title *institution*), where the search for money has taken on increasing importance.

Today, as we contemplate the explosive growth of history institutions large and small, their trajectory does seem, as Robert Janes writes, "inadvertent." Even though every one of these institutions has a founding story to tell and an initial reason for being, too few are truly unique or outstanding or add significantly or differently to the historical narrative. Yet miraculously they bob along, sinking some days, caught up on rocks other days, too often drifting, grateful not to be drowning altogether. They redefine the phrase *intentionally founded, inadvertently functional.*

The sheer number of history and cultural heritage museums is a double-edged sword: on the one hand, if you think of them as part of a large, layered, and intertwined history ecosystem, then, as in nature, numbers are critical to survival. On the other hand, numbers alone do not create the diversity necessary for an ecosystem to maintain a healthy and vibrant network that is able to withstand, and even thrive, in the face of significant new threats.[14] In fact, some of our colleagues make the argument right now that a big chunk of the historic house museum species—a long-standing bulwark of the history museum ecosystem—is headed for extinction primarily because of its sameness. By definition, ecosystems are complex and interactive, made so in part by their members' engagement with each other and with their environments. It's the interactions that make the whole thing work. So you could have a pretty dull historic house museum, but if the management figures out ways to keep the audience returning and engaging with one another, it may not be headed for the endangered list any time soon.

The following examples have challenged—and continue to challenge—the history and cultural heritage museum ecosystem: the state of social studies and civic education in our public schools, edutainment, heritage tourism, diversity, and consolidation. Has the field risen to these challenges? You be the judge.

HISTORY MUSEUMS AND HISTORY EDUCATION

For decades, many history and cultural heritage museums relied heavily on the influx of social studies students, who visited annually to learn about local or state history or to participate in National History Day competitions. However, as more and more school districts struggle to meet state and national testing standards and to reduce costs, humanities and arts programs have been reconfigured, reduced, or sidelined altogether, often in favor of science, technology, engineering, and mathematics (STEM) curricula. More than one museum has questioned whether its limited educational resources would be better spent on family programming rather than curriculum-based school programming. Yet in 2010 the National Association of Educational Progress reported that fewer than 25 percent of U.S. schoolchildren were proficient in civics, and three-quarters of high school graduates lack basic historical and geographical knowledge.[15] Retired Supreme Court Justice Sandra Day O'Connor has described the situation as a "crisis" in civic learning.[16] There seems to be no question that there is a widening need for quality civics/social studies education—education that history and cultural heritage museums have addressed, continue to address, or could address on a variety of levels. The scale of the educational challenge seems so great and the resources of history museums are so small by comparison. Can history museums make a significant impact on social studies/civics education, or, as social entrepreneur and *Harvard Business Review* blogger Dan Pallotta would argue, are the field's beliefs and aspirations holding it back?[17]

HISTORY MUSEUMS AND EDUCATIONAL ENGAGEMENT

In the 1980s and 1990s, the Disney concept of edutainment was considered by many to be a threat to history museum visitorship. Pioneered by the Walt Disney Company in the late 1940s, when it finally reached museums almost forty years later it was met with a combination of ridicule and fear. (In fact, you'll read about the reaction to one of our interviewees when colleagues saw the word *Disney* on his conference badge.) The logic went something like this: once the public got a dose of an animatronic Lincoln, who would ever want to go to his home in Springfield and look at a room full of static furniture? As it turned out, science centers and children's museums were among the first to see the value in edutainment. Their leadership understood the potential of entertaining education and using engaging, interactive, and project-based learning experiences to make it so. A quarter century later, leaders at many of the most successful history and cultural heritage museums, including many historic sites, have embraced narrative in all its guises and reaped the benefits from loyal visitors. Sadly, many more plod along, unable or unwilling to break from the old school model of "teaching" history where the past becomes a reverential spectator sport, reduced to a series of lifeless names, dates, and curious objects untethered to makers or users or reasons for being. Has the perpetual tardiness of history and cultural heritage museums to educational and interpretive advances widened the gap so far that it will be impossible for them to get out in front of the curve and be seen as innovators?

HISTORY MUSEUMS AND HERITAGE TOURISM

Heritage tourism, a long-recognized sector in the tourism industry, was aggressively promoted as the saving grace for history organizations and for communities with multiple historic sites. Indeed, it benefits museums and communities that are easy points of destination. But heritage tourism does not serve museums and communities that are off the beaten track, especially those that are open infrequently or those without the wherewithal to find their story. The National Trust for Historic Preservation, the leading advocate for and primary developer of the concept in the United States, identified five guiding principles for successful heritage tourism programs: collaborate, find the fit, make sites and programs come alive, focus on quality and authenticity, and preserve and protect the resource. It takes leadership to see the benefits of developing a museum or site to a high standard of quality, creating a visitor-centered experience, and finding the resources to achieve them. Even so, despite the money and marketing muscle tourism agencies, governments, and institutions themselves poured into it, visitation to historic sites has been on a long and agonizing decrease. John and Anita Durel point to an underlying reality that many politicians, developers, and history museum leaders fail to take into account: "Whatever the reasons, the old [cultural tourism] model is no longer viable. Efforts to make it work with new programs or better marketing will fail. The growth experienced in the 1970s and 1980s has tapered off and begun to decline. Unless something changes dramatically, the decline will continue and we will see more properties being sold or shut down."[18] Are history and cultural heritage museums driving the bus down the heritage tourism highway, or are they merely passengers along for the ride? This kind of reminds us of the movie, *Speed*, where a bus wired with bombs has to be kept moving at or above fifty miles per hour to keep it from exploding.

HISTORY MUSEUMS, DIVERSITY, AND EQUALITY

Demographic diversity in all its permutations—race, age, gender, economics, and so forth—is considered to be as critical to the history ecosystem as the diversity of types of institutions. This is true even in the wider world of nonprofits. As the authors of the 2011 report, *The Voice of Nonprofit Talent: Perceptions of Diversity in the Workplace*, wrote, "Nonprofit employees believe that their organizations do value diversity and inclusiveness but do not follow through on those values with actions to achieve results, and that the proof of true dedication can be found in the actual diversity of the organization."[19]

And then there is the issue of diversity, or lack thereof, in boardrooms, among staff, and in the audiences of history museums. Frequently interpreted as racial diversity, in reality diversity encompasses a myriad of factors, including race, gender, age, economics, education, sexual orientation, geography, ability/disability—it's the whole spectrum of race, class, and gender that marks our place and time in the twenty-first century. We find diversity in the digital divide, the unemployment line, among college acceptances, and the stock market average. For many museums school programming brings the most diverse audience through the doors—children representing broad socioeconomic, racial, and ethnic backgrounds who visit by dint of curriculum requirements or outstanding teachers. Few history museums have been able to replicate the broad diversity of school audiences in other parts of their programming, despite the fact that this has been a perennial topic since *Excellence and Equity*, if not before.

The role of gender in the museum workforce remains a stubborn conundrum. Women dominate the history and cultural heritage museum workforce as they have for the last several decades, causing researchers and pundits to believe they are the primary reason salaries and wages have remained low and benefits minimal in comparison to other educational institutions and female-dominated fields. The American Alliance of Museums's *2012 National Comparative Museum Salary Study* compiled salary, budget, and demographic data from four of its six affiliate regions, with 49 percent of respondents representing history museums and historic sites. Of the survey's total number of respondents, 82 percent of participating institutions reported operating budgets of $3 million or less. The survey found that "two-thirds of all museum professionals in the sample were women. Women outnumbered men in 40 of the 48 full-time positions." The overall sample size, the high percentage of reporting history museums/historic sites, and the very high percentage of operating budgets at the lower end of the spectrum are significant factors in the survey's findings: women more than hold their own against men in the CEO slot (57 percent female; 43 percent male) and far surpass men in the vice president/deputy director slots (61 percent female; 40 percent male).[20]

It would seem, however, that gender diversity in museum leadership runs parallel to that of all nonprofit and for-profit leadership in that the larger the institution, the fewer women are in the CEO's seat.

> Thirty percent of the "CEOs" (and odds are *very good* that this is, indeed, their title, as it makes them feel important) of nonprofits with budgets over $7 million are women. . . . Sadly, though, there is an inverse relationship between the percentages of women in CEO positions at these nonprofits the larger the organizational budget gets. (Only 21% of women in nonprofits with budgets over $25 million are women.) In organizations with budgets between $1 million and $7 million, the majority (52%) of the CEOs are women; and in those organizations with budgets under $1 million, 64% of the CEOs are women.[21]

We can't leave this part of the discussion without also mentioning pay equity. AAM's 2012 survey found that women museum directors/CEOs earn seventy-eight cents for every dollar earned by their male counterparts (comparing median salaries only).[22] The National Committee on Pay Equity reports that in 2011 (the year of most recent data), working women in the United States earned seventy-seven cents for every dollar earned by men. The earning power of women of color ranged from 60 percent to 85 percent. Additionally, the National Women's Law Center notes that the wage gap persists at all levels of education.[23]

The boardroom is still male (but just slightly so), and most of them are white. On this score, many directors and trustees remain puzzlingly defensive, saying things like "our small, rural community is not racially diverse" or simply "we just cannot find diverse people to serve on our board." Acknowledging diversity's shape-shifting nature helps us cease believing that one person of color on a board or staff means we have done due diligence. Our museums should reflect our communities. If 40 percent of our town's population farms for a living, but farmers aren't represented on our board or in our audiences, something is out of kilter. Board and staff leaders owe it to the future health of their institutions to put in motion strategies that create pathways to attract volunteer and paid talent that better mirrors the communities they represent.

Again, listen to the words of *The Voice of Nonprofit Talent: Perceptions of Diversity in the Workplace*:

> It's time for our CEOs and boards to exercise leadership by translating good intentions into concrete results. Addressing diversity and inclusion cannot wait until the economy fully recovers, until the budget is balanced, or until all of the other issues that are traditionally prioritized above an organization's "people focus" have been addressed. Creating a diverse and inclusive environment cannot be merely delegated to human resources or a chief diversity officer. Personal commitment followed by action—particularly from the highest leadership level—is the only way to make progress in advancing more people of color to senior roles. We cannot treat the diversity objective as something to "work towards" gradually, over decades. Time is running out. When the economy recovers, we will again be competing with organizations that offer more money, better perks, more resources, and, in many cases, concrete evidence that they value diversity.[24]

HISTORY MUSEUMS AND MERGER

Last, but not least, as the history museum ecosystem responds to a battered funding climate, there's much talk, but so far little evidence, among the nation's history and cultural heritage museums of full organizational or programmatic mergers or transfers of assets. As Rainey Tisdale documented in her 2012 session at the American Alliance of Museums (AAM) annual meeting and subsequently discussed in her blog, state-subsidized museums in Denmark and Norway embraced merger in the face of declining government support. The results were dramatic: By using mergers Denmark reduced its number of museums from 170 to 111 and Norway reduced its museums from 350 to 75.[25] Of course, this example is about state-supported museums helped to merge by governments, providing incentives to do so. It's an unlikely scenario in the United States, where the vast majority of museums are private nonprofits and, no doubt, one of the reasons why so few history and cultural heritage museums have merged. Some funders attempt to facilitate the merger conversation with the promise of grants and expertise to bring nonprofits to the table. Tisdale lists a variety of reasons why the merger pill seems hard to swallow: fear of loss and change are the primary drivers, to which we should add lack of vision about mission delivery coupled with a lack of understanding of audience needs. Here is another instance where leaders like the ones we profile here mitigate and lead change.

INTRACTABLE CHALLENGES?

While the Smithsonian, Colonial Williamsburg, and The Henry Ford continue to be the largest and brightest stars in the history museum constellation, smaller institutions, many too small to see with the naked eye, have joined them. Thousands have come into being in almost every county in every state, with a smaller but parallel presence in every province in Canada. In 2008, the Pew Charitable Trusts cited a minimum of fifteen thousand historic house museums in the United States.[26] Add to that history and cultural heritage museums, historical societies, historic landscapes, monuments, trails, and ruins, and the population likely doubles. The fact is there is no accurate count. What we do know, however, is that while all are rooted firmly by geography and nurtured by local populations, many share the same great expectations as North America's largest museums.

Those expectations include sufficient support to attract and retain qualified staff, keep the doors open, the signage intact, and the lawn mowed, and also to provide creative programming, ensure quality collections care, engender community engagement, and put money in the bank. Underlying those expectations is the notion that a spinning turnstile provides the requisite evidence that a museum has value, is valued, and will be valued despite the fact that many residents never visit. As interviewee Burt Logan, executive director and CEO of the Ohio Historical Society, observes, it's probably a given that small history organizations don't have the capacity to endure long term. How do you tell a community that its heritage does not have importance? On the other hand, how can we capture and remember a community in ways other than a museum? We need to think of documenting a community's history as a means, not an end.

Traditionally, the field considered support from for-profits, government, and individual philanthropy as critical indicators in proving an institution is

truly "community based." The fourth leg of this financial stool is the shaki-
est: earned income—the stuff of shops, events, and admissions—is always
subject to the vagaries of visitation, weather, the economy, school busing, or
the price of the gala ticket. The reality is shifting here, as well. Tisdale
summarizes several recent national studies underscoring the overwhelming
challenges facing all museums, including the American Association of Museums's "Museums and the American Economy in 2011" survey, which
found that among the 427 reporting institutions almost 72 percent reported
economic stress ranging from moderate (43 percent) to severe (16 percent) to
very severe (13 percent).[27] Tisdale writes:

> The 2005 Heritage Health Index warns that millions of objects held by US
> museums and historical societies are at risk from poor storage conditions as
> well as inadequate staffing and disaster planning. The 2009 Technical Devel-
> opment Corporation, Inc. white paper "Building a Sustainable Future for His-
> tory Museums" reports that significantly increased performance expectations,
> coupled with particularly high capital costs for maintaining collections and
> buildings, have set up many institutions for failure. At a time when everyone
> in the field is talking about sustainability, the future of museums, collabora-
> tions, and creative solutions, shouldn't we own the discussion of this contro-
> versial topic and have it on our terms, before more museums face closing their
> doors, and have to make tough decisions under duress?[28]

Sustainability of history and cultural heritage museums and their changing
leadership cannot be fully understood or addressed in isolation of these real-
ities and a rapidly evolving environment.

Let's take a moment, then, to get an even wider-angle view. Every history
and cultural heritage museum competes for attention and funding within an
expanding nonprofit cultural sector. Since the beginning of the twenty-first
century, arts and cultural organizations of all types, including history and
cultural heritage museums, grew by 49 percent according to the Americans
for the Arts (AFTA) National Arts Index Report—that's a rate greater than
all nonprofit organizations, which grew just 32 percent.[29]

As a follow-up to the AFTA report, Stephanie Riven wrote on its blog
that there are three core strategies all arts and cultural organizations must
embrace to stem the tide of waning attendance and funding: innovative leadership capable of communicating bold ideas broadly, consistently, and in a
wider context; developing a collective impact by speaking with a unified
voice; and engaging substantively with our communities and cultural partners. She expands upon the three core strategies with a list of her own:

- Putting aside our own agendas and our individual needs to be the authority
  in the room

- Taking more steps toward visionary and innovative thinking at the national, state, and local level
- Acknowledging that "survival" is not enough
- Taking risks to avoid the status quo
- Making a commitment to continuous dialogue
- Seeking collaborative learning experiences geared toward new options and potential for our sector[30]

We know from the *Nonprofit Almanac 2012* that the arts and cultural sector make up a remarkably expanding nonprofit universe, which grew by almost 50 percent between 2000 and 2010. There is now one nonprofit for every 175 Americans. Health care and higher education institutions dominate the 4 percent of American nonprofits, with expenses of $10 million or more. They account for more than 85 percent of the spending. In addition, the number of volunteers in social service and health care organizations is five times greater than the number of people volunteering in the cultural institutions.[31]

It is no longer enough to characterize the challenges of history and cultural museum leadership as difficult or complex. Certainly it is all of that, but it is also excruciatingly nuanced, existing on a persistent gray scale that rarely yields to black-and-white decision making. Leadership today is informed by hundreds, even millions, of data points that were simply not available when Tolles's book was published in 1991. For example, the Internet was not commercially available until the early 1990s when *Excellence and Equity* called for museums to combine "intellectual rigor with the inclusion of a broader spectrum of our diverse society."

One could argue that the ground has not only shifted for history and cultural heritage museums and their leaders but also that it has put them on a different playing field altogether: communities are in demographic flux, education is in uncertain flux, communication is in dizzying flux, economies are in global flux. History as an academic discipline has morphed from a single authoritarian voice to one where there are many voices. The wild growth of people pursuing genealogy, personal collecting, reenacting past events, coupled with the self-curation of personal heritage via scrapbooking, Facebook, and e-publishing have democratized the public's understanding of their place in the historical narrative.

SURVIVAL IS NOT ENOUGH

Now as we move into the second decade of the twenty-first century, North American history and cultural heritage museums have weathered a global recession, constricting support to greater or lesser degrees. Despite that scenario, too many continue to struggle or neglect altogether questions of leadership development, diversification, and succession. They have seen dramatic expansion of personal technology and social networking connecting people virtually, but at the same time isolating them. They have witnessed public education thrown into a whirlpool of budget cuts, curricula overhauls, and heightened pressure to perform. Given all the things that have happened—are happening—is it still rational to ask, "Why not?" A newly complex world demands a deeper reflection of why an institution exists in the first place.

It may be that the history and cultural heritage museum ecosystem is more forgiving than a biological one. There are many institutions that can and do subsist under the radar, barely open to the public, turning a blind eye to collections care, offering little more to its community than a half-forgotten attic. And there are others who may talk a good game and look pretty swell but are riddled with ethical missteps or are educational wastelands. They may be rudderless or leaderless or both, but it's not exactly dog-eat-dog, survival-of-the-fittest in the history museum world. At least for now.

NOTES

1. Edward P. Alexander, *Museum Masters: Their Museums and Their Influence* (Nashville: American Association for State and Local History, 1983), 17.

2. Stephen Weil, "Beyond Management: Making Museums Matter," Keynote Address at the 1st International Conference on Museum Management and Leadership—Achieving Excellence: Museum Leadership in the 21st Century. INTERCOM/CMA conference held in Ottawa, Canada, September 6–9, 2000, 8–9, accessed June 1, 2013, http://www.intercom.museum/conferences/2000/weil.pdf.

3. Vincent Moses, "Book Review: *Museums for a New Century: A Report on the Commission on Museums for a New Century*," *Journal of San Diego History* (Fall 1986), accessed June 2, 2013, http://www.sandiegohistory.org/journal/86fall/museums.htm.

4. Ellen C. Hirzy, ed., *Excellence and Equity: Education and the Public Dimension of Museums* (Washington, DC: American Association (Alliance) of Museums, 1992), 5.

5. Hirzy, ed., *Excellence*, 8.

6. Hirzy, ed., *Excellence*, 26.

7. Andrée Marie Hymel, "Museum Directorship: A Digest of Contemporary Opinion," MA thesis, Teachers College, Columbia University, 2000, 52.

8. Hymel, "Museum Directorship: A Digest of Contemporary Opinion," 182.

9. Sherene Suchy, *Leading with Passion: Change Management in the 21st Century Museum* (New York: AltaMira Press/Rowman & Littlefield, 2004), 5.

10. Gail Anderson, *Reinventing the Museum: Historical and Contemporary Perspectives on the Paradigm Shift* (Lanham, MD: AltaMira Press, 2004), 3.

11. Gail Anderson, *Reinventing the Museum: The Evolving Conversation on the Paradigm Shift* (Lanham, MD: AltaMira Press, 2012), 447.

12. Center for the Future of Museums, "Voices of the Future: Phil Nowlen," TEDTalks, 2009, accessed May 3, 2013, https://www.youtube.com/watch?feature=player_embedded&v=VzG1Iua_j7k.

13. Nina Simon, "On White Privilege and Museums," *The Museum 2.0 Blog*, March 6, 2013, accessed April 10, 2013, http://museumtwo.blogspot.com/2013/03/on-white-privilege-and-museums.html.

14. The ecosystem analogy was recently voiced by Dan Spock of the Minnesota History Center at the 2012 joint meeting of the Organization of American Historians and the National Council on Public History. His comments were noted by Phil Katz, "Some Notes on the Future

of History Museums," *The Center for the Future of Museums' Blog*, May 17, 2012, accessed January 15, 2013, http://futureofmuseums.blogspot.com/2012/05/some-notes-on-future-of-history-museums.html.

15. National Center for Education Statistics, "The Nation's Report Card: U.S. History 2010 (NCES 2011–468)," Institute of Education Sciences, U.S. Department of Education, Washington, D.C., accessed April 3, 2013, http://nces.ed.gov/nationsreportcard/pubs/main2010/2011468.asp.

16. Ginger Rutland, "In the Spotlight: Sandra Day O'Connor: Retired but Hardly at Rest," *Sacramento Bee*, March 3, 2013, accessed April 3, 2013, http://www.sacbee.com/2013/03/03/5229761/retired-but-hardly-at-rest.html#dsq-form-area.

17. Kate Torgovnick, "A New Way to Judge Nonprofits: Dan Pallotta at TED2013," *The TED Blog*, March 1, 2013, accessed March 17, 2013, http://blog.ted.com/2013/03/01/a-new-way-to-judge-nonprofits-dan-pallotta-at-ted2013/.

18. John Durel and Anita Nowery Durel, "A Golden Age for Historic Properties," *History News* (Summer 2007): 8.

19. Robert Schwartz et al., "The Voice of Nonprofit Talent: Perceptions of Diversity in the Workplace" (Commongood Careers and the Level Playing Field Institute, 2011), 16, accessed January 4, 2013, http://www.commongoodcareers.org/diversityreport.pdf.

20. American Association (Alliance) of Museums, *2012 National Comparative Museum Salary Study*, 2012, 13. The study's data is as of December 1, 2010. The data is a compilation of surveying by four of AAM's six regional museum associations. The Mid-Atlantic states and the West Coast states were not included in the survey. Accessed August 4, 2013, http://www.aam-us.org/resources/research/museum-salary-study.

21. Laura Otten, PhD, "It's a Man's World," *The Nonprofit Center Blog*, April 26, 2013, accessed April 26, 2013, http://www.lasallenonprofitcenter.org/its-a-mans-world/.

22. Philip M. Katz, "By the Numbers," *Museum* (May–June 2013), 8.

23. National Committee on Pay Equity, accessed April 26, 2013, http://www.pay-equity.org/.

24. Michael Watson, "Foreword," in *The Voice of Nonprofit Talent: Perceptions of Diversity in the Workplace* (Commongood Careers and the Level Playing Field Institute, 2011), 3, accessed January 4, 2013, http://www.commongoodcareers.org/diversityreport.pdf.

25. Rainey Tisdale, "Widespread Mergers. Could It Work in the US?" *The CityStories Blog*, May 4, 2012, accessed December 18, 2012, http://raineytisdale.wordpress.com/museum-mergers/.

26. Marian Godfrey and Barbara Silberman, "What to Do with These Old Houses," The Pew Charitable Trusts, April 30, 2008, accessed November 11, 2012, http://www.pewtrusts.org/our_work_report_detail.aspx?id=38618.

27. American Association (Alliance) of Museums, "Museums and the American Economy in 2011," April 2012, accessed December 18, 2012, http://www.aam-us.org/docs/research/acme12-final.pdf?sfvrsn=0.

28. Tisdale, "Widespread Mergers. Could It Work in the US?"

29. Americans for the Arts, *National Arts Index 2012*, accessed October 2, 2012, http://www.artsindexusa.org/national-arts-index.

30. Stephanie Riven, "The State of the Arts: The Arts Are in a State," *Artsblog*, August 15, 2012, accessed October 2, 2012, http://blog.artsusa.org/2012/08/15/the-state-of-the-arts-the-arts-are-in-a-state/?utm_source=rss&utm_medium=rss&utm_campaign=the-state-of-the-arts-the-arts-are-in-a-state.

31. Katie L. Roeger, Amy S. Blackwood, and Sarah L. Pettijohn, *Nonprofit Almanac 2012*, Urban Institute Press, October 2012, accessed October 15, 2012, http://www.urban.org/books/nonprofit-almanac-2012/.

Chapter Three

Leadership Training and Development Today

Learning leadership is an ongoing process of becoming more and more aware and vigilant. It is a process of continuously seeking to know yourself, to clarify your thinking, to take responsibility rather than to place blame, and to control only yourself.
—Julie I. Johnson, Getty Leadership Institute

It's important to understand that there is a critical difference between leadership training and leadership development. As Getty Leadership Institute faculty member Julie I. Johnson writes, leadership training is squarely focused on hard skills mastery, as she notes, the *doing* of leadership. Leadership development, on the other hand, is the evolutionary and experiential process by which individuals *become* leaders.[1] Leadership training, which is internal and personal, generally comes first as individuals learn tried-and-true methods to solve common workplace problems. Leadership development is more externally based, focused on how the individual relates to the environment as a whole.[2]

We know there is a growing and urgent need for leadership training and development in the history and cultural heritage museum field. Likewise, there are a number of variables in play meeting the need or ignoring it. Let's start with the individual: Before one can begin to contemplate leadership training and development needs, one has to acknowledge one has skill or experience gaps. Not surprisingly, most people think they're better at what they do than they really are; we tend to have positive illusions about our prowess. While these are perfectly natural yet mighty psychological forces to reckon with, they often prevent us from asking for help, learning new ideas, honing new skills, and ultimately becoming better leaders. What came through loud and clear in our interviews is the importance of individuals taking personal responsibility for getting the training and development they need to grow professionally. The notion of self-initiative cannot be underestimated, and this is especially true of leadership training and development precisely because they are neither widely understood nor appreciated.

Then, there is the availability factor. Assuming an aspiring or veteran leader is self-aware enough to acknowledge her strengths and weaknesses, can establish goals for leadership development, and can figure out some pathways and types of support to meet them, there are a variety of training programs but a lesser number of true development opportunities from which to take advantage. That said, beyond traditional graduate school programs, there are simply *not enough* leadership training *or* leadership development opportunities. Nor is there enough variety to allow working professionals to take easy advantage of them and, this is essential, for the ongoing cultivation of their leadership capacities.

In addition, there is not enough emphasis on the institutional value of leadership training and development overall. This blind spot almost always begins at the museum's top with its board of trustees. When a board fails to understand its own need for leadership training and development in order to govern better, it is not likely to understand how it applies to the director. Frequently, boards believe their quotient is better than it is. This attitude of having mastered a skill sometimes makes boards blind to the necessity of ongoing leadership training for trustees, director, staff, and volunteers. If a museum's decision makers don't make training and development a priority, understanding that access to it makes their institutions, not just staff, stronger, leadership development will never gain a toehold.

Leadership training and development for the history and cultural heritage museum field is traditionally found in four places: graduate and certificate programs; independent workshops and seminars for individual leaders; books and articles on leadership used by directors, board members, and team leaders; and in on-the-job experiential learning shaped by a boss, board member, or a mentor. When we asked our interviewees what prepared them most for their current leadership positions, the overwhelming majority cited previous positions where they learned from others, had a variety of responsibilities, established core competencies, and where they were allowed to experiment and fail. As business blogger Dan McCarthy writes,

> Too many companies spend too much time on [courses, books, articles and other means]. It's not only the least effective, it's lazy. The top companies understand it's all about learning through experience. When you think about it, it's a sunk cost—you might as well leverage it. Don't get me wrong—courses can be effective, when they are designed in ways that incorporate the other points. [3]

When you think about your career, as a beginner or a veteran, where did you learn your most valuable leadership lessons?

For many leaders in the trenches, access to formal leadership training and development is irregular at best, dependent on institutional philosophy and finances, while in a sort of catch-22, access to leadership literature and positive on-the-job opportunities are heavily dependent on strong existing leadership within an organization. Without this level of commitment at the top of the museum, new directors, department heads, and junior staff will not see a need to keep up with leadership trends and fail to understand that leadership is first and foremost the ability to make sense of an environment and adapt quickly to change. In addition, the understanding of who benefits from leadership training and development has not kept pace with the field's changing nature where even the smallest history museum is globally driven, and where the speed of change constantly demands adaptation.[4] Further, the field has been slow to define what leadership means and to address competencies for leadership development.[5]

As a result, the field's emphasis has more frequently focused on mastering management rather than leadership, yet the two are undeniably symbiotic halves of a whole. Since Bryant F. Tolles edited his collection of essays on the changing directorial roles in American history museums and historical societies, and Hugh H. Genoways and Lynne M. Ireland wrote *Museum Administration: An Introduction* in 2003, writing on museum leadership and management continues to grow, albeit somewhat sporadically. Tolles's essayists examined the director as the intellectual leader, the initiator of professional standards, the legal guardian, planning engineer, fund-raiser, and the critical communication link between the board and the staff. *Museum Administration* focused on the nuts and bolts of management, including budgeting, planning, programming, and collections and facilities management. Despite being written more than a decade apart, these two books can be seen as a companion set describing the hard and soft skills required of museum leaders and managers; however, both describe leadership as something people do, not something people know. They are based on the theory that if an individual responds in predictable ways and improves his or her problem solving or communication skills, then all will be well. Or at least better.[6]

By comparison, the quantity of leadership literature flowing from B-school and celebrity authors is overwhelming, perhaps implying that leadership in for-profits, the military, sports, or politics is more fascinating, more urgent, or somehow more necessary than leadership in the cultural nonprofit sector. The fact is that the bulk of these books are frequently more about knowing than doing. They trumpet leadership's soft skills—team building, listening, feedback, facilitating creativity, and the like rather than the hard skills of product development or budget analysis, which MBAs presumably learn in graduate programs.

A quick Internet search at goodreads.com of popular leadership books returns 2,002 titles ranging from Dale Carnegie's 1936 classic *How to Win Friends and Influence People* to Doris Kearns Goodwin's *Team of Rivals: The Political Genius of Abraham Lincoln* (2005) to Susan Cain's *Quiet: The Power of Introverts in a World That Can't Stop Talking* (2012). Based on our interviewees, today's museum leaders routinely read across the spectrum—nonprofit, for-profit, and biography, for example—adapting what they need to the museum environment. Their shelves contain books by such well-known leadership writers as Jim Collins and Peter Lencioni, in addition to Michael Watkins's *The First 90 Days*, Donald T. Phillips's *Lincoln on Leadership*, James A. Autry's *The Servant Leader: How to Build a Creative Team, Develop Great Morale, and Improve Bottom-Line Performance*, and *Leadership for the Disillusioned* by Amanda Sinclair.

As history museum leadership evolved in the twentieth century, we saw a shift from the erudite connoisseur with academic training in history, anthropology, or art history to a professional trained in the multidisciplinary work and craft of the museum. Throughout the United States and Canada there are now more than 125 degree-conferring and certificate programs in museum education, exhibition and design, collection management, and curatorial studies in addition to similar programs at the undergraduate level. While programs such as Winterthur, founded in 1952 by the Henry Francis DuPont Winterthur Museum and the University of Delaware, continue to offer a masters in American Material Culture built upon connoisseurship, by way of contrast, the twenty-plus museum studies masters programs available today provide general curricula covering a wide range of issues and fundamental skill development complemented by project-based learning and internships.

Richard Male, a Denver-based consultant to nonprofits, gets to the heart of what is often missing in these programs when it comes to leadership when he writes:

> We are too focused on training managers rather than leaders. Most college and graduate-level curricula about nonprofits do not include or require strategic thinking. Each emerging generation of nonprofit executives dutifully learns to write a budget, develop and evaluate programs, and engage a board of directors. The skills of considering complex external factors, along with learning to live with ambiguity, taking risk, and moving out of one's comfort zone, continue to be in short supply.[7]

Several programs, like the one at John F. Kennedy University, offer a combined Master of Arts and MBA for students pursuing careers in museum leadership and management, while Bank Street College of Education offers a Leadership in Museum Education Masters program that takes place on weekends during the academic year along with a weeklong institute in June. For the vast majority of masters programs, however, when they address forward-thinking leadership training at all, it is woven into existing curricula.

This year, however, a new graduate-level leadership program opens reflecting changes in the museum field as a whole and in its attitude toward leadership. Beginning in fall 2013, Drexel University will offer a new Master of Science in Museum Leadership with a focus on "educating tomorrow's museum leaders to meet the financial, technological, and programming challenges of the future."[8] Housed in Drexel's Department of Arts and Entertainment Enterprise, the program is promoted as a mix of leadership skills and development suitable for any type of museum.

The evolution of museum leadership training reflects the reality that a growing number of institutions hire leaders who do not possess discipline-based academic or museum studies degrees. Spurred by a desire to become more businesslike or to stanch red ink, some museums hire outside the field. Among small history and cultural heritage museums, where salaries often remain low and benefits nonexistent, staff may have no museum training or leadership development at all. While an institution always takes a risk when hiring, hiring outside the profession carries with it a mean learning curve. For some, the work of a museum is often a mystery (making the leader a questionable advocate for it and its standards); for others, especially those leaders who've migrated from the for-profit arena, the slower pace of decision making or the lack of performance standards can be a constant frustration.

FILLING THE LEADERSHIP DEVELOPMENT VOID

In order to address the varying skill levels of many history and cultural heritage museum professionals in leadership positions, a number of training programs exist offering immersive training for current and future leaders. The oldest among them is the Seminar for Historical Administration, sponsored by the American Association for State and Local History in collaboration with Colonial Williamsburg, the National Trust for Historic Preservation, and the Smithsonian National Museum of African American History and Culture. The three-week program addresses hard and soft skills through a combination of formal presentations by leaders in the field augmented with case studies, workshops, and field trips.

The Getty Leadership Institute (GLI) at Claremont Graduate University (CGU) is the umbrella for several leadership programs. Its flagship, the Museum Leadership Institute, began in 1979 as the Museum Management Institute, a month-long program aimed at mid- and senior-level museum professionals. A combination of hard skills training and leadership development, the Institute asks participants to think about the influence they wield within their institutions, as well as the ways their core values intersect with their museum and its success measurements. GLI also offers programs for first-time directors, board chairs in combination with their directors, as well as next-generation museum leaders.

These two programs paved the way for a number of others offered by national and regional museum associations, graduate programs, and independent organizations—from the Institute for Museum and Library Services (IMLS)-funded Institute for Cultural Entrepreneurship developed by the Cooperstown Graduate Program in collaboration with the New York State Historical Association and the Museum Association of New York, to the recently inaugurated leadership academy of the Association of Midwest Museums, to the Center for Curatorial Leadership focused on the creation of "a new kind of curator" (that's one who masters curation and handles critical management responsibilities in his or her institution).

Citing the enormous challenges faced by staff throughout museums, not just at the top, George Washington University's (GWU) museum studies program is developing a leadership program for midcareer museum professionals that would kick off in 2014. Faculty member Martha Morris says initiating such a program is a direct response to the needs of alumni, many of whom participated in a 2012 survey revealing their desire for training in change management, leadership skills, strategic planning, board development and fund-raising, visioning, team building, entrepreneurship, and facilitation. What form this training will take is still in discussion, but Morris believes it is a necessary complement to the current curriculum.

In 2004 the Cooperstown Graduate Program (CGP) celebrated its fortieth anniversary. That same year it decided to survey twenty-one museum leaders from across the country in an effort to understand the criteria used to hire new professionals. The survey began as an assessment of the program's curriculum but also included data about the field's needs for training. Designed by a social scientist, the survey asked participating museum leaders to define the requisite knowledge and skills entry-level professionals need, not only to be successful but also to climb the leadership ladder. The study's data, published in the Autumn 2004 issue of *History News*, served as an important catalyst for a dialogue between professional training programs and practitioners on the front lines of museum work.[9] The museum leaders were selected based on conversations with staff at the American Alliance of Museums (AAM) and the American Association for State and Local History (AASLH) and represented a variety of museum sizes, disciplines, and locations. Most were in history or general museums, the traditional focus of the Cooperstown program. A range of institutions was included to determine how requisite skills varied with size of staff and budget.

The study revealed that museum professionals, even at the beginning of their careers, need to understand and participate in development, fund-raising, community relations, and program assessment. In addition, new staff, like everyone else, must see themselves as critical to increasing revenue on the one hand and in delivering mission on the other. As now-retired Virginia Historical Society director Charles Bryan stated, museum work requires "an entrepreneurial approach on the part of all staff."[10]

In recognition of the impending retirement of museum professionals of the baby boom generation, the Museum Association of New York (MANY) published a white paper in 2006 titled, "Who's Next: Questioning the Future of Museum Leadership in New York State." Research began with three regional focus groups of professionals from twelve museums and historical societies, as well as with graduate students and faculty from five of the state's nine museum studies programs. Individuals who have left the field and key staff people from the New York State Council on the Arts also participated. The most significant finding from these meetings was that

> mid-career training was a recurring theme in all the regional discussions. Participants felt it was and is an unaddressed need. Too few organizations value leadership training, fewer still value ongoing leadership development, failing to recognize these experiences produce a ripple effect that ultimately aids the organization. Apart from the obvious benefits of providing new knowledge, mid-career education gives participants mentors and a peer group that are worth the price of admission.[11]

Through this initiative, it became clear to MANY that training midcareer professionals at all levels of the organizational hierarchy may provide answers to questions about the upcoming leadership void.

Following up on the "Who's Next" white paper, CGP and MANY administered a web-based survey to midcareer museum professionals in February 2007. Of eighty-eight respondents, the survey found:

- 52 percent indicated that leadership, advancing organizational effectiveness through vision, mission, and values, team building, and leading from within would be the most useful type of training to them
- 55 percent noted that leading and supporting organizational change would be the most useful skill needed to do their job better

Based on the results of these two surveys and the findings published in MANY's white paper, midcareer professionals (people with graduate degrees who now find themselves in leadership positions), as well as their museums and communities, would benefit from greater access to leadership training and ongoing leadership development to equip them with the knowledge and skills to become innovative and entrepreneurial in their approach to museum work.

A 2012 survey by the Bridgespan Group of more than 225 nonprofit leaders found that despite attempts to develop leaders, many organizations fall short. Among the nonprofits surveyed, the overwhelming majority of senior leaders and their organizations fully supported the idea of leadership development, but only 42 percent invested sufficient resources in leadership development. Most of the surveyed organizations admitted to a lack of understanding about future leadership needs, making it virtually impossible to maintain or grow organizational momentum as leaders change.

> Given our lack of understanding of future needs, it's not surprising that few of us—less than 29-percent—report that we have development plans for individuals. . . . the good news is that almost 65-percent of us report that we have ample on-the-job opportunities for development. We are less positive about our capabilities to secure access to training, and to coach and mentor future leaders.[12]

It must be said (and it cannot be overstated), if a person is not self-aware enough to see on-the-job-training as an opportunity rather than just another workplace requirement to be endured, he or she is likely to develop risk-averse behavior that could short-circuit leadership aspirations.

In her recent dissertation, Julie I. Johnson reminds us that in the cultural sector, despite all these programs, there is plenty of anecdotal evidence but precious little longitudinal evidence that leadership training and development sticks.[13] She also points out that institutions tend to believe that when they send a director to a program like Getty the entire organization benefits. We must remember that what's learned in the bubble of a museum studies class-room or leadership seminar is put to the test in the institution once the newly enlightened return home and are reimmersed in the issues they left behind. If the institution itself is not open to developing leadership and making the space for new or different approaches to work, newly honed skills and experiences will be dulled, forgotten, or taken elsewhere.

THE CROSSROADS

History and cultural heritage museums and their leaders are at a crossroads. Many struggle mightily to move beyond their four walls, expanding their community presence through relevant programming, working collaboratively with multiple audiences to create a shared understanding of the past, and injecting an entrepreneurial twist to partnerships across sectors. This last idea is sometimes the most fraught, as history and cultural heritage organizations don't always mesh easily with either their nonprofit siblings or their for-profit cousins. Outside the rotary meeting or a chamber of commerce com-mittee, history museum leaders sometimes find themselves isolated from a community's flow. Nonetheless, as directors and board members understand their museums in relation to their communities, it is also clear that leadership must be comfortable sharing authority with an ever-expanding array of stakeholders from elected officials to real estate developers to the preschool around the corner. A generation ago, leadership training built on a personal skill set emphasizing the individual as the hero leader. Today's training places leadership in relation to the group as something relational, collectivist, and nonauthoritarian.[14] This emphasis on the leader as a team member changes leadership from something that comes with a position to a set of behavioral characteristics, making the whole enterprise more democratic. Anyone can possess those characteristics and use them for the good of the organization.[15]

At the 2012 joint annual meeting of the Organization of American Historians and the National Council on Public History, George Washington University museum studies professor Laura Schiavo challenged her colleagues, asserting that history and cultural heritage museums aren't doing enough to "disrupt and transform current museum practice" but instead resort to well-worn and overworn traditions.[16] Interviewee Van Romans echoed these sentiments, saying most museums don't know their audiences and haven't the faintest idea of what to deliver to whom or why.

After being asked by peers and stakeholders to articulate their value, many history and cultural heritage museums still cannot do so. Many have not done even the most basic research to understand their external impact, nor have they engaged in the type of original research or raised resources to reinvent their programming, brands, and relationships, much less overhaul their physical plants. Many organizations and their leaders operate with a scarcity mentality that leads to small-bore thinking, operational blind spots, and a deep resistance to change. Few of these organizations have the type of professional development funds that open opportunities for experimentation, collaboration, or evaluation. On the other hand, one wonders: If such funds were readily available, would these organizations take advantage of new knowledge, different perspectives, and, ultimately, change that is at the core of leadership development?

History and cultural heritage museums don't evaluate themselves rigorously enough. The fact is that thanks in large part to the concentrated prodding of funders, programmatic evaluation developed by leaps and bounds but organizational self-assessment, benchmarking, and strategic goal setting, coupled with tough success criteria, are far less pervasive. Boards and staffs do not demand them. And too few funders provide organizational capacity-building support over the long haul to bring about sustained change in organizational behavior.

Finally, as a field we are late to the game of defining what leadership means for the long-term health and well-being of history-based institutions, and because of that, we have failed to address the full range of competencies necessary for leadership development. As the twenty-first century rolls forward, history and cultural heritage organization leaders need a unified effort to get ahead of the monster curve threatening to sideline history and cultural heritage from economic development and mainstream education.

Beginning in the early twentieth century we hear John Cotton Dana's clarion call for museums to be servants to the public, a call that is echoed and expanded upon with increasing persistence in the late twentieth century by Stephen Weil and in the twenty-first century by interviewee Nina Simon. The time for focused, creative, intentional leadership is now.

NOTES

1. Julie I. Johnson, "Museums, Leadership, and Transfer: An Inquiry into Organizational Supports for Learning Leadership," PhD dissertation, Antioch University, 2012, 6, accessed May 23, 2013, http://aura.antioch.edu/etds/13.

2. Johnson, "Museums, Leadership," 42.

3. Dan McCarthy, "A CEO's Guide to Leadership Development," *SmartBlog on Leadership*, February 28, 2013, accessed March 10, 2013, http://smartblogs.com/leadership/2013/02/28/a-ceos-guide-to-leadership-development/.

4. Johnson, "Museums, Leadership," 32.

5. Johnson, "Museums, Leadership," 5.

6. Johnson, "Museums, Leadership," 33.

7. Richard Male, "Nonprofit Weaknesses Start with Too Few Leaders and Too Many Managers," *Chronicle of Philanthropy*, February 10, 2013, accessed February 19, 2013, http://philanthropy.com/article/Nonprofit-Weaknesses-Start/137189/.

8. Drexel Now, "New Drexel University Graduate Program Will Prepare Students for Museum Leadership," March 5, 2013, accessed March 11, 2013, http://drexel.edu/now/news-media/releases/archive/2013/March/Museum-Leadership/.

9. Gretchen Sullivan Sorin and Dr. Martin Sorin, "Museums, Professional Training and the Challenge of Leadership for the Future," *History News* 59, no. 4 (Autumn 2004): 17–20.

10. Sorin and Sorin, "Museums, Professional Training and the Challenge of Leadership for the Future," 19.

11. Joan H. Baldwin, "Who's Next? Questioning the Future of Museum Leadership in New York State," Museum Association of New York, 2006, 7, accessed October 5, 2012, http://manyonline.org/2006/04/whos-next-questioning-the-future-of-museum-leadership-in-new-york-state/.

12. Bridgespan Group, "The Challenge of Developing Future Leaders: Survey Results Say . . . ," 2012, 1–5, accessed March 12, 2013, http://www.bridgespan.org/getattachment/6d0a44b3-a794-444e-b6a4-7594b825f659/The-Challenge-of-Developing-Future-Leaders-Survey.aspx.

13. Johnson, "Museums, Leadership," 48–49.

14. Johnson, "Museums, Leadership," 39.

15. Johnson, "Museums, Leadership," 4.

16. Phil Katz, "Some Notes on the Future of History Museums," *The Center for the Future of Museums Blog*, May 17, 2012, accessed January 15, 2013, http://futureofmuseums.blogspot.com/2012/05/some-notes-on-future-of-history-museums.html.

Chapter Four

Intentional Leadership: Four Fundamentals for the Twenty-First Century

Intentionality is the inside-out interplay between the current state and the future focus. Intentional leaders become instruments of change. Leaders and organizations need to set their cultural intention as clearly as other goals and metrics. Intentionality is like an internal compass setting; it maintains the courage and commitment to hold true to the course.
—Center for Creative Leadership, "Inside Out: Transforming Your Leadership Culture," 2008

Once considered solely a scholarly and social pursuit, leadership in history and cultural heritage museums is now a multidimensional game where the playing field is in continual flux. Today's successful leaders are not just willing to challenge their institution's status quo if disrupting inertia will create positive change for the long run, they consciously mix and match skills, experiences, values, and vision to continually shifting internal and external environments. They are hungry for community engagement and know they need it in order to understand how their museum fits into the larger picture. They create galvanizing institutional visions, and through them they energize, enable, and empower others, and they constantly nurture their institutions through self-assessment, goal setting, formal and informal learning, experimentation, and teaching by example. They are intentional about their leadership.

Twenty-first-century leadership is not about reshuffling the same frayed set of people, projects, time frames, and deadlines. While quick fixes are caffeine to sleepy institutions, it is momentum quickly lost if it is expended without an underlying strategy. As the authors from the Center for Creative

Leadership wrote in their white paper, "Transforming Your Organization": "Organizations seeking to adapt during turbulent times—like now—cannot force change through purely technical approaches such as restructuring and reengineering. They need a new kind of leadership capability to reframe dilemmas, reinterpret options, and reform operations—and to do so continuously."[1]

We know that leadership is a constant rethinking of the entire deck of resources to find the fulcrums—those things that supply capability for action—that can initiate positive change. Often the fulcrums for change are small or simple and, therefore, overlooked. When our interviewees Janet Carding of the Royal Ontario Museum and Anne Grimes Rand of the USS *Constitution* Museum encourage their staffs to experiment by casting it as simply "beta testing," they relieve the pressure and anxiety of trying new approaches and feeling it has to be right the first time. In this example, the fulcrum for creativity is in the language Carding and Rand use to describe it. They reframed it! The twenty-first century leader understands that small changes yield big results, in part because small changes are within our grasp—they're controllable and they usually don't cost much.

In spite of their museum's subject matter or their love for the past, today's history and cultural heritage museum leaders have to be futurists. This is leadership that is about keeping one eye on the future, the next move, and the endgame. Today's leaders need to be comfortable with the "what if's" and the "how can we's." As Tynesia Boyea Robinson notes in her essay on managing to outcomes, these leaders are also bilingual and comfortable with nonprofit and for-profit language and ways of doing business. They are fully engaged with their missions, use metrics to measure improvement and impact, and they understand the importance of internal and external accountability.[2] They seek possibilities, they are attuned to what's next, and they look for connections that may not currently exist, making their institutions deeply valuable to the communities they serve. They are curious. In this regard, they step outside the museum walls to listen to a community's issues and needs before strategizing approaches to address them. They ask powerful questions of themselves and others. They are seekers. They adapt and apply ideas from across the nonprofit and for-profit sectors. They simply don't buy into the "Aw, gee, we're just a poor nonprofit" scarcity mind-set. Indeed, they are willingly, openly, and unapologetically abundant thinkers.

Interviewee Rob Kret knows how to think abundantly. As head of the Hunter Museum of American Art, he worked with three other nonprofits and the city of Chattanooga to raise $120 million to fund a new waterfront plan that included a $23 million expansion for his museum. The project was among eight finalists nationwide for the Lodestar Foundation's Collaboration Prize.[3] This collaboration also produced significant back-of-the-house mergers of human resources, IT, and financial management functions (among others), which provided access to necessary expertise that otherwise was being duplicated at each institution.

FUNDAMENTAL #1: CONVERGENCE OF LEADERSHIP

Along with these qualities of futuristic and abundant thinking, experimentation, and risk taking, today's leaders represent an about-face from the traditional, hierarchy-preserving, top-down thinking of a generation and more ago. We live in a world where the openness and equality of the Web leads to the free-flow exchange of information and ideas. We expect to have a voice and to tap into expertise from around the globe. Hierarchy is flatter, thanks to this kind of access. In an effort to spread authority, encourage development, and up the ante of creativity among standout staff and volunteers, the twenty-first-century leader is comfortable sharing leadership in what interviewee Kent Whitworth of the Kentucky Historical Society describes as "leading from the chair instead of the front of the room." Whitworth takes great satisfaction in seeing his staff exert ideas and influence. He considers himself to be their chief cheerleader.

As important as shared authority is to strengthening a workforce, it is equally necessary for nurturing external relationships, including audiences. One of the most visible proponents of audience nurturing is Nina Simon of the Santa Cruz Museum of Art & History. Simon's commitment to integrating audiences into a museum's work stems from her "community first" approach to program development that involves regular convening of residents for focused brainstorming and experimenting with all sorts of audience feedback activities. Sticky notes in bathrooms? Chalkboard insights from program participants? Simon tries all of it to give audiences a real voice, and thus a real stake, in *their* museum. "I love it [the image of being the conductor of a community-based orchestra]," Simon told a reporter recently. "Not controlling everything, just helping steer the way and keep us moving forward."[4]

This new convergence of leadership is a radical departure from command-and-control, top-down decision making of the past, and it represents our first fundamental element of twenty-first-century leadership. As Julie I. Johnson points out,

> The changing nature of society and work along with the speed of change has underscored the need for new forms of leadership. Whereas previous goals of leadership and measures of leadership effectiveness resided in the ability of designated leaders to influence actions of followers, recognition is growing that managing change is a primary function of leadership. To that end, process-oriented and collective approaches may be more appropriate for enacting leadership. With the shift towards a more process view of leadership, the

nature and quality of workplace relationships become increasingly important. Leadership is seen as an activity available to staff at all levels of the organization and not limited to just a few in positions of authority. [5]

We believe our selection of interviewees epitomizes the first element of twenty-first-century leadership: convergence. While the CEO/director interviewees we profile here fully embrace their responsibility for shaping and making decisions and for being the final arbiter of a given course of action, none enact this element of leadership alone. Our non-CEO/director interviewees equally value shared authority as a way to build and strengthen their own leadership skills and experiences, as well as those of their staff. "I want people to feel like they have a voice," says Mattatuck Museum interviewee Bob Burns. "When you're willing to share success with your team," says interviewee Jamie Bosket of George Washington's Mount Vernon, "It blossoms into pride—it's like wildfire."

FUNDAMENTAL #2: MULTIDIMENSIONALITY

As Johnson states,

> There is and will continue to be less of a need for the "Lone Ranger" type of leader and more need for an individual who can motivate, coordinate and connect within a continually changing environment. The work of leadership will be done in contexts of ambiguity and uncertainty and this will require different roles for leaders at different times during an organization's lifecycle. [6]

Clearly, twenty-first-century leadership demands this and it brings us back to Robinson's notion of the bilingual leader, one who can speak the language of the for-profit and nonprofit worlds, who has a quiver full of hard and soft skills from both sectors, and most importantly knows when and how to use them. Twenty-first-century leaders must also bring a broad range of personal interests and opinions to the table; they live and thrive in multidimensional environments, seeing the interconnectedness of themselves, their institutions, and their communities in time and space. Interviewee Jim Enote weaves his wide-ranging interests and skills in art, language, cultural mapping, and agriculture with the beliefs and traditions of his Zuni culture to form a seamless whole that is his life and work. The second fundamental element, then, of twenty-first-century leadership is multidimensionality.

You may recall the scenario we described in the introduction of the museum director jumping from issue to issue using, to greater or lesser degrees, skills learned in formal settings or more likely through on-the-job experience. Our harried leader juggles long- and short-term challenges, almost all of which depend on communication with a variety of stakeholders ranging from the board president to staff to a major donor to the accountant. Each stakeholder was looking for something slightly different from our leader—an idea, a question, a piece of information, an analysis, an impassioned case for support, a vision for what could be.

The leader's typical day is filled with multidimensionality—demands for both right- and left-brain thinking and for grasping the big picture and the significant detail: strategic directions, finances, crisis management, team building, and donor engagement. Leaders must move facilely back and forth among these dimensions, often without skipping a beat, and many times without a clear solution or ready response. Leaders who routinely approach their museum's work from a tried and true or safe vantage point run the risk of suffocating growth. That kind of pattern blocks the organizational oxygen necessary for multidimensional work.

Likewise, the difficult, seemingly intractable, issues history museums face aren't successfully addressed by using a sky-is-falling approach. As the authors of *Switch* point out, "Most of the big problems we encounter in organizations and society are ambiguous and evolving. . . . To solve [them] we need to encourage open minds, creativity, and hope."[7] This is exactly the tack interviewee Sally Roesch Wagner, the founding director of the Matilda Joslyn Gage Foundation, took as she nurtured her museum from idea to reality. A veteran educator, Wagner is skilled at asking questions and seeking understanding. As a founding museum director, she entered what she admits was uncharted territory for her. She began with not only a grand vision but also with plenty of questions and an open mind.

When multidimensionality is mastered by doing and knowing, it begs the question of pigeonholing oneself early in one's career. Understanding the issues and emotions in play within institutions and between institutions and audiences evolves when a leader is aware of where he or she is. "There's been a lot of balancing and coming to grips with who I am," says interviewee Dina Bailey, director of Exhibitions and Visitor Experiences at the National Underground Railroad Freedom Center, "and I've needed to find the balance between my academic training and my natural abilities."

When considering a new leadership model for the field, Jeanne Liedtka and her colleagues at the Getty Leadership Institute saw successful leaders as those who synthesize and internalize multidimensionality. They are the people who can hold two opposing thoughts in their heads at the same time; they preserve distance while developing connection; they dig deeper while developing breadth; they are pragmatic while remaining optimistic. In applying multidimensionality to the way today's leaders learn, Liedtka summed it up this way: "Overall, it seems that any new leadership education model should focus on developing an understanding of: relationship to self AND the relationship to others; relationship to expertise/learning AND the relationship to emergence/learning; and relationship of the present AND the relationship to the future."[8]

A New Leadership Education Model

Developing distance	Vs.	*Developing connection*
Inquiry Skills		Empathy skills
Emphasis on learning/testing		Understanding how to work with others
Asking questions/inquisitive		Knowing when to lead vs. delegate
Open to multiple answers		Ability to build teams/open to shared leadership
Flexible/ adaptable		Comfortable with conflict
Intellectually nimble		How to build trust/social capital
Active Listening		Working/open to difference (global/generational/political)
Self-awareness		Connecting with audience
Coping with ambiguity / chaos		Cultural sensitivity
Developing Depth	Vs.	*Developing Breadth*
Technical Skills		Innovation Skills
Deep knowledge/expertise		Intellectual playfulness
Connoisseurship		Creativity
Getting it right		Tolerating failure/taking risks
Telling the truth about current reality	Vs.	**Envisioning a new tomorrow**
Pragmatism	Vs.	Idealism/optimism
Analysis		Synthesis
Present/constraint-focused		Possibility/future-focused
Managing affordable loss/prevention		Realizing potential/achieving ideal
Financial flows connected to current realities		Big vision connected to details

Overall, it seems that any new leadership model should focus on developing an understanding of:
- Relationship to self AND the relationship to others
- Relationship to expertise/learned AND the relationship to emergence/learning
- Relationship of the present AND the relationship to the future

Table 4.1 A New Leadership Education Model

FUNDAMENTAL #3: AGILITY

What does the skill set look like for leaders who embrace convergence and multidimensionality? The Institute of Museum and Library Services (IMLS) 2009 report, *Museums, Libraries, and 21st Century Skills*, emphasized skills leaders needed to successfully steer institutions through the shoals of shifting economies, societal needs, and audience expectations. These skills were clearly moving (or had moved) toward treating institutions as organic and interconnected systems existing within concentric circles of dynamic communities, informal learning, and accelerating social interaction. IMLS's *21st Century Skills Framework* identified three overarching skill sets: learning and innovation skills; information, media, and technology skills; and life and career skills.

Of the twenty skills listed, the majority fall into the museum leader's wheelhouse, among them critical thinking and problem solving; creativity and innovation; communication and collaboration; cross-disciplinary thinking; basic literacy; information and media literacy; flexibility and adaptability; initiative and self-direction; social and cross-cultural skills; productivity and accountability; leadership and responsibility; global awareness; financial, economic, business, and entrepreneurial literacy; and civic literacy.[9] With little exception, these are "knowing" rather than the "doing" parts of leadership. They are difficult to teach or master in the classroom. They are ever evolving and lead to the third fundamental element of twenty-first-century leadership: agility.

Agility on the part of history and cultural heritage museum leaders assumes that museums are not precious specimens preserved in amber, unchanged and unchanging. Agility across a broad swath of knowledge and skills allows leaders a breadth of strategic options that single-mindedness simply does not. When you read one day that a major history museum suffers its lowest walk-in visitation in forty years and another day hear that a tiny start-up museum receives the government funding your established institution counted on, you need to have more than one plan of action, more than one set of vocabulary, and more than one way to evaluate and articulate success. "If you're the kind of person that needs a structured environment to survive," interviewee Pam Green muses, "I don't think you can be a [successful] director."

Green, who is executive director of Weeksville Heritage Center in Brooklyn, New York, knows about agility. Taking the reins from an iconic founder, Green knew she had to adapt the institution in order to sustain it. But one week after she started her new position at Weeksville, September 11 changed the landscape and made sustainability seem like an impossible goal. There were more questions than answers, but one thing was clear: a continual recalibration of priorities was necessary to navigate the world September 11 left in its wake. It was to be a totally organic process, Green says, that ultimately realigned the mission, board, staff, programming, and the site. "If you focus solely on challenges," Green says, "you will not survive. In the end, it was all about leaping out on faith and building on the courage and conviction of those that went before and on whose shoulders you stand."[10]

FUNDAMENTAL #4: IN TUNE AND IN TOUCH

In 2010, the Wisconsin Society of Association Executives formed a task force to think about innovation in nonprofit associations. It began its work by looking at the for-profit sector for clues about how business fostered and resourced environments that routinely made space for creativity resulting in new ways to achieve mission. It published its research in a white paper titled "Innovation for Associations."[11] What the task force found was echoed by many of our interviewees: leaders remove obstacles; they see; they act. These leaders are listeners. They pave the way for staff to take calculated risks; they encourage and reward creativity, and in so doing help staff to learn from failure, not fear it. They live in the customers' world. They know what their constituents want and don't want because they ask and they listen, and they apply what they hear.

Leaders of innovative organizations facilitate collaboration across diverse teams knowing that there's a clear advantage to having more perspectives than too few. They foster human connections. They know that successful initiatives start and grow from the roots, not from top-down mandates, all of which is largely accomplished by listening. We call this fourth fundamental of twenty-first-century leadership *in tune/in touch.* "There is a difference between someone believing I don't respect them, and me slowing down to make them understand [me]," interviewee Tonya Matthews says. "Then I feel more authentic." Interviewee Anne Grimes Rand adds, "People should feel valued, listened to, creative, and respected at work." Rand, who is the president of the USS *Constitution* Museum in Boston, is deeply devoted to the audience experience at her museum. It is the bottom line for her and her staff, and it is the bedrock value the museum works from every day.

In tune/in touch institutions make place and space for people. They support learning and skill and knowledge acquisition for staff, volunteers, and audiences. Stakeholders have a voice here, and because they do, these museums are able to deepen community engagement, allowing them to stay one step ahead of the curve. They are aware of a myriad of professional and external trends, whether it's about collection management or popular culture. In tune/in touch institutions build trust by meeting or exceeding individual and community performance expectations. There is internal trust to be found among board and staff, among all levels of staff, and among staff and volunteers. Christy Coleman, president of the American Civil War Center at Historic Tredegar in Richmond makes a point of bringing people together around a sense of shared purpose, one that she works hard to shape. "[It] takes time to help them see what I am seeing," she says. She relies on her background in history interpretation to gather input, talk it through, reach common ground, and act. In tune/in touch museums are nurtured by in tune/in touch leadership.[12]

Together, the IMLS framework, the four fundamentals as we see them for leadership, and Liedtka's leadership education model offer a clear and compelling road map for identifying and nurturing the kind of leadership that is critically needed to meet challenges now and in the future. They form the basis from which the history and cultural heritage museum field and its training and development programs can refine, teach, and build competencies for staff and board leadership. As a field we must do a better job of integrating training and development at every stage of a museum professional's career. There is simply not enough emphasis on nurturing leadership nor enough value placed on making leadership development widely available to those interested in pursuing it.

Convergence of Leadership + *Multidimensionality* + *Agility* + *In Tune/In Touch* characterize the interpersonal skills needed for successful organizational leadership as much as they characterize twenty-first-century institutional culture itself. Against the backdrop of these four fundamentals, we present the stories of thirty-six leaders. Despite being at varying stages in their leadership journeys, we are struck by how committed they are to facilitating convergence in their daily work (and how much joy they get from it, too), how they balance multidimensionality to reap its rewards, and how deeply they embrace and use the concepts of agility and in tune/in touch.

Since leadership is as much knowing as doing, our leaders share four deeply seated personal qualities that have facilitated their career success and the success of their institutions. Those personal qualities are: self-awareness, authenticity, courage, and vision. We believe that these particular personal qualities are necessary correlations to the interpersonal fundamentals, and that successful history and cultural heritage museum leaders must have all eight at their disposal.

But are these personal qualities in a person's DNA, or can they be learned? "Tests have shown there is no leadership gene. While studies might find a certain trait to be significant, there always seems to be considerable evidence that fails to confirm that trait's importance. Context is often more important than traits," writes Joseph S. Nye, former dean of the Harvard Kennedy School and author of *The Powers to Lead*. "We talk about leaders being more energetic, more risk-taking, more optimistic, more persuasive, and more empathetic than other people, but these traits are affected partly by a leader's genetic makeup and partly by the environments in which the traits were learned and developed."[13] Noting that leadership is a combination of personality and behavior, interviewee Burt Logan, executive director and CEO of the Ohio Historical Society, believes he's a product of determination and a lot of hard work, stating, "I'm a product of behavior. I've enjoyed leadership because I always wanted to be a leader. I've enjoyed the opportunities I've had, but I've had to work for them."

Our leaders bear this out. Despite our call for greater intentionality, many of our leaders admit to developing these qualities somewhat accidently or more likely as a by-product of pursuing another quality or fundamental or by responding to an external reality. There are many ways to learn to be more self-aware or more agile, for example, or to hone existing proclivities and talents, but the desire to do so must first come from within.

Let's meet our leaders now.

NOTES

1. John B. McGuire et al., "Transforming Your Organization," Center for Creative Leadership, 2009, 3, accessed November 15, 2012, www.ccl.org/leadership/pdf/solutions/TYO.pdf.

2. Tynesia Boyea Robinson, "Managing to Outcomes: Mission Possible," in *Leap of Reason: Managing to Outcomes in an Era of Scarcity*, edited by Mario Morino et al. (Washington, DC: Venture Philanthropy Partners, 2011), 107.

3. For more about the Lodestar Foundation Collaboration Prize: http://www.lodestarfoundation.org/collaboration.html.

4. Georgia Perry, "Innovator Drives Museum's Success," Santa Cruz.com, March 19, 2013, accessed March 20, 2013, http://www.santacruz.com/news/2013/03/19/innovator_drives_museums_success.

5. Julie I. Johnson, "Museums, Leadership, and Transfer: An Inquiry into Organizational Supports for Learning Leadership," PhD dissertation, Antioch University, 2012, 39–40.

6. Johnson, "Museums, Leadership," 45.

7. Chip Heath and Dan Heath, *Switch: How to Change Things When Change Is Hard* (New York: Crown Business, 2013), 123.

8. Jeanne Liedtka appeared in *The Compleat Leader* blog post, "Name the Beast!" published by the Getty Leadership Institute at Claremont Graduate University, April 30, 2012, accessed February 18, 2013, http://compleatleader.org/2012/04/30/name-the-beast/. Chart used with permission.

9. Institute of Museum and Library Services, *Museums, Libraries, and 21st Century Skills* (Washington, DC: Institute of Museum and Library Services, 2009).

10. Pamela E. Green, Unpublished Case Study for the Institute for Cultural Entrepreneurship for Museum Leaders, a professional development program of the Coooperstown Graduate Program, 2010. Contact Gretchen S. Sorin, director of the Cooperstown Graduate Program, for information and access to this case study, sorings@oneonta.edu.

11. Wisconsin Society of Association Executives, "Innovation for Associations," white paper, 2011, accessed December 20, 2012, http://cdn0.pathable.com/attachments/797028403/1295640503___Innovation_for_Associations_White_Paper.pdf.

12. This paragraph about in tune/in touch institutions has been informed by the trend research of the LitLamp Communications Group in Chicago. LitLamp's "13 Things Breaking through in 2013," at PatriciaMartin.com, can be found here: http://patricia-martin.com/13ThingsBreakingThrough.htm, accessed January 10, 2013.

13. Joseph S. Nye, "Nature and Nurture in Leadership," *The Harvard Crimson*, June 2, 2009, accessed March 12, 2013, http://www.thecrimson.com/article/2009/6/2/nature-and-nurture-in-leadership-as/.

Chapter Five

The Self-Aware Leader

Find out who you are and do it on purpose.
—Dolly Parton

Your visions will become clear only when you can look into your own heart.
Who looks outside, dreams; who looks inside, awakes.
—C. G. Jung

Leadership seems as though it is about the organization, about knowing it through and through, but successful leaders spend equal amounts of time studying themselves. The profiles of these thirteen leaders demonstrate how they do that, making leadership a personal journey of reflection, discovery, reevaluation, and even reinvention. If being offered the corner office, a comfortable salary, and a bucketful of perquisites feels like the end point, think again. Each of these stories shows us that leadership is a learning process. And perhaps one of the most important things about self-aware leadership is that leaders who live it model behavior that works organizationally too. As long as leaders and followers are engaged in an ongoing process of self-understanding, then it is natural for museums to engage in the same process of experimentation, reflection, and recalibration.

Learning can take many forms. Some of our interviewees were lucky enough to participate in leadership training, such as Ryan Spencer and Kent Whitworth, who attended AASLH's Seminar for Historical Administration, and Gonzalo Casals and Janet Carding, who attended the Getty Leadership Institute, are avid readers, as are most of the interviewees.

One of the things about self-knowledge is that it keeps you humble. As our interviewee Catherine Charlebois reminds us, the path to leadership is a step-by-step process that requires time to build good reflexes. Her desire to become a director someday is tempered by her assessment that her "toolbox is not complete yet." Along with humility, the leaders interviewed here are kind. They care about their staffs. For Melissa Chiu being a leader is about relationship building, with her staff as well as her colleagues at other museums. All of these leaders understand that influence is easier than control. Casals characterizes his way of working with staff as a series of questions, describing his direct report meetings as an opportunity to bat ideas back and forth.

For some in this group, work is defined as service. These leaders serve their organizations, and they find the act humbling. When Ryan Spencer at The Henry Ford talks about his love for his work, for where he works, and for the people he works with, you hear his unabashed gratitude in every word. He is very centered, grounded in values, and guided by a sense of purpose that overshadows ego and personal gain. This is a love affair we hope never grows old. And then there is Ilene Frank, who remarked, "Your position is not you," adding that she loves the idea of saying *we serve* our museum.

The leader as a servant to others, and to institutions, is a particularly apt appellation for the nonprofit sector. First coined by Robert K. Greenleaf in a 1970 essay titled "The Servant as Leader," the notion of a leader who serves is currently popular in business and leadership literature. As Greenleaf writes,

> The servant-leader *is* servant first. . . . It begins with the natural feeling that one wants to serve, to serve *first.* Then conscious choice brings one to aspire to lead. That person is sharply different from one who is a *leader* first, perhaps because of the need to assuage an unusual power drive or to acquire material possessions. . . . The leader-first and the servant-first are two extreme types. Between them there are shadings and blends that are part of the infinite variety of human nature. [1]

Perhaps most important in each of these stories is the individual's willingness to turn the spotlight on themselves, acknowledge strengths and weaknesses, and move forward. Jennifer Kilmer was disarmingly frank with her future historical society board, reminding them that her skill set wasn't history. She was an administrator. She had never done a capital campaign, but she led and learned along with her board.

As the authors of "Inside Out: Transforming Your Leadership Culture" write,

> By giving attention and weight to internal dimensions, leaders introduce the possibility of new thinking and new beliefs—and therefore new decisions and new behaviors. Leaders practicing together in the leadership culture enlarge the mental and emotional space for change, allowing them to make unexpected and innovative decisions. The bigger the operational change, the more the

cultural space needs to expand. We call this the inside-out approach to trans-forming an organization. And it starts with you.[2]

Edward R. Bosley, Director, The Gamble House, Pasadena, California

- MBA, Anderson Graduate School of Management, University of California, Los Angeles, and Ecole Supérieure des Sciences Econo-miques et Commerciales, France, 1980
- In an age when historic houses are on shaky ground, he helped build a $5.5 million endowment.
- Quote: "You need to humble yourself and listen."

Edward "Ted" Bosley made a lot of changes at age thirty-five. He moved from the East Coast to California; he left the high-powered world of Manhattan advertising for a nonprofit; and he inadvertently stepped onto a leadership path. Bosley, the director of Gamble House, one of the country's preeminent Arts and Crafts homes for the past twenty-plus years, was originally hired because of his corporate advertising experience. "I was hired to do PR and to be the assistant director," he explains. "Advertising is a corporate pyramid," he continues. "And I chafed at that." He adds that the behaviors necessary to survive corporate life—stabbing your way to the top—were an anathema to him—so even before he made the move to Gamble House, he had begun to look for a smaller agency.

Gamble House is owned by the city of Pasadena, but the University of Southern California operates it, and ultimately Bosley reports to the dean of architecture at the University. "The Dean was probably quite skeptical," Bosley says about his hiring. He had only been there two years when he was asked to step into the director's position. "There was no curator at the time," Bosley remembers, "so the director's position incorporated that as well." He was asked and accepted all without a search, something he still seems amazed about almost twenty-five years later. "Either they were too busy [for a search] or I was doing a good job of keeping my head above water," he remembers, recalling that the thing that scared him most was the idea of stepping into someone else's shoes, particularly someone for whom the director's position had become something akin to a cult of personality. "I had to work hard to win over some," he says, recalling how he had to assure his board and staff he wasn't going to make changes overnight.

Serendipitously, Bosley was an art history major as an undergraduate. He also has an MBA from the University of California. "It's a good combination," he says, of the content-driven BA combined with a graduate degree that taught him to read a spreadsheet and speak the board's language. When Bosley stepped into the director's position, he had not seen the institution's financial statements. "There was no maintenance endowment," he recalls, "and no relationship with any foundations." The whole endowment was $400,000. "I had to get the wheels rolling right away," he says, adding that the relationships that ultimately brought in the money were all about people. "You're real, you care, and you're listening," is the Bosley development mantra, and it is one that has worked. Today, Gamble House has a $5.5 million endowment and a significant maintenance program.

Bosley is frank about the fact that his workplace success has come at a price. "If you're doing a job you love, you don't always see the boundary clearly," he says. For Bosley, failing to see the boundary cost him a marriage. He is better at cordoning off work from the rest of his life now. Thursday and Sunday evenings are sacred, and he frequently escapes to a weekend cabin where he can indulge his love of hiking.

He does believe, however, that courage is a key leadership ingredient. "It's easy to recognize a problem," he says, "but much harder to *do* something or to recognize how things will look with or without a change." He also describes himself as an innate listener, a quality that has served him well not only in development but also as a mentor and leader. "You're so much more likely to move a project forward when you listen with respect and compassion," he says. "You need to humble yourself and listen." Hearing that, it is no surprise that James Autry's *The Servant Leader* is on the bookshelf in his office.

Ask Bosley whom he admires, and he will tell you about Milt Schroeder, his graphic arts teacher in seventh grade. Bosley was both mystified and in awe of Mr. Schroeder's passion not only for typeface but also for trying to make typeface matter to middle school students. "I wondered, how *does* he make us care?" In the end it isn't the subject matter that stuck with Bosley— although he did begin adult life in advertising where typeface sometimes matters a great deal—but his teacher's passion. He also remembers the minister at his childhood church. "He was firm; he knew what he wanted; he was self-effacing," Bosley says. "I hope that's how people see me."

Although he says he's not a techno geek—he does own an iPhone, but its many bells and whistles are underused—Bosley is a fan of the Internet and the role it plays in networking. He checks Frank Vagnone's *Anarchist's Guide to Historic House Museums* weekly, sometimes commenting, and he cites it, among other places, as a source of thought-provoking conversations. "Conferences are expensive and take up a huge block of time," he says, adding that the time to recover is punishing. But for him, the Internet allows thought-provoking interaction on his own time.

Then there is the role of face-to-face networking. Like many leaders interviewed for this book, Bosley sees it as key. "It has a huge role at important moments of leverage, and you don't know when it's going to happen," he says. He tells a story about being at the Grove Park Inn in Asheville, North Carolina, a mecca for arts and crafts devotees and museum folk that takes place annually. The cost of the conference for a small organization from the West Coast was big for what seemed like a small payoff. Bosley found a trustee who was willing to pay travel expenses, and off he went, standing for the best part of each day by his table talking about Gamble House to anyone and everyone. One of his random conversations resulted in a very large donation. With hindsight, he acknowledges he was at the right place at the right time. "You just never know," he says. "You talk with anyone who will listen and you assume everyone is capable of writing a million-dollar check."

And how does this one-time-ad-exec-turned-servant-leader want to be remembered? "If, in fact, I'm fortunate enough to close out my career here," Bosley muses, "I'd like to complete the Gamble House's landscape initiative. That might be my swan song." But that's not how he would like his community to remember him. Not exactly. "I'd like to be remembered as someone who saw moments of leverage and took advantage of them for the benefit of the organization," he concludes.

Colin G. Campbell, President, Colonial Williamsburg Foundation, Williamsburg, Virginia

- JD, Columbia University School of Law, 1960
- He believes strongly that history teaching—whether through the classroom, the university, or a museum, has to be more than just about the rights of the individual people but also about citizenship.
- Quote: "In the absence of a collaborative style," he says, "you're going nowhere; going it alone is not an option."

In more than four decades of public service, Colin Campbell has been a CEO three times. He is not the typical history museum director who climbed through the ranks from lowly intern to curator to administrator to the corner office. Currently, he is president of Colonial Williamsburg, among the most quietly experimental and yet the most iconic of American historic sites.

Campbell previously served as president of Wesleyan University, a position he held from 1970 to 1988 when he became president of the Rockefeller Brothers Fund. An attorney who was once vice president of the Planning and Government Affairs division of the American Stock Exchange, Campbell's skill set is sophisticated, and given the breadth of his career, it is predicated more on his experience in governance and management than subject-specific knowledge in American history or decorative arts.

Campbell's connection to Williamsburg began in 1989 when he was asked to serve on its board. "I did that for several reasons," he begins. "President Chuck [Charles] Longsworth asked me to; my wife's family has long-standing Virginia connections; and I really did feel that Colonial Williamsburg's mission interested me a lot, particularly since I feel there is often shallow attention paid to American history."

Campbell became Wesleyan University's president at the shockingly young age of thirty-four. It was the late 1960s, and Wesleyan, like many American campuses, saw its share of tumult. And that was only the beginning. Through the years Campbell has honed a leadership mantra that goes something like this: he believes in openness; he tries to say it like it is regardless of the constituency; and he believes in walking the talk, something he says a leader must do if he (or she) expects people to follow his (or her) lead. He is also a big believer in making sure that the director and the governing board are on the same page.

Ask Campbell about a workplace success and he looks back almost to the beginning of his leadership career, telling a story about becoming president of what was then the most highly endowed institution in the country. That ended almost as soon as Campbell's tenure began. Wesleyan had sold its press to Xerox in exchange for stock, which it found it couldn't unload. That left the university at the beginning of a period of exponential growth with a hugely devalued endowment. "Change was necessary," Campbell quips, explaining that persuading a wealthy university community of the notion that it was suddenly in a very necessary fund-raising mode was challenging. But Campbell prevailed. Gradually the community responded, raising new capital essential for its well-being. In retrospect, however, Campbell says he rushed his first campaign. "We weren't internally ready," he remembers.

Reflecting again on his mantra of openness, Campbell adds that age has its benefits. "Today I am in a position to make judgments in perilous times." And given the news from Colonial Williamsburg where visitation continues to fall, it needs Campbell's confidence. He meets with the foundation's nine officers every Monday, followed by a meeting with Williamsburg's leadership team of directors, curators, and hotel managers. Every quarter he also meets with as many of the full-time staff as possible, upward of 250 people. He also schedules regular meetings with divisional vice presidents and their senior leadership team. And last, in the spirit of walking the talk, Campbell has a one-hour monthly breakfast for nonexempt staff. He reports for fifteen minutes and takes forty-five minutes of questions. "They are wonderful," Campbell says.

And who are Campbell's mentors? He interjects to point out that in forty years of non profit work, he has had only six board chairs. The first name he mentions is Ronald "Ron" Daniel. A fellow Wesleyan alum, who Campbell describes as a truly remarkable human being, Daniel was CEO at McKinsey and Company at the same time he was Campbell's board chairman. "He provided leadership for the board and support and counsel for me," Campbell says. "And he was not afraid to raise the tough questions." Another star in Campbell's constellation is David Rockefeller Sr., now ninety-seven years old. "I only knew him as the outgoing chair of the Foundation," Campbell recalls, "but he was graceful, thoughtful, and generous to everyone, no matter what their station," he says, adding that his own engagement with employees at Colonial Williamsburg is based on the David Rockefeller model. More recently, Campbell finds himself learning from another trustee, Forrest E. Mars Jr. "He is very engaged," Campbell says. "He gets behind the superficial to what really matters."

The owner of an iPad and an iPhone, work always calls to Campbell. Not surprisingly, he is a bit of a workaholic. His willingness to let go is an ability he attributes to his wife, Nancy. "She assures that the balance is there," he says. For him, her partnership has been extremely important. "I'm not laden with hobbies," he says without irony, although he does have a fierce interest in international politics. He does not tweet, and while he reads blogs and occasionally contributes to others, he does not have one of his own.

Campbell sees his legacy in three distinct areas: higher education, grant making, and historic sites. He believes a liberal arts education is sustaining. "It is preparation, not for a job, but for life," he says. Second, he underscores his belief in collaboration. And last, he says that before he leaves, he would like to solidify Colonial Williamsburg's commitment to its proposed center for history and citizenship. He believes strongly that history teaching, whether through the classroom, the university, or a museum, has to be more than just about the rights of the individual people, but also about citizenship.

And the future? Campbell riffs on two topics. "Museums, symphonies, and other institutions are under stress," he says. He includes historic sites such as Colonial Williamsburg in that group. "It's quite clear that more can't be sustained," he continues. Asked if there's an antidote, Campbell has a one-word answer: collaboration. "In the absence of a collaborative style," he says, "you're going nowhere; going it alone is not an option." Campbell's other thought about the future involves technology. "We have to master it, but not be controlled by it," he says. As an example, he describes Colonial Williamsburg's new game *Rev Quest*, created for school-age children and smart phones. The game that debuted last summer attracted adults and families and will reappear this summer. While he questions how colleges and universities can sustain free online teaching and learning, Campbell is a fan of exhibit space on the Web and is justly proud of Williamsburg's e-museum.

Janet Carding, Director and CEO, Royal Ontario Museum, Toronto, Canada

- Masters, History of Science and Medicine, with distinction, University of London, 1992
- Worked in museums on three continents: Europe, Australia, and North America
- Quote: "Some think museums and galleries need to be more business-like, but I think we instead need to be better nonprofits, say clearly why we make the world a better place, work closely with our users, and demonstrate the impact we make."[3]

The arc of Janet Carding's museum career seems to have touched upon almost every facet of museum activity (collections, exhibitions, programs, capital, planning, etc.) to the point one wonders if this was by design. Was it intentional? Carding laughs and then says no—none of her career has been intentional. She wanted to go into the sciences, hence the degree. Then, she saw an ad for a job at the The Science Museum in London, which she applied for and got. That pretty much sums up her career, she confides. "It's been a happy accident."

Carding says she had no burning passion to work in museums before actually working in them. What turned the switch? She's always enjoyed the semiacademic nature of museums—how they cross boundaries between research, learning, and the public—and the way they foster lifelong learning opportunities.

The Royal Ontario Museum (ROM) is her first director's position, although she's held significant leadership positions for most of her career. While she didn't enter the field knowing she wanted to lead, since her college days she has had a bias for coordinating, delivering, and generating ideas, which is . . . well, leading. She says, "I always got things done and enjoyed leading projects and teams and departments." So, in a way there was an intentionality about her leadership over time, with each stage allowing her to evaluate and look ahead. "I have a track record of delivering," she states. "I can articulate issues in strategic terms; I can lead people. I had built a track record for accomplishment." As a result, leadership opportunities came her way.

When asked what it's like to be the first woman director of the Royal Ontario Museum, an encyclopedic institution that celebrates its centennial in 2014, she admits she doesn't quite understand what the fuss is about. She gets this question a lot, and while she finds it fascinating, it's one she doesn't dwell on. First off, she's always been a woman. For her what is new is being the director. But Carding allows she's probably not what people expect when they meet the director of the ROM—not that she looks excessively young (she's forty-eight), but it's her gender and her style. She's conscious that people are looking for continuity from past directors as well as for change.

More to the point is what her hiring says about the public's perception of the ROM. It's by no means the first museum in Canada with a woman director. But it is seen as a jewel in the crown of museums, and her choice as director has made her pleased and proud. However, although there are more women in the field even in Canada, the gender balance on her management team is not fifty-fifty. Yet.

Where she sees a substantial lag within the museum is in ethnic diversity. Toronto, by contrast, is ethnically diverse, but the ROM is not. The museum is looking at a diversity strategy for the organization as a whole right now.

Despite the lack of intentionality in her leadership journey, once Carding was tapped for the ROM job she says, "I quite self-consciously prepared for this role. I took time out to prepare for this role." Because she was moving not just to a new job but to a new environment on a different continent (from Australia to Canada), she adopted a questioning approach to understand key parts of the organization—its users, its programs, and more. She tapped into her coursework from the Getty Leadership Institute in 2005, rereading some of that material. Another big plus was having worked with an able museum director in Australia, which helped her reflect on what she might emulate at the ROM. Also, several board members in addition to colleagues in Toronto provided off-line advice. She says she tried quite consciously, with some success, not to make assumptions that just because a situation looked like one she had experienced in Australia or the United Kingdom, it was not the same.

At the beginning, she recalls an intense period of learning, resulting in a process of articulating how the organization could move forward under her leadership, subsequently resulting in a strategic plan.

When thinking about how her leadership has changed over time, Carding notes that there's a lot of positional power that comes with being a director—people defer to you and they do not always give you honest appraisals—but a director must transcend that, getting people to talk openly and honestly. At the ROM, as elsewhere, relationship building takes time.

She's still surprised that power has to be wielded with a light touch. She's also growing into the role of chief spokesperson with opinions, someone who assimilates lots of information about the museum. These are situations that must be eased into, and she is relatively comfortable with them now.

She feels it's a bit early in her tenure to judge what will endure, but she's very pleased with how the staff thinks about the audience, creating new programming for families and young adults. She encourages them to keep experimenting. They've brought in Kathy McLean, principal of Independent Exhibitions, a museum consulting firm specializing in exhibition development, design, programming, and strategic planning, to do workshops with staff on rapid prototyping and figuring out how to take risks in the right places. Strategic planning also builds capital among staff by developing honest, transparent communication that helps when all the news isn't good.

Last summer, Carding wrote about the importance of organizational change in an article for *museum geek* blog. When identifying the need for organizational change, Carding advises leaders to use all channels available—online, social, print, and broadcast—to look externally for information to bring to bear on the current situation. She suggests paying attention to trends in economics, politics, and technology (for example, how the music industry and print media have adapted to technology and user-generated preferences is one way to think about how museums can share authority with audiences), and looking for disruptive trends, too. It's critical to gain input from outside the organization, too, she says.

She also suggests setting up advisory groups and partnerships and experimenting with specific projects. Once you've gathered this information, get conversations going inside the building. Carding is a big proponent of bringing cross-disciplinary teams together to generate a variety of perspectives. A Strengths-Weaknesses-Opportunities-Threats exercise is a good tool for assessing how an organization stacks up against trends and competition. Look at short-term tactics *and* diverse longer-term strategies. Be both opportunistic and keep your eye on rapid changes. Then, she says, "The question is, 'What can we make out of it'?"

She used the example of how the ROM is becoming a resource for visitors and others to access collections online. It took internal, cross-discipline dialogue (curatorial, front of house, audience research, IT, etc.) and planning. She facilitated the conversations, encouraging realism and listening to the staff's hopes and fears. Because she's occupied so many positions within museums, she understands and is comfortable with different points of view. She'll often encourage staff to look on some new project as a work in progress. "Being in perpetual beta lowers the fear factor," she says.

When asked about aligning work, family, community, and self, Carding admits that she thinks about this a lot. She is single at the moment and has no children, which is beneficial since the ROM needed someone with stamina and commitment to work demanding hours. She's conscious that her work limits her community participation, so she tries to give back by focusing on contributing to the museum community by writing, presenting at conferences, and serving on boards.

The more work demands, the more she feels it's important to do something completely different. She sets a premium on enjoying the singular moment or activity—not multitasking, but reading a book or watching a film or just going for a drive.

Carding counts among her role models Kathy McLean for what she's done with exhibitions; Seb Chan (at the Smithsonian Cooper-Hewitt National Design Museum) for what he's doing with digital space; and Max Anderson (at the Dallas Museum of Art), who she thinks is one of the opinion formers in the field right now. "He's thrown down the gauntlet for what we should be doing," she says. She also admires Arnold Lehman (at the Brooklyn Museum), for being in the forefront of community engagement. Of course, she quickly adds, there is no one museum doing everything right. Last, but not least, on her list of role models is the actress Helen Mirren because of her incredibly flexible talent, exemplary work ethic, and her authenticity.

As she reflects on how museum leadership is changing, Carding responds, "For me, that is a question between how museums deliver on their missions and how they put together their support to meet their missions." She comments that there has been government retraction of support for museums (except for Asia), resulting in less of a public sector–public service attitude among people who work in them. She sees the pendulum swinging more toward social profit enterprises. "Museum leaders need to be more like leaders of NGOs and some educational institutions. They must be able to talk about relevance and relationship building—these are becoming more important."

Gonzalo Casals, Deputy Executive Director (COO), El Museo del Barrio, New York, New York

- Immigrant Civic Leadership Program, Coro New York, New York City Mayor's Office of Immigrant Affairs, 2011
- Museum Leadership Institute, Getty Leadership Institute, Getty Museum, 2010
- MA, Museum Studies and Art History, City College of New York, CUNY
- Believes in the power of art to ambush us, to capture our imaginations. Is a huge fan of experiential education
- Quote: "I take the lead as a result of being impatient."

Gonzalo Casals is an introvert. At least that is how he describes himself. He laughs as he explains his need for time alone, so it is difficult to know if he means it. But he swears he does, saying he can be social when he needs to be, but then he needs his own space.

Casals is the deputy executive director at El Museo del Barrio in Manhattan, where he supervises several departments. Ask him if he entered the field with any notion of leading, and he chuckles. "I didn't know anything about leadership," he says. A native Argentinian, Casals has a musical voice that rolls through a thought. He began college believing he wanted to be an architect, but by the time he finished he had moved away from buildings and more toward architectural theory and design, and it was design that brought him to museums.

In fact, he had his moment of epiphany while getting ready for an exhibit. He and the other designers were there late at night. They were behind schedule, nothing was hung, and in the middle of the room were huge crates containing some of the exhibition's artwork. As the crates were opened and a sculpture appeared, Casals remembers it as a magical experience. "I still get goose bumps thinking about it," he recalls. For him, that was one of those this-is-what-it's-all-about moments: the serendipity of art and being ambushed by the creative process. It took him by surprise, and the memory still makes him want to give others a similar experience.

His goal when he arrived in the United States and more specifically in New York City was to find a museum job. It soon became apparent that he would need a graduate degree to get the kind of job he wanted. Working as an architect by day, going to City College at night, Casals completed his coursework and went looking for a job. With twin interests in education and technology, he cast his net widely, but when friends told him about an opening at El Museo del Barrio, he resisted. "I said, 'Why? Because I'm Latino?'" he remembers. He didn't want to be pigeonholed, but he went to the interview. "The minute I got there, I saw challenges and complexities," he remembers. He was offered a job first as public programs coordinator. Two years later he was appointed as director of education and public programs. And now he is deputy executive director.

In retrospect, one of the things Casals prizes about El Museo del Barrio is its emphasis on art. He sees art as a tool for social change. "The center is for people, and art is the tool," he says. He isn't so sure that history museums operate the same way. Recently he visited a Civil War museum. "I told them they should be teaching leadership, not the Civil War," he says, adding that he thinks too often a museum's interpretive goal is in the wrong place.

Somehow in his frantic life Casals managed to cram in two leadership training opportunities, one national and one local. In 2010 he was accepted to the Getty Leadership Institute, and a year later to the Immigrant Civic Leadership Program run by Coro New York, specifically its Immigrant Civic Leadership Program. In both instances he credits the programs with giving him a network and with providing the opportunity to think about his work. Of his experience at the Getty, Casals says, "You're out of the office for three weeks with your peers and you're forced to look, to take time to reflect." Then he adds that he's a huge fan of experimental education, but that even experimental learning requires time for reflection.

Casals appreciates the art of networking. His two leadership programs taught him that. "It's how you learn," he says, adding that with a network, when you need something you pick up the phone. As a mentor himself, he says he is extremely humble, but he tries to encourage his staff to use the power of their networks.

Ask Casals about his leadership style and he responds that he is all about questions. "I give my direct reports the tools, and it's their p·oject; if they don't do it, it won't happen," he says, adding that his one-on-one meetings with staff are often a series of questions, bouncing ideas back and forth. "I ask why they are doing what they're doing and what is their thinking," Casals explains. Looking back, he says he is much more patient as a deputy director than he was when he first began his museum career. "I think before I execute," he says, "and I'm a little more grounded." He adds that his type of leadership looks at a variety of different points of view.

Mention the word *courage* and Casals laughs. "I take the lead as a result of being impatient," he responds, adding that he has no fear about making decisions. Institutionally though, he adds that El Museo is the kind of institution that thinks about what it could and will be in a decade; to Casals that is courage.

It turns out that Casals is a workaholic. "I'm an immigrant," he says, as if that explains everything, adding that his personal and professional networks are mixed. For him it is more the world and himself rather than work and personal life. And yes, it is no surprise that he's very technology conscious and very plugged in. "I am constantly checking my cell phone," he confesses.

Ask Casals about museum leadership and how it is changing, and he is puzzled. He is sure it is changing; he is just not sure how. "A lot of people are talking about it, but there aren't a lot of answers," he says. In the old days Casals says museum directors were subject experts who became directors. "Then the director was the business person with a vision," he adds. "And now I sense something is changing and it has to do with the humanization of museums. Museums have become the human center—the public living room for the community."

And how would he like to be remembered? Casals says he wants to be the person who changed existing practices in order to understand museums in another way. At El Museo, he says the organization needs to combine the qualities of community center and mini-MOMA (Museum of Modern Art in New York) at the same time. He believes "museums are morally obliged to help society make sense of the changes happening around them." But he says, at the same time, that museums need to know their own limitations. "Art is a tool to make change," he concludes.

Catherine Charlebois, Curator of Exhibition, Collection and Oral History Programs, Centre d'histoire de Montreal, Montreal, Canada

- MA, History Museum Studies, Cooperstown Graduate Program, 2000
- Knows firsthand the power that personal stories and images can have on audiences and institutions
- Quote: Said the tortoise in the movie *Kung Fu Panda*: "Yesterday is history, tomorrow is a mystery, but today is a gift. That is why it is called the 'present.'"

Catherine Charlebois grew up in a very old house with very old objects. Her first memory of a museum visit was going to see a Picasso exhibition at the Montreal Museum of Fine Arts as a child. But she didn't know until she was nineteen or twenty years old that she could actually work in museums. She was on a track to be an architect, but doing the technical stuff was not what she wanted. Her first love was history and geography, yet she didn't want to be a classroom teacher. Her father told her to do what she loved because it would have a domino effect on everything else in life—"it will fall magically into place" are the words she says her father used. And sure enough, that's what happened.

Charlebois is not only philosophic and grateful when describing her career path and where it led her, she is downright joyful. When she understood she could get a history degree and pursue museum studies, she proclaims, "It was like an alleluia—this is what I have to do in life!" A native Quebecois, she wanted to take her graduate studies somewhere that afforded her an immersion in English. In her search for options, she stumbled on a book that recommended the Cooperstown Graduate Program (CGP), so she researched it on the web. At the time, she was into material culture, and she wanted to be a curator. She thought CGP would be a good fit.

She took a lot of American history courses hoping to get a job in the United States and immigrate, but even though she worked for a brief time at an upstate New York museum, she returned to Montreal when she married. While working at the McCord Museum (where she volunteered before graduate school), Charlebois fell in love with education and the possibilities of teaching history to the general public. Since 2009, she's been with the Centre d'histoire de Montreal, where she's amassed an impressive amount of managerial and programmatic experience.

Now in her late thirties, her career goal is to be a museum director. "It would feel right to me," she says. She believes she can do it, but she thinks she may need more experience. She might not take a directorship now even if it were offered because she thinks her natural exuberance needs tempering. She's discovered that it's important not to skip steps but to take the time to build good reflexes. She even entertains the notion that she would like to be the director of the Centre d'histoire someday. "But I'm having too much fun right now," she says, "And my toolbox is not complete yet."

She fell in love with her current museum long before she ever worked there and speaks of it with care and pride. Her position is a tremendous boost for her next career step, whatever that might be, because the institution is in an intense period of redefining, rebuilding, and repositioning itself, with Charlebois in the thick of it. Thirty years old, the Centre is executing a plan to take it to the next level, shedding a long-standing inferiority complex and finding its niche. "The museum is a good one and deserves this growth—this place in the sun," Charlebois says.

As a result of this institutional transformation, Charlebois's responsibilities expanded. She is in many ways the de facto deputy director, allowing her boss to focus on the overall transformative game plan, which means she's building experience in exhibition and curatorial practices, as well as financial management. She also manages a big staff in addition to volunteers. She believes her actions have more impact because she's influencing the future of her organization. "I'm at the crossroad in the history of the institution," she says. "I feel I'm making a difference, and that's a good feeling."

Her director helps her to expand her skills, but she says he's learning, too. Since the institution is going through this period of reinvention, everyone is learning new things. "He trusts my instincts," she says. "He gives me big projects, and he gives me the space to make my mark." As a result, she has undertaken a lot and amazed herself in the process. Her first exhibition broke new ground for the museum and garnered public praise and professional recognition. Called "Lost Neighbourhoods," it used photography and was based almost entirely on oral history. Charlebois had no institutional model to follow for the project, so she relied on her previous knowledge to invent a new methodology for it. "I have that in my backpack," she proudly states.

"All experience is good, even the ones you suffer through," she concludes. "You have to be creative when things don't go well—they test you." When she makes a decision, she says she doesn't have regrets; she lives with her decisions and accepts the consequences. Knowing she has to be true to herself, she makes decisions with all that she knows at that moment. "Since *I* made the decision, why would it be a bad choice?" she asks. With that attitude, it's unlikely there's much of anything that will prevent her from achieving her professional and personal goals.

Charlebois also has a brief stint of board service under her belt. With hindsight, she now understands it gave her an important life lesson: "I learned that when you have one person that gives an organization its personality, such as a founder or strong director, it does not work—it's not a good situation, because when that person leaves, the organization can collapse, and when that person is around, he/she can dominate in good and bad ways."

After some thought she says that her father is one of her chief role models because he always treated her as an equal—listened to her opinions, gave her confidence, and taught her that her ideas were pretty good, and that she had good reflections and reflexes. "He would be impressed with my thoughts," she recalls. "He thought I had a lot of wisdom." When asked whom in the field would she most like to meet, Charlebois quickly responds, "Lynn Dierking and Nina Simon—wow!"

At this stage of life and career, Charlebois feels she doesn't have to juggle work, family, community, and self, although she thinks that's partly due to the fact that she and her husband don't have children. Aligning her schedule with her husband's takes effort, but it is not overwhelming.

Networking is something Charlebois doesn't feel she does enough of, but she feels it hasn't prevented her from advancing her career. She leads a fairly unplugged personal life, although she knows that when she becomes a director, she will have to do more of it to be more in touch with stakeholders and politicians. She also expects that as her current responsibilities continue to expand, her director may want her to get out more, but she concedes she'll need his help to do that and to make introductions for her.

True to form, Charlebois offers the following simple pieces of advice to up-and-coming leaders: Do what you love (she hopes she'll actually have the chance to say that to somebody someday and that it will have an impact), truly believe in yourself and what you can do, be true to yourself—"you're the only guardian of your personal integrity," have fun, and enjoy the present moment. She quotes a line from the tortoise in the movie *Kung Fu Panda*: "Yesterday is history, tomorrow is a mystery, but today is a gift. That is why it is called the 'present.'"

"I feel so lucky in my life. I'm at the right place at the right time."

Melissa Chiu, Museum Director and Vice President for Global Art Programs, Asia Society, New York, New York

- MA, Arts Administration, College of Fine Arts, University of New South Wales, 1994
- PhD, Art History, University of Western Sydney, 2005
- Believes in the power of relationships
- Quote: "The best prompts come from a negative place."

Melissa Chiu's voice has long vowels of her native Australia. She ponders questions and could never be accused of rambling. The result is an amalgam of precision laced with a dose of Australian pop culture. Dr. Chiu is museum director and vice president for Global Art Programs at the Asia Society, a position she's held since 2001. Prior to that she was the founding director of the Asia-Australia Arts Centre in Sydney, Australia, so she knows a thing or two about leadership.

Leadership wasn't at the top of her to-do list when she left college, however. "I wouldn't necessarily say that I was intent on leading an institution," Chiu says, "but I wanted to work with artists." Frustrated by the lack of opportunities for young curators in Australia at the time, Chiu saw herself slipping into a mix of multiple-arts-related jobs, but no career. "It was really unhappiness that prompted me," she remembers about founding the Asia-Australia Arts Centre, adding, "The best prompts are those that come from a negative place." Coincidentally, the organization's founding came at a moment when Australia was primed for trade with Asia, allowing Chiu and her fledgling institution to ride a wave of economic development.

"I'm fairly philosophical about the way your life goes," Chiu says about the beginnings of her professional life. Reflecting on her early career, she says, "On some level I would have loved to work in museums and even better in New York City, but it was a dream more than a goal."

In addition to being a founding director, Chiu also managed to earn both an MA in arts administration and a PhD in Art History. She is open about the fact that Australia's support for her while she was in graduate school made the entire process if not easy, at least debt free. Given how far ahead of the curve she was, it is no surprise that she is a leading authority on Asian contemporary art, having organized more than two dozen exhibitions of artists from across the Pacific rim. She gave the first retrospective exhibition of Chinese artist Zhang Huan and a historical exhibit of art from China's Cultural Revolution.

Given Chiu's depth of exhibition planning experience, when she is asked about a workplace success, it is not a surprise that what comes to mind is an exhibit. A loan exhibit, to be precise. What made it problematic was that it was coming from Pakistan. The exhibit, "The Buddhist Heritage of Pakistan: Art of Gandhara," contained many objects that had never been seen outside of Pakistan. Chiu's negotiations played out against a background of the murder of Osama bin Laden and news reports about American CIA contractor Raymond Davies, accused of murdering Pakistani civilians. With exhibition press releases out and the exhibit furniture built, negotiations broke down. It was Chiu who waded in to broker a new agreement with the Pakistani arts ministry. "We never knew whether we would get the show until the planes took off," she says, explaining that there had been no major exhibit of Pakistani art in the United States in forty years. "With this type of exhibit, it's too late for Plan B," she concludes.

Asked about her leadership philosophy, Chiu confesses, "I feel awkward about leadership as a concept." She adds, though, that for her, leadership is about relationships. "If you create sound relationships then positive things will happen." In addition to the relationships created at or through work, she has built relationships through serving on boards. Currently she serves on the boards of the Museum Association of New York and the Association of Art Museum Directors and feels that board membership has taught her a lot. "You get a strong sense of the lay of the land," she muses. "New York City has a different ecology, and we [Asia Society] have a niche audience, and with that niche role we can explore areas others aren't inclined to or can't." Her networking helps her to forecast trends and establish where the museum fits in the landscape. She describes the museum side of Asia Society as very mission driven, saying she and her staff spend most of their time on ideas.

Chiu acknowledges that the issue of balance—work and personal life—is a concern. "It is one of the hardest things in the realm of the art world—the public and private life, because they are often one and the same." She suggests that if the modus operandi is about building relationships, it is often difficult to separate her role as museum director from private citizen with a passionate interest in contemporary Asian art. And if you add children to that mix, it can reach a tipping point very quickly. "I actually thought I would go back to work a week after having my baby," Chiu says, laughing. Needless to say she did not. She suggests that for her, and perhaps for others, it becomes a question not of balance, but of time management. "I would be surprised if anyone [who has children] said it was easy or not foremost in their minds," she says.

Perhaps it's the work/life/balance thread that leads Chiu to think about her sister, and to confess that if she had to pick an individual she admires the most, it is Elisabeth, her twin. Why? The answer is simple. "She gave up a successful career to raise her two children."

Chiu believes the museum field is undergoing a sea change, although perhaps not quickly enough. "There is a shifting of the guard," she says, "from the baby boomers to Generation Y." But it isn't just a generational shift that Chiu has noticed. It is one of gender as well. "In the last five years a number of senior curators have retired or resigned, and most of their replacements have been women." That sounds like it might be a good thing, but Chiu is alert to life's nuances and suggests something counterintuitive: "You have kind of a sense that job value is diminished." While she applauds women in positions of leadership in the museum field, she acknowledges that men still head the top ten American institutions. In other words, she says, "While there has been a great shift in numbers, the larger museums are still thought of as positions for men."

Chiu is unequivocal about courage as a necessary ingredient for leadership. For her it's a must-have. "Great leadership requires courage," she says simply. "Leadership requires you to do things that go counter to what others say you should be doing." And, she adds, underscoring her faith in relationship building, you can't do it on your own.

Ilene Frank, Director, Rensselaer County Historical Society, Troy, New York

- MA, History Museum Studies, SUNY Oneonta, Cooperstown Graduate Program
- Sees herself as evolving and loves the "aha!" moments that come with self-discovery
- Quote: "To me, I'm not here to stand on top or have it all be about me. We're here to work on a common purpose."

Ilene Frank has been going to museums all her life. Currently the director of the Rensselaer County Historical Society (RCHS) in Troy, New York, Frank is a long way from her childhood home in the Washington, D.C., suburbs where trips to the Smithsonian happened frequently enough that she felt a sort of little-girl ownership over parts of the museum's vast collections.

The daughter of a school principal, Frank assumed she might teach. She majored in history in college, only to discover that combining history with an elementary education major as an undergraduate wasn't possible. "I kind of fell back into museums," she explains. Her first job was at Historic St. Mary's City, home of Maryland's first capital and a living history site, where her director was Candace Matelic. Frank credits Matelic with helping her realize museums could be a career. "She told me they combine all the things I love," Frank recalls. "She wrapped it all up in a box and said 'See, here's a great present.'"

Frank says she knew she wanted to be a leader from the moment she went to graduate school. "Leadership was something that interested me," she explains. She credits her mother, the school principal, as the person who paved the way for Frank's own career. "She became a principal when I was eight," she remembers, "and seeing her run a school was really formative." She adds that her initial idea of what leadership looked like—women's roles, working with a team, and being a facilitator—were shaped by watching her mother.

Ask Frank about a workplace success and she tells a story about her tenure at the Schenectady Museum and Suits-Bueche Planetarium in Schenectady, New York, where she served as director of education from 2005 to 2010. "In my interview," she begins, "I was told that the education department was the most dysfunctional department at the museum." She pauses for a moment before adding, "And I still took the job."

Everything Frank's interviewer said turned out to be true. Her department felt disrespected and disconnected. "They were fearful I'd swing the axe and clear them out," she says. But since this is a success story, it has a happy ending. "Within two years," Frank explains, "they were integrated and grounded and felt like a team." It wasn't simply a matter of positive reinforcement, although that helped. "We grew together; I didn't just say 'You guys are great.'"

Frank is self-aware enough to recognize strengths can also be weaknesses depending on the circumstances, and before she finishes her story she adds that it has a darker side. "The institution was really messy politically, internally and externally, but we [the education department] had become so strong as a team that people took everything too personally," Frank says. She feels culpable in that, saying that she wasn't always as clear minded as she could have been. She riffs briefly on what she now realizes is a necessary distance that a leader must maintain. "Sometimes you can't be a friend, you have to make decisions to save the organization," she says. Speaking about RCHS, her current museum, she says, "We are a family; we support one another and there are never enough resources, but we sometimes forget it is still a business." Frank speaks about how important language is when talking about work. She is not a fan of people who talk about "my collection" or "my exhibit." "Your position is not you," she concludes, adding that she loves the idea of saying *we serve* our museum. "How healthy that is," she says.

It's not a surprise that Frank has a workplace mantra, although she's no longer sure where she got it. It's one of many quotes that surround her desk. "I'll read it to you," she says. "Leadership is not a job or a position, but a way of influencing others towards ends recognized as valuable and fulfilling." It's a line from Amanda Sinclair's *Leadership for the Disillusioned* that Frank took from an article she liked about how everyone should be a leader regardless of their position. "To me, I'm not here to stand on top or have it all be about me. We're here to work on a common purpose." For Frank, staff and director must share a common understanding and communication; that helps them meet goals, assessments, and to keep budgets under control. "I also believe people should enjoy work," she says. "There should be time for fun, and we should remember to applaud ourselves when things go well."

Like many leaders in this book, Frank responds in the affirmative when asked if she is a different leader now than when she began. "Oh, my goodness, yes," she says. "I am always evolving; I love the 'aha' moment of discovery." She thinks too many people find themselves in the rut of believing they are done and they are perfect. "As I age and learn more about myself, I'm not as brash. I'm more tolerant," she explains, adding that she doesn't know if she'll be the same in another decade. Here she references a leadership program sponsored by her local Chamber of Commerce that she took in her first six months at RCHS. Calling it an MBA lite, Frank says the course cost $1,800, paid for in part by a scholarship and in part by a board member. Early in the course, she and her fellow participants took the Myers-Briggs personality test. As always, Frank tested as an introvert. "I've never understood that," she says. "I like people." But her instructor explained it this way: Extroverts begin the day with an empty purse. They spend all day putting coins in their change purse. Introverts begin the day with a set number of coins. They give them away all day, and when they are done, they're done. That was an "aha" moment for Frank, who said she has often felt guilty about her need for alone time. But no more. "Those moments of quirkiness— they are something you can build on—they can be a strength," she says.

Ask Frank who her heroes are and she names Joan of Arc. "I know, it's kind of funny for a nice Jewish girl," she quips. "I'm intrigued by those who live lives by values and belief systems," she adds, and then she deadpans, "plus she's a woman in armor and a sword."

Frank says she works on work/life balance every single day, saying she could easily find herself at work six or seven days a week. As a result she plans ahead to have one weekend free each month and two nights open each week. "You have to plan for balance," Frank says. She is also a person of faith, and that coupled with family always comes first. No surprise, though, Frank is a big networker. "There are two things it does," she says. "It keeps you in touch with colleagues, and you never know where a contact will lead." Frank says her network makes her laugh and keeps her grounded. She also sees her network as a series of relationships that may blossom into something benefitting either her or RCHS. "It has to connect naturally though; it doesn't work if it's forced," she adds.

Frank is certain she's living through an interesting time in the history museum field. Although she has witnessed the beginning of succession as baby boomers begin to retire, she believes her generation isn't that interested in leading. "My class [at Cooperstown] had sixteen people," she says. While many are in senior positions, she believes she may be the only executive director, and yet she remembers Gretchen Sorin, Cooperstown's director, telling her class that they were tomorrow's leaders. At the time, they were all enthusiastic. Today, however, many of her classmates say they never want to be directors, certainly not at small history museums. While she can't speak for all of them, she suggested part of the answer might lie in not wanting to deal with the huge financial issues plaguing many directors.

Apart from her mother and Joan of Arc, there is no single individual who serves as Frank's role model. "I see snippets in people, and say that's what I want to do or be," she says. Frank admires those who are successful, but also authentic, who don't sacrifice relationships for the sake of work. She also respects individuals who stand up for their beliefs and who are confident enough to take on something larger than themselves. And if that's a little reminiscent of the Maid of Orleans, maybe all Frank needs is armor and a sword.

Timothy Grove, Chief of Education, National Mall Building, Smithsonian National Museum of Air & Space, Washington, D.C.

- MA, Applied History, George Mason University
- Understands that you can learn by observing even when the person you are learning from isn't perfect
- Quote: "More success breeds confidence, which makes you want to take on a challenge."

Tim Grove has a resume many museum graduate students might envy. Currently curator of education for the National Museum of Air & Space, Grove has spent most of his career with the Smithsonian, with the exception of a three-year stint at the Missouri Historical Society.

Grove's career path is all the more remarkable because he didn't plan it. A journalism major, Grove found himself in a career counseling office toward the end of college. "I'd had a passion for history from early on, but the area of public history escaped me," he remembers. "And there were all these cool jobs!" Eventually he attended George Mason University with a major in Applied History, serving his graduate internship in Colonial Williamsburg's Department of Interpretive Development. "I kind of fell into education." Describing himself as a natural educator who needs people contact, Grove says, "I didn't know museums had education offices."

Grove is almost an accidental leader. "I didn't plan my career," he says. "I took jobs that would make me more marketable for the next position." If he has a mantra it might be: When a job ceases to be a challenge, it's time to move on. He does attribute at least some of his leadership skills to lessons learned in graduate school, particularly critical-thinking skills, the ability to process information, and knowledge of the research process. What he terms "the people part," the myriad issues of personnel and staff management required of anyone in a leadership position, Grove says he learned in part during his internship and in part by observing good and bad managers along the way. "They taught me a lot about managing," he says, emphasizing that there is just as much to learn from a bad manager as a good one.

"I didn't consider myself a leader at the beginning of my career," Grove says, although given that his first real museum job found him managing exhibits with a single co-worker and a troop of sixty docents, he was certainly in a leadership position from the very beginning. And he did well. "More success breeds confidence, which makes you want to take on a challenge," he says. He is currently participating in a leadership class offered internally to Smithsonian staff, something he was both interested in and encouraged to apply for. The class requires participants to have a mentor—Groves's is James Gardner, recently appointed executive for legislative archives, Presidential Libraries and Museum Services at the National Archives and Records Administration—and to meet for two to three days each month. Grove finds the class challenging, but he acknowledges that an institution as large as the Smithsonian can provide opportunities not available at smaller, independently run museums.

Sometimes, however, the Smithsonian's size is a negative. Grove recognized this early on when he created the Smithsonian Grass Roots Educator's Exchange. Drawing educators from the nineteen Smithsonian museums, the Exchange provides a framework for individuals in similar positions but different museums in order to exchange ideas. Grove has stepped back from his founder's role now, but the group continues to meet. In fact, it's spawned similar exchanges for Smithsonian exhibit developers and for docents. "I'm proud of it," Grove explains. "It's not a novel idea, but the fact that it is still going means it meets a need."

Grove credits his three-year stint outside the Smithsonian as a career energizer. At the time he felt his career track had plateaued, but a colleague had told him that if he ever had the opportunity to work on a national bicentennial project to grab it. So when the educational director position for the *Lewis & Clark: The National Bicentennial Exhibition* came up, Grove applied and got it. Although it meant leaving a very secure position, there's no doubt Grove made the right choice. You can hear the enthusiasm when he describes his work as a member of a five-person team responsible for amassing, exhibiting, and interpreting all manner of objects, paintings, and documents associated with Meriwether Lewis and William Clark's 4,600-mile journey. "It was an amazing collection from more than fifty institutions," Grove says, "and they will never be together again." Grove describes the experience of moving from a gigantic organization to participate as one of five as wonderfully freeing, one where he was able to put all his knowledge and skills together. Ultimately, the exhibit lives on at lewisandclark.org, where students, teachers, and the general public can access it. "I'm very proud of that," Grove says. "It's quite a process to get an organization that's more regional in nature [the Missouri Historical Society] to think intentionally."

Ask about work/life balance, and Grove almost laughs. "I live in an area where people are workaholics," he explains. He is very aware that a job can swallow one's life, and he always has been. He says he has colleagues who work too much, but for the moment he has got it under control, devoting free time to travel and various outdoor pursuits such as hiking, biking, and white-water rafting.

Looking back from somewhere near his career midpoint, Grove is clear that working at the Smithsonian is working in the bubble. And not just the bubble of Washington's bureaucracy. "It's its own country," he says, with its own procedures and processes, but he adds that the flip side of the insularity of a large government institution is the feeling that programs and exhibitions are constantly under the microscope. That results, Grove says, in a risk-averse staff who hesitate to experiment. "*The Enola Gay*," he says, "still resonates," referencing the 1995 Smithsonian exhibit that caused such a controversy by exhibiting the fuselage of the plane used in the Hiroshima bombing.

Asked who in the field he admires, Grove hesitates, before coming up not with names but characteristics he treasures. Top on his list was the ability to think outside the box and push boundaries. "I admire creativity," he says. "Creative and innovative people inspire others."

Here he referenced Colonial Williamsburg. "Their leadership allowed the re-enactment of an eighteenth-century slave sale in order to teach the horrors of slavery," he explains. "It showed great courage and drew international attention."

"A strong leader has to have vision," Grove says, adding that he's seen organizations falter when a leader doesn't have vision. Last, he believes integrity is crucial. "Without it there's no respect or trust; a leader must be honest and transparent."

"I know where things are," Grove says, describing the uncontrolled chaos of his desk. He considers himself tech savvy: he blogs, uses a smart phone, but confesses Twitter is something he does not understand. The longtime author of the American Association of State and Local History's (AASLH) *History News* column "History Bytes," Grove continues to grapple with museums and technology. A veteran of the annual Museums and the Web conference, Grove says it always bothers him that history museums are consistently underrepresented among conference participants. "I have a passion for history, but I also want people to think critically about technology," Grove says. As he noted in a 2012 "History Bytes" column: "Don't feel alone when making any decisions about technology because we're all in the raft together. Learn from others, ask questions, and by all means hold onto your paddle."

Jennifer S. Kilmer, Director, Washington State Historical Society, Tacoma, Washington

- MA, Politics, University of Oxford, Oxford, England

- Believes what goes around, comes around, and that having visitors interact with unique objects may supersede interactive technology someday soon. Says that where she drank the Kool-Aid was in believing in the importance of learning through interaction.
- Quote: "Every year I am almost a different leader. Audiences are changing so fast, I can't afford to get stuck as an administrator."

Jennifer Kilmer believes in the "aha" moment. In her short tenure in the museum world—she is currently director of the Washington State Historical Society in Tacoma—seeing visitors experience history firsthand is what gets her up in the morning. "I've always had a passion for community or local history," Kilmer says. She's been in her current position since 2011, managing a thirty-five-person staff, the flagship state history museum, along with the State Capital Museum in Olympia and the State Research Center.

Kilmer's learning curve has been steep and fast. A decade ago she was a grants manager at the Paul G. Allen Foundation in Seattle, a family foundation with more than a billion dollars in assets. Now she heads the state's largest history organization. For Kilmer, the four years of foundation work offered a window into what makes successful nonprofits tick. "It was probably a better training ground than graduate school," she explains, adding that her experience and interaction was almost entirely with the Foundation's cultural applicants. Asked if she felt the Foundation funded leaders or organizations, she replied that it was a mixture. "It was obvious some were funded because of their leadership. Even if a project was risky, an organization with strong leadership was more likely to be funded than one with unknown leadership." Kilmer thinks there is another factor though: money. "To be honest," she says, "it was more about financial capacity." She pauses before adding, "Whatever you do, better manage your money or you are going to fail."

Kilmer left the Allen Foundation in 2003 to become executive director of the Harbor History Museum in Gig Harbor, Washington. Describing it as a fledgling organization that was ready to take a big step, the position offered Kilmer a shorter commute and a chance to try out what she had learned about nonprofit governance at the Allen Foundation. The first thing she focused on was financial capacity. There really wasn't any. "The board had never asked for a gift," Kilmer says, adding that 65 percent of the organization's budget came from a single donor. She and the board cut their teeth with a membership drive. "That gave the board the opportunity to tell the organization's story and build membership." They were quick learners. About $11 million later, they built a new museum.

Kilmer was clear from the moment Harbor History Museum hired her that apart from her personal passion for community history, she was not a "museum person." "I look at myself as an administrator, a fund-raiser, a human resources person," she says. She does admit that when she began there were more than a few things that were peculiar to museums, including a language and a culture about audience, programming, collections, and exhibits that she had to master. "I rely on curators and staff to provide me with guidance," she says. But she didn't need a museum studies degree to understand what was happening opening day in Harbor History Museum's one-room schoolhouse packed with children and parents trying to master the skills of a late-nine-teenth-century education. "They were learning, but not knowing they were learning," Kilmer remembers. She says it still gives her goose bumps.

It's no surprise that when Kilmer is asked to describe a professional success, she references Harbor History's hugely successful capital campaign. What she remembers, however, is what a colleague said to her the day the waterfront building was complete. "She said, 'You only get to do this once in your career. Be proud, but realize it's unique.'" If she has a regret, Kilmer says, "There is one thing I've had to learn across time, you have to work effectively with the board." She reflects that it took a while for her to under-stand the give and take that comes with director/board relations. "You're educating them about how the museum works, but you're also seeking their support," she says. For Kilmer, part of the process was learning when to stop talking and listen. "I needed," she recalls, "to shut up and try to learn." She concludes by saying she is now at a point where she recognizes the board is there for her and that they all want to make the museum a better place.

Although Kilmer professes not to have a work mantra, saying she is still figuring the museum world out, she realizes she does have one: *It is what it is.* "It's so easy to get bent out of shape, getting wrapped up in how some-thing happened," she explains. She says that sometimes people spin in place, asking variations of the same question, when what they really need to do is move on. She does say that she is not the same director she was ten years ago. "I hope I am [different] because I was completely green and inexperi-enced," she says, laughing. She describes the process of learning leadership as transformative, and says, "Every year I am almost a different leader. Audiences are changing so fast, I can't afford to get stuck as an administra-tor."

Kilmer says she learned a great deal from her parents, who are both behavioral analysts. "I admire the way they have maintained their curiosity across their professional lives," she says. She also is grateful for the fact that they modeled lives that were about helping others, something she tries to emulate through her work at Harbor History and now the State Historical Society. Kilmer says she also learned a great deal from her former boss at the Paul G. Allen Foundation, Susan Coliton. "I could present something to her and within ten seconds she would zero in on what was important and what needed to be changed," she says. "She taught me about processing information and getting to the point." While Kilmer has mentors, including Coliton, she does not see herself as a mentor. At least not yet. "I don't know if I'll ever get to that point," she says. However, she is quick to add that as director of the State Historical Society, the Society itself is an institutional mentor for a number of smaller organizations in the state, interactions that she enjoys.

Kilmer may be a young director who has climbed a steep learning curve, but she sounds as though she has the work/life balance conundrum licked. "I don't worry about it from home," she says about the Historical Society. That's something she feels is particularly important for her daughters, ages seven and three. Kilmer says that when she is home, she focuses on her children and checks her email infrequently. "When I leave work, I leave," she says, adding that she's told her staff, "We have to be good stewards, but we're not an emergency room."

And what does Kilmer think about the future of her adopted field? "I think we're having to fight harder and harder to get people to understand our value," she says. "The day when it was a given that museums were important is over." She compares the issues museums struggle with to those of libraries, saying there was a time when you went to the library to do research, now you go to Wikipedia. "Museums are exactly the same," she says. "You can go online and you can have an equal if not a similar experience [to being in a museum]. So we have to be better at what we do." She concludes by suggesting that it isn't enough for a museum to do what it has always done. "[It's like] we're serving a meal," she says. "You can't just say 'It's good for you.' You have to stop and think and understand how what you're doing impacts life to make sure visitors come."

Nathan Richie, Director, Golden History Museums, Golden, Colorado

- MA, Museum Studies, John F. Kennedy University
- Chairs the AAM Standing Professional Committee on Education
- Quote: "A sense of self-awareness is critical."

Nathan Richie's been around. He's been a curator of collections and programs in an Indiana art museum, a director of exhibits and programs at a Chicago museum dedicated to the First Amendment, and a program assistant in a West Coast arts organization that presents work by visual artists suffering from life-threatening illnesses. He finally returned home to Colorado to become director of the Golden History Museums, a move he believes was instinctual, because he likes small institutions—lots of variety, never boring—and because he thought it would help build his experience base, making him more well-rounded and marketable. It's been a good fit.

Based on his career trajectory, taking on a directorship seemed like a natural progression. His previous positions honed his managerial, human resources, and budgeting skills. Graduate school provided him with the theoretical underpinnings for what museums mean. And he keeps involved with issues in the field through his chairmanship of the American Alliance of Museums' Standing Professional Committee on Education (EdCom).

Having spent years thinking EdCom was the coolest of committees, he can hardly believe he chairs it today. Now that he is a museum director, he feels he's able to bring a different perspective to the education discussion. And given the loneliness at the top, something Richie wasn't prepared for, the committee provides a key network of colleagues, friends, and mentors.

"I have a great admiration for the work of an organization's leader," he says. "I understand the roles and complexity of it. I'm also fascinated by it." He understands leaders have to make difficult decisions to stay the course, measuring results before recalibrating. In fact, he's putting that very methodology to work every day, particularly when it comes to strategic planning.

Having a vision for an institution is also critical to leadership. Richie's own vision for the Golden History Museums is an evolving one, but some areas have solidified. He operates from three guiding principles: don't dwell in the past; history must inform the present; and make connections to community now. He says, "Everyone knows when historic moments happen, but we don't always take the time to document them. However, these historic moments are opportunities to do something awesome. We can do things the way we always have or take the chance to set ourselves apart. Ask yourself, 'Why is it relevant; what can we learn?'"

"Golden is a unique destination for families on the western side of Denver," he continues. "I want our historic house museum to be a model for kid's interaction at a historic site, not a velvet ropes tour. It's not always about the objects."

With just a few years under his belt as a director, Richie thinks he's a different leader now than when he began. For one thing, his responsibilities have grown. He's mindful of the fact that his voice carries "outsized" weight because of his position. "I know when to be the bull in the china shop," he says. "I know when things need a decision."

This sense of self-awareness is critical, Richie feels, and to remind him of what he needs to be successful in his work, he keeps a sticky note nearby that reads "clear, direct and confident." "It gives me affirmation," he explains. When asked what he considers to be the elements of his leadership style, he quickly ticks off the following characteristics:

• Would like to be a mentor

- Hopes to be clear, direct, and confident
- Tries to be flexible
- Embraces experimentation; doesn't punish failure
- Plans, goals, and evaluation are in place with direct reports

Richie winces when asked about handling the work/life balance. "The 'total leader' is superman—he/she doesn't really exist," he says dismissively. Despite the fact that he and his wife have a young child and share a car, he admits he sees his staff more than his family sometimes. He's fortunate to have flexibility in his work. "There is something to be said for making the other things in life an obligation," he says, but he admits that maintaining a balance may help him decide where he wants to take the "leadership thing."

When he reflects on how museum leadership is changing, he muses, "There are museums that continually face an identity crisis. Ten or fewer years ago, the trend for institutions was to hire business leaders for directors: that hasn't worked out so well for many of them, but there are more people like myself who want to be change agents and have the skill sets to do so." But he admits he hasn't seen much leadership succession take place yet.

"How I learned what I know I got from observation, trial, error, consultation, gut instinct, improvisation, action, and recalibration," he says. His advice to the next generation of museum leaders: "Diversify your skill set; be a sponge out there."

Rebecca M. Slaughter, Director, Branigan Cultural Center, Las Cruces, New Mexico

- MA, Cooperstown Graduate Program, 2005
- Seminar for Historic Administration, AASLH, 2009
- Believes in the importance of mentors (including family) and networking
- Quote: "Sometimes it's not the program that is wrong, but the way we got there."

Rebecca Slaughter describes life in southern New Mexico as life in the land of mañana. But she does not say it unkindly. "It makes life interesting," she adds with a laugh. A graduate of the Cooperstown Graduate Program in Museum Studies, Slaughter is the director of the Branigan Cultural Center in Las Cruces. She moved west to become assistant director of the Branigan's sister museum, the Las Cruces Railroad Museum (both are city-owned operations) in 2006. She served briefly as its director before assuming the leadership position at the Branigan.

Slaughter says she had no plans to be a museum leader. Ever. "I attended the Seminar for Historic Administration in 2009 and I *still* didn't know," she says, adding that while she is not objecting, she honestly believed her route to a directorship might take a little longer. If you wanted the perfect story of how a young professional found the museum field, you don't need to look any further than Rebecca Slaughter. She started working as a museum volunteer in her hometown between a job teaching overseas and the rest of her life. Docent training led to volunteering in various departments, and eventually to being asked to catalog some 1,200 objects in the museum's vault. "It was two months of really cool stuff," Slaughter remembers. Then the museum's receptionist left, and Slaughter was offered the job. Before she knew it, the grant writer left, and she was asked if she wanted that job, too. This unexpected beginning that sent her from curatorial to development in a few short months was also a tantalizing training ground, giving her experience in a variety of departments in an organization that did a little bit of everything. When Slaughter finally decided on graduate school, she chose Cooperstown for the general nature of its programs. "We did have a leadership class [there]," she says, "but it wasn't what I expected it to be. It focused more on personality." Later when Slaughter found herself actually working in a development office, there were moments when she wished her graduate program had focused a little more on the business aspects of running a nonprofit. "You can't come up with fuzzy little numbers and hope it works out," she quips.

At the Branigan, Slaughter does not have a board of trustees. Because it is a city organization, the city council functions as the board. "I knew I needed board experience," she says, "so I joined several local boards." She currently serves on the board of the San Cruces symphony along with the boards of Habitat for Humanity and the Dona Ana County Historical Society. She's found that not only does this experience give her cross-community connections but also it provided a crash course in reading profit/loss statements.

Slaughter came to New Mexico from Connecticut, where she was the curator at the Mattatuck Museum in Waterbury, another general museum, for a little over a year. It's her experience there that Slaughter references when asked about a workplace success or failure. She describes how in her excitement over being offered a real job she failed to ask some important questions. When she arrived, she discovered her position as curator also included being curator of exhibitions, registrar, and a technology person. In retrospect, Slaughter says, "I can't say I was young and dumb, but if I hadn't been so excited about taking a job, I might have asked some more pointed questions." Other than that, she has no regrets. "I left the job having accomplished a lot," she says. She adds, however, that it did take two people to replace her once she moved on.

Ask Slaughter about a workplace success and she immediately speaks about her work at the Branigan Cultural Center in Las Cruces. For the first time in her museum career Slaughter is not in a general museum. The Branigan is hybrid, part cultural center with strong ties to the local arts community and part history museum. One of her charges when she took the directorship was to professionalize and legitimize the exhibit proposal procedure and to build public programming, which during her brief tenure has grown from twelve annual programs to over thirty. She describes the Branigan's former exhibition process as random, a sort of my-daddy-has-a-barn-let's-put-on-a-play approach. She suffered a few slings and arrows in the local paper when her more formal approach to community-based exhibitions took effect, but she says she did not react. Now, two years later, the community is supportive. "I firmly believe that you can still be professional with amateur art," Slaughter says.

Despite her ambivalence over whether she wanted to lead, Slaughter knows she is a different sort of leader today than she was five years ago. "I think about things more," she says. "I stop." She describes a more self-aware leader as one who questions how things happen. "Was it the process, was it me, was it the timing?" she asks rhetorically. Recently she had an event planned for one hundred people maximum mushroom to a crowd of three thousand. And she let it, but she acknowledges her old self might not have, insisting that a one-hundred-person event was a one-hundred-person event rather than staying on top of a process as it unfolds. That ability to keep her distance meshes well with Slaughter's work mantra. Asked to explain, she hesitates. "I don't know. Can I say this?" she asks. With encouragement she says, "Shit happens." Then she goes on to add that people are human. "I don't ask people to do things I won't do unless it's welding," she quips. "But I do let staff make their own mistakes." Slaughter says she supports her staff, giving them space to grow and follow their passions, acknowledging that sometimes people fail. "Sometimes it's not the program that is wrong, but the way we got there."

Ask Slaughter whom she admires and the answer comes quickly: her mother. "She's never gone back on what she believes," Slaughter says, describing a single parent with three children, collecting welfare, who managed to put herself through college and graduate school. "She fed us real food and took us to every free educational opportunity," Slaughter remembers. "She did what she had to do. I'm not sure I could do it. She's a cool lady."

Slaughter has her own mentors, a group that includes her mother and consultant John Durel, someone she says she admires for his ability to listen and to think outside the box. She also has two large networking pools that she taps into frequently, her graduate school network and the Seminar in Historical Administration alumni. "Even trustee work here in Las Cruces makes connections," she adds.

Slaughter describes herself as moderately plugged in. She has an iPhone, uses Facebook, and while she is on Twitter, she doesn't tweet. "I know more about Richard III's skull than the Super Bowl," she jokes about two events from the week's news. From technology, the conversation shifts to changes in museum leadership. "We're definitely seeing the end of the director keeping a job for forty years," Slaughter says. But she explains that she believes it's not only because people are more mobile, they are more mobile mentally. While she sees the field changing, she acknowledges that there are many who still want to keep the status quo. "I am on the edge of that," she says. "We're still trying to figure that out and yet we're in a constant state of flux."

As she thinks about her own legacy, Slaughter says she hopes she is remembered as someone who sparked imagination in others. "Nothing is more exciting than the 'aha' moment," she explains. She recalls one of her first exhibits in Las Cruces on artist Frieda Kahlo, where she watched a woman react emotionally to Kahlo's paintings. Telling Slaughter that this was the first time she had been to a museum and seen herself, she left to get her mother and show her the exhibit. "That's why we do it," Slaughter says. "It's those moments of perfect alignment."

Ryan Joshua Spencer, Manager, Firestone Farm and Equine Operations, The Henry Ford, Dearborn, Michigan

- Master of Letters: Museum and Gallery Studies, University of St. Andrews, Scotland 2008
- Has the museum's mission statement memorized and recites it regularly with his staff
- Quote: "I knew I wanted to make a difference and be the steward of something great. I think that's what leaders do."

Ryan Spencer is the epitome of a servant leader. A rapid-fire talker, this thirty-year old is brimming with gratitude for the opportunities he's been given and the people with whom he works. Words such as *privilege* and *stewardship* pepper his conversation, and they carry personal weight and meaning. He is deeply committed to The Henry Ford and unabashedly in love with his career. His love and gratitude are at the core of who Ryan Spencer is as a museum professional and as a human being.

As with so many of our interviewees, Spencer began teaching after college. "I wanted to do something in history," he recalls. "I was teaching at the same time I was volunteering at a local history museum. I loved the museum experience so much that I decided to move in that direction." So he left the classroom behind for a stint as an interpreter and livestock handler at Greenfield Village before heading off to graduate school in Scotland.

"I decided to go to Scotland for my masters because I wanted to broaden my experience and bring something new to the table," Spencer says. "I knew people who had gone there." When he returned to the States he returned to The Henry Ford, where he's been on a track for rapid promotion, first as educational coordinator of special projects, then to manager of the Firestone Farm, and now the farm and equine operations. He is emphatic that he entered the field knowing he wanted to lead. "I knew I wanted to make a difference and to be the steward of something great," Spencer says. "I think that's what leaders do. I wanted to improve that part of an institution for which I would be responsible."

Growing up about an hour away from The Henry Ford, Spencer knew he wanted to work there even before he ever visited it. "My parents went there on their dates, so I heard about The Henry Ford from the time I was very young," he says. "I finally got here on a school field trip—it made me fall in love with history." This special connection was augmented and nurtured by his parents and a grandfather, who read history and instilled in him an appreciation for it. His dad works in a steel mill and has a high school education. His mom went to community college. His grandfather retired from the same steel mill where his dad now works. Spencer is the only one in his family with both bachelors and masters degrees.

When asked about his attraction to agriculture and agricultural history, Spencer says, "My relatives grew up on or have farms. My best friend's family had a dairy farm. I come from a long line of farmers, and my great-grandfather's farm is still in the family, although it's not farmed anymore. I feel like I'm tapping into my past when I'm at the Firestone Farm."

He's had the privilege of knowing wonderful people who have been his mentors, including his predecessor at The Henry Ford, many of his professors, and the director of The Henry Ford Museum & Greenfield Village, John Neilson. "I try to learn from people all around me," he says. "I have very good friends who could be role models." But a lot of his inspiration and wisdom comes from his grandpa, who grew up very poor in the south. He was always reading and taught Spencer about leadership.

As a result, Spencer aspires to lead by serving, believing that he has simply been entrusted with resources to nurture. He knows that investing in people who work for you is critical, and he is certain that your staff is "the perfect fit" for you. "As a leader, we ought to do what we ask our staff to do," he says. "We are on the same team," adding that only then can one lead in good conscience.

Spencer's staff consists of about thirty union and nonunion full-time and part-time members. He invests in them in a variety of ways: he gives raises when he can, but since that's not always possible to do, especially in this economy, he spends a good percentage of his time relationship building. He makes it a point to show appreciation for his staff and their work, to be concerned about their personal lives, to provide opportunities for professional development, and to be honest with them when things aren't going well. His two assistants are old enough to be his parents. How does he deal with the age difference? "I'm willing to learn from them, I engage in dialogue with them, and I show respect. I acknowledge they have value and experience. Ultimately, I have to understand that I was given this job for a reason, and I take confidence in that."

Spencer believes that if staff knows they are stakeholders in the mission, they do incredible things. "We hold each other accountable, accept people's mistakes, and grow as a group," he says. Right before the farm opens each day, there's a ten-minute staff meeting, which consists of updates and tasks for the day. For Spencer's team, the group also recites the mission statement, and they're asked to reflect on their roles as part of a bigger idea. He asks them to contemplate what they're going to do that day in terms of passing on the concepts of ingenuity, resourcefulness, and innovation to guests. (Spencer's email signature block carries The Henry Ford mission statement, with these words highlighted.) As far as he knows, he is the only program manager who does this. He laughingly admits that this sounds like an opening employee huddle at Walmart, but he's convinced it works.

At the beginning and end of each season, the Farm and Equine Center staff gather to go over all the goals for the year and to discuss what's been successful and what hasn't worked well and to review policies, and they cap it off with a potluck, where "we sit and chat about all the new information."

He thinks that theory in museum classes prepared him the least for his current leadership position, noting that "simply because until you've had a chance to put the theory into practice, you just don't know how to deal with the real situation." Spencer says the Seminar for Historical Administration (SHA), which he attended in 2012, came at a perfect time because he'd had enough experience under his belt to understand the theory. SHA has given him a group of peers he's stayed connected with, so he continues to learn. And ongoing learning is critical for Spencer. "I always imagined how I wanted to recreate the past as accurately as possible at the Firestone Farm, down to the smallest detail," he says. "So I did a lot of research and learned new skills in the process. I have a couple of Amish friends who are experts with horses and farming, and I consult with them."

Does he see his leadership style changing? Spencer laughs. "I've been in a management role for three years. I knew some things and I've made a few mistakes. But I understand that I'm constantly being made and improved." He's not going to stay at The Henry Ford forever, he thinks. He doesn't want to settle and become complacent; he knows he'll need to find a new challenge in a history museum. But, who knows? It may be at The Henry Ford.

He is driven, which he admits is a double-edged sword. It propels his career, but he has to keep it in check, lest it cause his expectations for staff to be too high. He has a passion for what he does, which is clearly evident when he talks about his work. He feels his empathy for others has been critical to his success thus far.

He tries to be quite strict about maintaining balance among work, family, community, and self. For example, he makes a point of visiting or calling extended family frequently. He makes an effort to go to church each week. And he looks for opportunities to spend time with people he cares about. He tries to be careful to limit how much work he takes home, although on a recent vacation day he did spend some time reading an article for work. On Saturdays, he almost always has breakfast with his grandparents.

Not surprising, he's technologically plugged in. "I use the i-gamut," he says. He sees younger visitors wanting to take out their phones and manipulate what they're seeing, scanning QR codes and the like. He's tempted to do that when he visits museums, too. "I'm amazed that seven-year-olds have phones!" he exclaims. He's very interested in new media and how it affects the visitor experience, and he writes regularly on The Henry Ford blog, in concert with the public relations department. "It's a lot of fun to do," he says, noting that visitors come after reading his posts.

"I really hope that we're getting past the idea that museums are just great repositories," he says. "Museums can be causes for good, but they must be relevant in order to do good. We can't get stuck in the 'good enough' mentality."

Among his advice for other aspiring museum leaders, Spencer says, "Be willing to learn and to keep your eyes open. Remind yourself about the magic that got you interested in the profession, because if it ever becomes just another job, there are more lucrative businesses to get into. Make time to reflect and know that we're here to inspire."

Kent Whitworth, Executive Director, Kentucky Historical Society, Frankfort, Kentucky

- MA, History with an Emphasis in Historic Preservation, Middle Tennessee State University, 1989
- Is definitely *not* a maintenance director
- Quote: "Leadership isn't for the faint of heart, nor is it something you can do alone."

"The director title is not the title it's cracked up to be; many times I still had to take out the trash!" Kent Whitworth exclaims with a warm southern accent. "If a person is all about the title, it's probably not the person you want to emulate. Don't talk it; live it." Whitworth is also quick to note that he's not interested in what he calls a maintenance directorship. He wants a challenging give and take with his board and staff. For that to happen, he is aware that, for him, at any rate, the board-staff fit is critical to the success of a director. There needs to be a mutual commitment to the mission and to taking an organization forward. Whitworth knows from experience that it takes more than luck to find the right combination.

He began his career thinking he wanted to be a curator. In fact, a directorship was the furthest thing from his mind. Fortunately, a couple of internship experiences, one at the National Trust for Historic Preservation's Decatur House, and the other at the American Association for State and Local History, dispelled that notion and moved him to the public side of things. "Everything has prepared me for my current leadership position, in and outside of the field," he reflects. For example, he worked for a few years at his *alma mater* (the only anomaly on his resume), and his boss there was a model of someone who delivered organizational clarity. "He talked about stewardship in meaningful ways," Whitworth remembers. "Leadership and management lessons came from there."

Thoughtful and practical, Whitworth's assessment of his leadership role, and leadership in general, is laced with references to books and authors that hold important lessons for him. Jim Collins and Peter Lencioni are two touchstones that sprinkle his conversations. In fact, he's a huge proponent of Collins's *Good to Great* model, which advocates first getting the right people on the bus, and then getting them in the right seats. "Figure out *who* first, then what," Whitworth agrees. "Because of this approach and my team, we're doing things I never imagined."

After almost a decade at the Kentucky Historical Society, Whitworth admits he loves his work just as much if not more than he did when he started, citing a genuine passion he draws on. He recalls he was told that the longer you are in the field, the more you move away from doing what you love, and he's found that is true. But he counterbalances it with a leadership team of ten people who spend more than 30 percent of their time together, allowing him to vicariously experience things.

Whitworth says that his leadership team is always asking, "And then what?" He believes they're tuned into opportunities, a lot of which bubble up from conversations. Whitworth recalls an exercise where each member of the leadership team identified an organization to benchmark. Next they had to justify their choice to the team. Since they're now starting to look at outside industries, a staff member suggested they visit the Toyota plant about thirty miles away. He had taken his family there on the factory tour and thought it would be great for the team to go. Whitworth describes this as leading from the chair and not the front of the room. He loves the notion that an organization can encourage and reward leadership from anywhere in the room.

"That visit changed our vocabulary," Whitworth describes. "When we take an approach we learned from our visit we now say we're 'Toyota-ing.' An example is prototyping. We used to think we had to have resources to prototype, but we learned that Toyota does a lot of their prototyping with cardboard and duct tape. We figure if it's good enough for Toyota, it's good enough for KHS. Innovation doesn't have to cost tons of dollars."

Whitworth sees his role as assembling a strong team, helping to resource and equip it, creating enough overall clarity so that people can follow and do without too much managing, and trying not to micromanage. "I'm the chief cheerleader," he exclaims.

Whitworth explains that the strategic plan helps to keep everyone accountable, especially him. "Being a director is hard work," he says. "It doesn't get you out of the fire." Each week he completes a five-over-five matrix, where he lists his top five accomplishments for the week as they relate to the top five goals of the plan. It takes time to put the matrix together, but he feels it's time well spent. It feeds into his performance review, which is a 360-degree evaluation, something he describes as an out-of-body experience, noting that it has been very constructive once he got used to it. He looks on it as an important professional development experience.

When he attended the Seminar for Historical Administration in 1990, his biggest takeaway was that life can't be all about work, because life is short. Whitworth talks about his vertical life with God and his family life. He feels he has a handle on the vertical, but he struggles with getting priorities straight consistently with family. "It's like navigating a stream," Whitworth reflects. "Being self-aware is critical, and having a family and a spouse who can talk and laugh about it is good." As a reminder, he keeps a picture of his family in his office with the following quote from Rick Warren's *Purpose Driven Life*: "The best use of life is love. The best expression of love is time. The best time to love is now."

When asked about how he sees museum leadership changing, Whitworth replies, "The field is very different now even from four to five years ago. If we're not meeting real needs, our game is over. It's incumbent upon us to figure out those needs and let the rest go." He suggests that the recession brought a needed recalibration. "The smoke-blowing days are over for both the public and private sectors," he says. "Now the focus is on critical-thinking skills, which is right up history's alley."

He continues, "When confronted with the choice of hiring younger professionals or more experienced professionals, we haven't regretted hiring younger people. They've been so invigorating, which I think bodes well for the future of museums." But then he admonishes, "We're not playing a nostalgic game—history museums need new, forward-looking perspectives."

SUMMARY: LESSONS LEARNED

Lesson one: Successful self-aware leaders are continuously learning and reflecting.

So what do we learn from our self-aware leaders? Clearly being uber-competent isn't enough. Achievers are sometimes self-protective rather than self-aware. Yet honesty and transparency give this group of thirteen self-aware leaders a humility that is clearly important. Janet Carding admits that she was quite deliberate in preparing for her new role as CEO of the Royal Ontario Museum. Carding realized that joining one of Canada's most venerable institutions, assuming leadership that had always been held by a man, and moving to a country with a common language and political system as her native United Kingdom but with different mores meant that she needed to assess her strengths and address her weaknesses.

In today's global, Facebook-driven world, nothing is static. Our leaders know that context is everything, and context drives change, both internal and organizational. Leaders who know who they are apply different skills in different situations. A consummate learner and regular reader of leadership and management literature, Kent Whitworth applies what he learns. He lights up when he sees or hears about new approaches he can adapt to the Kentucky Historical Society. Ted Bosley's tenure at the Gamble House is a study in applying skills. When the historic house needed a public relations man, it hired him, but his ability to anticipate change and grow with it has kept him there and helped make Gamble House a dynamic museum. Jennifer Kilmer sees herself as a sponge, soaking up ideas and ways of being. She believes she is a different leader every year.

Lesson two: "Surrender, Dorothy." Recognize that influence matters more than control.

Control may give the appearance of leadership, but it doesn't get the job done. Gonzalo Casals admits he is a workaholic, but when it comes to his staff, he surrenders control. "I give my direct reports the tools, and it's their project; if they don't do it, it won't happen," he tells us. Ryan Spencer knows this, too. He invests himself in his staff, saying, "We hold each other accountable, accept people's mistakes and grow as a group." That is grounded in surrender, in recognizing that as a leader there is only so much you can control. You can control whom you hire, but not their work pace; in turning over responsibility you create a responsible and self-aware staff.

Lesson three: Listening provides lessons.

Self-awareness means listening to others, to colleagues, direct reports, and even family by not reacting but listening. Comments that come up frequently are likely true. They don't make you a bad person, but if you are listening they provide opportunities for change. Again, it is Jennifer Kilmer who reminds us that one of her biggest lessons learned was to stop talking. As Ted Bosley explains, "You're so much more likely to move a project forward when you listen with respect and compassion," he says. "You need to humble yourself and listen."

NOTES

1. Robert K. Greenleaf, "The Servant as Leader," The Robert Greenleaf Center for Servant Leadership, accessed February 3, 2013, https://www.greenleaf.org/what-is-servant-leadership/.

2. John B. McGuire, Gary Rhodes, and Charles J. Palus, "Inside Out: Transforming Your Leadership Culture," Center for Creative Leadership, January–February 2008, 3–4, accessed November 15, 2012, www.ccl.org/leadership/pdf/publications/lia/lia27_6Inside.pdf.

3. Janet Carding, "What Can Museums Learn from Nonprofit Leadership?" *museum geek* Blog, August 2, 2012, accessed August 9, 2012, http://museumgeek.wordpress.com/2012/08/02/guest-post-what-can-museums-learn-from-nonprofit-leadership/.

Chapter Six

The Authentic Leader

Authentic leadership often comes unsolicited, the result of achievements that inspire trust in others. If you put those achievements out in the world, whatever your intention, you need to take responsibility for the possibilities they create. If what you put forth meets a need in the world, you must do whatever you can to help others find a way to fulfill it.
—Sally Helgesen, "A Journey to Authentic Leadership"[1]

In many ways this is one of the most important chapters in this book. Authenticity can't be learned. Imitating anyone in this book won't make you a leader; it will just make you a lesser version of someone else. Calling someone an authentic leader may not have the panache of visionary or courageous leader, but you can be sure whoever she is, she is exclusively herself.

Our format, using interviews, isn't unique. Our format is similar to CEO Bill George's, whose *True North* was published in 2007. Like George we believe that storytelling is a powerful learning tool. We weren't so interested in what our museum and heritage organization leaders had to say about leadership itself. What is revealing—and here is where the authenticity part comes in—is how they draw on their own stories to describe and interpret the leaders they are today, and how they use their stories to relate to others.

When we asked Beth Grindell, the longtime interim director of the Arizona State Museum, to talk about leadership, the first person she mentioned was her father, a career military officer. "A lot of what I know about the outward appearance of leadership, I learned from him," she told us. "You stand up straight, you have a good handshake, you listen, and you issue clear instructions." She is not alone. Ellen Rosenthal, president at Conner Prairie, said something similar about her father. "More than anything, he's my leadership model," she explained, adding that her father is who she thinks about when she struggles with workplace issues. The point here is not that everyone needs a father story, but that part of being an authentic leader is incorporating the truth of autobiography into work life.

Leadership, and more particularly authenticity, is based in true life. Sprinkled throughout all of these interviews are references to experiences in Sunday school, high school, farm work, and family. As Anne Cathcart, one of our youngest interviewees, points out, "You take a little bit from every job, including learning to work with people and absorbing feedback." These biographical moments build passion, and passion is what every authentic leader possesses. Interviewee Rosenthal describes taking a leadership course at the Wharton School. After listening to her speak, one of her classmates commented on her passion, adding that until listening to her, he had not really understood what being passionate about work was like.

Authenticity isn't about confession, however. It is not about oversharing or becoming the Dr. Phil of history museum leaders. Instead, it is about understanding why you are where you are today. In understanding what drives you, you know what brought you to the museum field in the beginning. Having a sense of where you are and a confidence in whom you are allows authentic leaders to fully focus on others. They are openly and willingly invested in the people, the institutions, and the communities with which they are involved. A service ethic runs like a deep vein of gold through them.

Take Christy Coleman, for example. Her background in theater and living history interpretation at Colonial Williamsburg established her strong affinity for and allegiance to the visitor and the visitor experience. In an interview for Richmond (Virginia) television, Coleman described bringing the people she portrayed to life as an awesome responsibility. As president of the American Civil War Center at Historic Tredegar in Richmond, Coleman nurtures a small museum with a big story to tell. "Theater is really about emotional truth," she said. And so is bringing great history to audiences. In order to do it well, she believes in giving consideration to what audiences want.[2]

Authentic leaders' lives are values based. As people, they are kind, bighearted, and compassionate. And they love their work. In the individuals whose stories you read here, it is hard to miss the gratitude and the passion. Hopefully, your own passion aligns with your organization's purpose.

Dina A. Bailey, Director of Exhibitions and Visitor Experiences, National Underground Railroad Freedom Center, Cincinnati, Ohio

- Masters, Anthropology of Development and Social Transformation, University of Sussex, England, 2007

- Graduate Certificate, Museum Studies, University of Cincinnati, 2009
- Met and gave a tour to First Lady Michelle Obama
- Quote: "I didn't know I wanted to lead, but I felt confident I would lead in whatever field I chose."

Dina Bailey is from a family of teachers. She just knew teaching was what she was going to do, too. And for nearly three years she taught English and substituted in schools in Indianapolis and Cincinnati. Her teaching experience was mostly with Advanced Placement students, which was great, Bailey admits, but she longed to work with more "normal" kids. It was after graduate school in England and a stint substitute teaching back in the States when it became clear that she didn't want to be stuck in formal education. What to do? It was her aunt who suggested that she get a job in a museum.

The National Underground Railroad Freedom Center opened when Bailey was in college. Later, as her substitute teaching was winding down, she pursued and received a curatorial fellowship there. At the time, she still wasn't sure if she wanted to work in a museum, but she felt her choice was between museums and teaching. Would she continue with what she knew—teaching—or would she take the plunge and move into a field with a big learning curve? Bailey chose the museum.

It's a choice she does not regret. Since her fellowship, Bailey has had a rapid two-year succession of job titles and experiences at the Freedom Center: associate curator, director of exhibitions and collections, and now director of exhibitions and visitor experiences. She admits she's on the fast track, in part because the Freedom Center is unique, relatively new, and in need of her leadership skills. She has been a key player on the transition team in the Freedom Center's merger with the Cincinnati Museum Center in 2012, in part because she is a good gauge of staff.

Her fast-paced career trajectory has had its share of hardships, too. For one thing, she looks younger than she is, which is sometimes a source of resentment among her colleagues who've been in the field longer. As a younger woman she's also experienced her share of negotiating leadership among older men. She has had to work very hard to build trust and push herself to prove that she deserves her position and responsibility. She currently has twenty-three direct reports, plus volunteers, and she says, "I've gained a deeper of understanding about being a supervisor of people. There's been a lot of balancing and coming to grips with who I am, and I've needed to find the balance between my academic training and my natural abilities."

Bailey credits her parents with teaching her about responsibility and maturity. "They gave me a lot of self-confidence," she says. That, combined with a variety of leadership responsibilities in high school, college, and church, formed the basis of her current leadership skill set. "I didn't know I wanted to lead, but I felt confident I would lead in whatever field I chose." But as a "natural leader," Bailey knew she had to draw on her own motivations to find the resources to fill gaps in her skills. As far as Bailey is concerned, networking is a key to everything: it increases her toolbox; it introduces her to a wide range of people and ideas; it is the source for jobs, board service, and next career steps; and it helps her to stay on top of her game and be innovative.

A life learner, Bailey always wants to know what is next. She is constantly reading for inspiration and cross-pollination of ideas, while looking for new partnerships to engage in her work at the Freedom Center. One example of her entrepreneurial spirit can be found in an exhibition on human trafficking, *Invisible: Slavery Today*. The exhibition offered the Freedom Center the opportunity to partner with not-for-profits and government agencies and work with academics who are studying and creating policy about contemporary slavery movements. While it took a look at slavery in the modern world, it also examined contemporary sex trafficking in Ohio, asking visitors to take action by becoming modern-day abolitionists.

Among her role models are her mom; many Freedom Center board members; AASLH vice president for programs, Bob Beatty; and Spencer Crew, the former director of the Freedom Center.

Maintaining a work-life balance is also a challenge, which she tries to mitigate by keeping track of her time. "It makes me conscious about time when I do that," she says. She admits that maintaining a balance can be really difficult early on in a career. As a teacher, she recalls that there were plenty of long days and little outside life. She still works a lot of hours, but outside of work she relies on family (she has a standing dinner date with Mom) and her international and national friendships, which she devotes time to nurturing.

When asked about how she sees museum leadership changing, Bailey ponders, "I hope to see a younger generation of leaders; I hope leaders will bring younger people in. The world is changing too quickly, partly due to the impact of social media—just look at how it's changing traditional forms of interpretation. Museums need innovators at higher staff levels and at the board level."

Her advice to the next generation of museum leaders?

- Keep pushing yourself and your institution.
- Recognize your sphere of authority and learn when to push it and when to pause it; that way, you'll be less frustrated by the system.
- Have a sense of experimentation and encouragement.

- Learn to be aware of yourself and your environment, and where you're coming from. This is critical in dealing effectively with the people you work with.

"Leadership is always a challenge," she says, "The moment you become complacent, you get into trouble. You can become manipulative or arrogant. I never want to take leadership for granted. Just because you get to one place doesn't mean you can't go further."

Jamie O. Bosket, Vice President, Interpretation and Events Division, The Mount Vernon Ladies' Association of the Union, Mount Vernon, Virginia

- MA, Museum Studies, The George Washington University, Washington, D.C., 2008
- Includes divisionwide "principles" in all job descriptions
- Quote: "No one else is going to be strategic for you."

When it comes to Mount Vernon and his work there, Jamie Bosket wears his heart proudly on his sleeve. He feels deeply that doing so is the key to success. He credits the steady stream of promotions he's had during his short tenure in no small measure to his passion for working at George Washington's bucolic Potomac River estate. With its national mandate and profile, he knew Mount Vernon was where he wanted to be, a feeling that's only grown as he's developed as a professional.

Mount Vernon offers everything Bosket loves about museums. In addition to the Washington story, it's been in the forefront of preservation since its inception; it's financially stable; and it's getting ready to build Washington's presidential library, which will take the museum into a new phase. It provides Bosket with many learning opportunities, continuously challenging his abilities. As far as Mount Vernon is concerned, Bosket sees his passion as "the gravy."

Bosket knew he wanted to work in museums since he was a child. A school visit captured his imagination, and he became increasingly fascinated by museums, so much so that he found five dollars to join his local history museum, which in turn allowed him to volunteer. He was twelve years old and giving tours to adults. "What felt natural has now become an imperative," he muses.

Between college and graduate school Bosket served as site manager of a small local history museum and a programs and collections department assistant in a large outdoor museum, both in upstate New York. Bosket believes there is no one particular experience that prepared him for his current leadership position. Rather, it's a combination of experiences at a variety of museums large and small that created a snowball effect. Throughout, he has stayed focused on his goals; his passion for work is the constant that runs through his career.

What continues to evolve, on the other hand, is his understanding of how people work—group dynamics—especially as the numbers of people he supervises grows. He manages what Mount Vernon terms the "Total Guest Experience" delivered by a 150-member action team, a team to which he tries to be as accessible to as possible. "I prefer to talk with people person-to-person. Sneakers are my technology!" he laughs.

In suggesting Bosket as a possible interviewee for this book, a staff member wrote:

> In his time at Mount Vernon, Jamie has proven himself an irreplaceable leader amongst staff—most of whom are over a decade older than him. His ability to visualize everything on the Estate from the guest's perspective has led to a wide range of changes with how our front line interpretive staff interact with guests and teach them about George Washington. What makes him a real leader, however, is his ability to blend this advocacy for the guest (and often for his staff) with the ability to see the "big picture" of budget, timing, and internal politics. He has sacrificed a great deal of his personal life to make sure that he lives up to the examples set by George Washington and his own mentor, Mount Vernon's President Jim Rees—which sounds incredibly corny, but really is true.

How about that for a ringing endorsement?

While he puts in his share of eighty-plus-hour workweeks—he did a lot of that the first three years to show he wasn't above hard work—Bosket notes, "There's a difference between ever present and ever involved." Understanding and making that distinction has also been evolutionary. Balancing life and work is within your control, he says, adding, "but I've gone all work." However, he is trying to establish a new balance, a peaceful place for a total life using those eighty-hour weeks as groundwork. He wants to live up to expectations, being willing to do what needs to be done, believing that he is primarily responsible for making his example a sound one.

When asked about creating change within a large workforce, Bosket quickly replies, "You first have to be able to accept change in order to create a culture for change. I'm constantly creating a fresh workforce as people come and go."

"Sharing and communication are key," he says. "Getting the team together and socializing are important." It underscores something his mentors taught him: It is critical to connect people with the institution's impact. "Never stop reminding staff that you're all in it together."

Bosket is so committed to developing his team toward a common goal, he created a set of overarching division principles that appear on all 150 job descriptions (including his own). The principles, which state that team members will exceed guest expectations, encourage a meaningful appreciation of Washington, personally engage themselves in Mount Vernon's mission, and take responsibility for their professional development and collaboration, are not found in any other divisions at Mount Vernon.

As a result, Bosket gets high marks from team members and a lot of credit for new and exciting work. Bosket's team looks for strategic actions. As he explains it, the team is always leaning forward, adding, "When you're willing to share success with your team, it blossoms into pride—it's like wildfire."

At twenty-nine, Bosket says he is Mount Vernon's youngest vice president by a long stretch. He's exceedingly mindful that he's been the beneficiary of many opportunities, creating a sense of great obligation to foster a creative, nurturing environment for his team, or as he puts it, to pay it forward and pass it along. His advice for aspiring museum leaders: "Constantly search for ideas and people who will develop you. Seek out mentors and people to help (young and old); constantly collect other perspectives; be open to techniques. Find ways to assert yourself to receive opportunities."

How does he see museum leadership changing? "Museums need to be far more willing to be flexible; far more open to nontraditional audiences (for example, nonvisitors, but who are nonetheless interested) and to technologies," he replies. "Technology moves faster than museums normally do. Objects stay the same but connectivity with audiences change. We must be willing to adapt ourselves and our institutions."

Anne Cathcart, Associate Manager of Collections and Programs, Chesterwood, National Trust for Historic Preservation, Stockbridge, Massachusetts

- BA, Art History, Bowdoin College, Brunswick, Maine, 2008
- Helped manage the campus tour program at college
- Quote: "We all get curve balls. Having a sense of humor helps."

Can you remember starting out in your career, the excitement of working in a field you love, the energy and enthusiasm that came with new experiences, and the sensation that all was possible? You were a sponge soaking up information, using fresh eyes to examine organizational traditions and relationships, and seeing potential everywhere. If you remember that, then you're standing in Anne Cathcart's shoes.

After a brief, postcollege stint with Teach for America teaching kindergarteners in the Bronx, she's found herself in a sylvan, storied setting: Chesterwood, home of the sculptor Daniel Chester French, now owned by the National Trust. In 2009, she began as an intern on a four-month Institute of Museum and Library Services grant, and she "got the bug." Her pathway from the Bronx to the Berkshires was guided by a series of informational interviews (she talked to fifty to sixty people), a generous supply of encouragement from her close-knit family, and her belief that you've got to know when to change your plans in midstream, if necessary. By contrast, many of her friends working in the arts were more decisive about their careers early on, which she thinks short-circuited the benefits from the soul searching and research she's done.

Now in her midtwenties, without prior museum experience or a masters degree (yet), she's fully immersed in a museum small enough to afford her a wealth of opportunities to learn and experiment, while honing her natural leadership abilities and technical skills. Her current title of Associate Manager of Collections and Programs (a recent promotion from curatorial assistant) belies the true breadth of her responsibilities, which include grant writing, training staff and volunteers, managing seasonal staff and interns, and contributing to exhibitions and programs. "It's exceeded my expectations," she confides about the experience. As a result, she's become passionate about French, Chesterwood, and bringing the site to life.

Much of her leadership foundation was laid in college, where Cathcart managed a part of the campus tour guide program. In addition to managing and scheduling her peer guides, she gave tours herself, which offered her insights into customer service—"The tour guide either makes or breaks a campus visit." She was also a writing advisor and tutor, helping students with writing and editing their papers and mentoring one through a semester-long writing partnership. At Chesterwood, she writes all press releases, website content, and curatorial materials.

As she reflects on her trajectory from college to first job to Chesterwood, a definitive learning-by-doing philosophy emerges. "You take a little bit from every job, including learning to work with people and absorbing feedback." In fact, she says she learns almost on a monthly basis how to delegate and work with others, something that is important given that most of her coworkers and direct reports are thirty to fifty years older than she. "We all get curve balls," she laughs. "Having a sense of humor helps."

Even though her lack of prior museum experience gave her a pretty steep learning curve, she's mitigated that with a combination of professional development and networking. She's used networking to learn about careers, employers, and job opportunities, and says, "It helps me to fine tune my elevator speech." Right now, she's got about twenty to thirty young professionals in her network, and she makes a point of reaching out to widen her circle of contacts. In addition to participating in local networking groups, Cathcart is involved in several national and regional museum associations.

Among her professional role models are curators at the Metropolitan Museum of Art and Olana State Historic Site (New York), staff at the National Trust, and Chesterwood's director, Donna Hassler, who believes Cathcart will be running her own museum in the near future.

While Cathcart sees herself as a director someday, perhaps of a museum that's preserving a historic site, she believes she has a ladder to climb first that includes graduate school and working in at least one larger institution (just for comparison's sake). But she's taking her boss's advice that she needs to be open about opportunities that can come from out of left field. So at this point, she's not ruling anything out.

Her critical thinking and problem solving are the skills she uses with staff and decision making in general. She feels that her ability to analyze and synthesize situations and options, and, not inconsequentially, execute the ideas and plans of others, are key strengths that have moved her toward greater responsibility at Chesterwood, as well as built trust with Hassler.

She also has the opportunity to wrestle with Chesterwood's long-term issues. Although she doesn't know what might eventually happen, she's comfortable with not having all the answers. Not always knowing how a direction or decision might pan out requires her to be flexible and think on her feet, another learning opportunity she relishes.

It can't be emphasized enough that Cathcart's parents and siblings are central to her success. Her parents introduced her to the arts at a young age. They encourage her resourcefulness, and they are important sounding boards about life and career. As the youngest in the family, she's been able to watch the careers of her siblings unfold, giving her lots of practical pointers.

Her advice to peers in the museum field: take initiative; don't fear making a wrong move. "Our parents are known as the helicopter generation, and we're shaped by that. Many of us are not particularly resourceful, yet there are tons of resources available."

"There are many different ways to be a leader," she observes. Luckily for her, she's getting the chance to prove that every day.

Christy S. Coleman, President, American Civil War Center at Historic Tredegar, Richmond, Virginia

- MA, Museum Studies, Hampton University, 1996
- As a screenwriter, her most recent work, *Freedom Bound*, won an Emmy in 2009 for Outstanding Educational Programming for the Colonial Williamsburg Foundation.

• Quote: "Information gives you the ability to lead change."

There's a note on Christy Coleman's computer that reads: "Have you talked with a board member or donor today?" For Coleman, her role as president of the American Civil War Center at Historic Tredegar is all about bringing people together—whether it's her board, staff, or a group of museum leaders in her city—to support a shared sense of purpose. While it's critical to understand the balance sheet and take the calculated risks to realize a healthy institution, none of it will be meaningful if stakeholders aren't engaged.

Coleman's youthful sights were trained on a career in theater, not museums. Raised in Williamsburg, Virginia, her first brush with living history was a frontline stint in the historic village as a high schooler. By her own admission Coleman has a knack for working with people, along with "intense" ideas about what living history can do. Drawing on her interpretive experiences at Colonial Williamsburg, where she held several positions that blended her talents as an actress with history, she quickly moved through the interpretive ranks, ultimately becoming head of interpretive programs development prior to her move to Detroit. Coleman sees the museum visitor as the critical element in why museums do what they do and is a staunch champion of the visitor's perspective. As a result, she often approaches organizational assessment from the visitor's point of view before she even digs into the numbers. Knowing what's happening to the visitor gives her grounding to then challenge staff-held or board-held assumptions.

Her leadership at the Charles H. Wright Museum of African American History in Detroit provided her with valuable lessons about bringing an organization and its people through a funding crisis, and it allowed her to come up with solutions and use some risk taking. "Detroit was an amazing place for learning new ideas about fund-raising and financial management," she recalls. She immediately dove into needs assessment by benchmarking financial information and fund-raising—no surprise that some of it was aimed at cost/visitor ratios—and that resulted in clarifying the vision and mission, testing assumptions and shifting staff resources and program focus. "Information gives you the ability to lead change," she says.

Coming home to Virginia from Detroit was a goal for Coleman and her family. She and her husband agreed that whoever got a job first, that would be where the family would go. As it turned out, she was the one who "stumbled" into the job at the American Civil War Center. Once she learned more about the institution, she was "flabbergasted" about what this museum was trying to do and how important the mission of the museum was to both the community and the nation. As the first museum to explore the causes, course, and legacies of the Civil War from Union, Confederate, and African American perspectives, its mission and its promise cinched the deal for her.

She's now experienced leading a large institution (Detroit) and a much smaller institution (Richmond), and she enjoys the time flexibility of the small museum, which helps her manage her busy work and family schedules. Coleman makes no excuses about the fact that her family comes first. However, she is quick to point out that no matter an institution's size, the leader has the opportunity to adjust policies and practices to make life/work balance better for everyone, and if they see a need and can do it, they should do it.

Size doesn't matter either when it comes to understanding board dynamics. "A leader needs to know why each and every one is on the board. She needs to know about competing visions. These are things that can't be learned in a classroom," Coleman says in answer to what prepared her least for leadership. Although she considers herself to be a Type A personality, she respects the authority of the board. "However, there is a difference between governance and management. It is my role to lay out parameters that can bring boards to decision—this takes time to help them see what I am seeing."

Here's where building from a shared purpose comes in. Helping others see what the leader sees requires sharing information, ideas, and dreams. "Add to it and build it. It's not so much consensus leadership, but it relies on input from stakeholders," she says. "Work with your board champions."

One news article credited Coleman with "a remarkable talent for building partnerships with the Richmond community." When asked about the importance of partnerships to her work, Coleman replied, "Too often museums think they're in competition with each other, but if you work together you've got something special (another Detroit lesson). All boats rise when museums work collectively on issues." She cited her participation in a group of Richmond museum directors who met regularly to share program information about what each museum was doing. Coleman saw greater long-term value in the directors working together to become proactive advocates for their work rather than just reporting to each other what each was doing. The shift in their focus now allows them to stay out in front of the issues that could affect their institutions and, if needed, band together quickly in times of crisis.

Another example is her own institution's partnership with its neighbor, the National Park Service. "Respect and communication make partnerships work, and it takes commitment to make it happen," she says. "It's required that each gains an understanding about the other's organizational cultures and perspectives." Only then can shared purpose be achieved.

In thinking about the future of museum leadership, Coleman reflects, "Strong leaders must be entrepreneurs—venturists, really—as well as risk takers—it's a different mind-set. It's more than simply being business minded."

In many respects Coleman has come a long way from her high school interpreter days at Colonial Williamsburg, when carving out a career in the museum field was the furthest thing from her mind. In so many other ways, her convictions about communication and understanding and her passion for the possible are themes she's sustained throughout her career.

Is it any wonder that her ability to assess needs, articulate vision, and build shared purpose are at the top of Christy Coleman's resume?

James Enote, Executive Director, A:shiwi A:wan Museum and Heritage Center, Zuni, New Mexico

- BS, Agriculture, New Mexico State University
- Enote considers his career an odyssey of hitchhiking, watermelon picking, writing, and advocacy for indigenous peoples.
- Quote: "The all-nighters don't end. If you see something that needs to be done, then do it."

To say Jim Enote is one with his institution is not an overstatement. The Zuni tribal member, high-altitude farmer, and artist has had a long and deep relationship with the A:shiwi A:wan Museum and Heritage Center (AAMHC) stretching back to the mid-1980s, when it was still in the conceptual stage. Enote recalls that as the museum's architect moved forward with building plans, it became apparent that the cart was before the horse: Enote's committee was exclusively focused on building a space, with no idea what purpose the museum would serve. That prompted him and a few others to begin a conversation about what the museum might mean to the Zuni people. "The word *museum* carries a lot of baggage in Zuni," Enote says, referencing the colonial past. "We wanted to redefine it. We knew the museum would have a profound effect on Zuni people, and it would require a full-time effort to serve them in a meaningful and truthful way."

The museum incorporated as a nonprofit, independent of the tribal council, a different choice from some other Native American museums. Enote eventually found himself serving on the board and taking a turn as board chair. Even when he rotated off the board, he maintained an interest in the museum's programs and exhibits. But after being named director in 2004, he discovered the museum's original mission had been compromised. Instead of being a center for Zuni people to access and share knowledge and values, it served a largely non-Native, tourist audience. Enote set out to reclaim the institution by engaging diverse and respected individuals in the community searching for important "denominators" or themes shared by all Zuni, such as religion and sacred spaces, language, agriculture, and art. Working with a small staff, a handful of volunteers, and a large number of Zuni religious leaders and cultural advisors, Enote steered the museum back to its mission.

Today, he believes people know the AAMHC is fulfilling an important purpose. "It's reflective of Zuni people and culture," Enote says. "It serves as a forum and a safe place to come together."

This is how Enote approaches life and work. Whether it's about the museum, preserving his own and other Native cultures, land and water conservation issues around the world, farming, art, or any number of other concerns, Enote is motivated by the belief that society can always be better, and it's his obligation to help. For him, part of finding his personal truth is by working to make things better.

His leadership creates an enabling environment, or as he puts it, "That's what being a leader is all about." He works diligently to build and maintain networks—"the web," as he describes them—and relationships to Zuni language and protocols. In fact, he's just returned from a week on the floor of the Grand Canyon with Zuni religious leaders that strengthened relationships and the web of knowledge and culture that surrounds them. Similarly, he has developed programs for Zuni artists to travel in the Grand Canyon and across the Colorado Plateau. These experiences are at the core of Enote the man and the museum director. "It's wonderful work, and I really enjoy it," he says. "I will never leave it because it's so important to society."

Enote lapses into a discussion that begins with how Zuni kids learn about themselves and their culture online. Not all of the information found online is correct, of course. This is especially true of the descriptions other museums apply to Zuni materials in their collections, and there are many Zuni collections all over the world. This led Enote to think about how the AAMHC could use the power of knowledge and information to shape digital media. He recounts that by working in formal partnership with eight major museums, including Cambridge University's Museum of Anthropology and Archaeology in England, the Smithsonian National Museum of the American Indian, the Denver Art Museum, and the National Museum of Ethnology in Osaka, Japan, the AAMHC became a leader in the field by creating digital collaborative catalogs with museums worldwide holding Zuni collections. It used to be when Enote contacted museums where he knew Zuni material was, few responded. "NAGPRA (Native American Graves Protection and Repatriation Act) jump-started things," he says, describing how his institution now has access to material held in other collections, can correct information, and can enhance context. There's a sense of satisfaction in Enote's voice when he describes this power shift from large, far-flung institutions to the little museum in Zuni.

Born in Zuni, New Mexico, where more than 90 percent of the Zuni live, Enote is surrounded by family, friends, and acquaintances he's known all his life. Most Zuni never leave this place. He believes there is great advantage in working close to home because that is where you can make the biggest impact. His water and agricultural work takes him to consult as far away as

Africa and Asia, but he is quick to point out that everywhere it is local people who know what is really going on; they are the ones with deep knowledge and are critical to any solution. He believes in investing in local people whether it's in Zuni or halfway around the world. With this in mind, he advises aspiring museum leaders to work as close to home as possible. Where you are grounded, you are good.

He also emphasizes the importance of tending to one's web of relationships. Building and maintaining them requires constant work, but the web connects you to the past, the present, and the future. Lastly, he reminds aspiring leaders that the all-nighters don't end with youth. At age fifty-six, he admits he still works around the clock if he has to, saying, "If you see something that needs to be done, do it."

"There's a petroglyph of a spiral that symbolizes the migration of the Zuni from the Grand Canyon to the plateau," Enote explains. "It's about searching, moving, testing, exploring and finding individual and collective truth." It's also a graphic metaphor for Enote's life and for the leadership he carries deep within him.

Beth Grindell, Senior Curator, Arizona State Museum, Tucson, Arizona

- PhD, Anthropology, University of Arizona, Tucson, 1998
- A museum director who is also a court-appointed advocate
- Quote: "I try to keep the bigger picture in mind. It's about inclusion, remembering everyone's needs, and treating them with respect."

Beth Grindell describes her museum career as purely accidental. Grindell, who spent the last five years as interim director of the Arizona State Museum at University of Arizona until recently being appointed as senior curator, began her professional life—she has a doctorate in anthropology—believing she would teach at the college level or do research or both. "The museum as a career hadn't entered my mind," she remarks. All that changed when Grindell was asked to join the State Museum as associate director, and it changed again when the then-director died. Grindell stepped into his office expecting to hold the fort during the search. But the search was postponed and then put on hold.

Ask Grindell what prepared her for what sounds like accidental leadership, and she will tell you about her career-military father. "A lot of what I know about the outward appearance of leadership, I learned from him," she says. "You stand up straight, you have a good handshake, you listen, and you issue clear instructions." Grindell says that in the early days of her directing tenure it almost felt as though she was acting the role of director, something she could turn off at the end of the day. She used a personal counselor and a job coach to help with her transition to the leadership position, and she recruited two members of the museum's staff—the head of daily operations and the head of collections—to serve as a back-up team. And she read a great deal. On her bookshelf: Warren Bennis's *On Becoming a Leader* and Jim Collins's *Good to Great* along with Elaine Gurian's book on *Institutional Trauma*, especially when of the ten crises Gurian and her writers cite, Grindell experienced three in two years: the death of a leader, a huge (delayed) project, and the financial blow that came with the 2008 budget crash.

It has not been all bad, though. On the external side, Grindell is happy with several of the new exhibitions the museum opened, and internally, on the personnel side, she is even happier. "The morale is good and I've had good feedback," she says, adding that it isn't just staff who tell her things are better. Visitors also remark on the museum's climate change. Grindell attributes some of that to her very deliberate effort to open lines of communication. "Ten times a year we meet as a full staff," she says. That means bringing together as many of the fifty staff members as possible. She also established a committee of collaboration and cooperation, which vets every project before the museum. "Everyone is free to bring ideas," Grindell says. Although she adds the committee had trouble in the beginning saying no to colleague's ideas, in the long run it has built collegiality, and she is pleased with the process.

Grindell's swift passage to leadership means she had to develop a personal mantra or two to help guide her. "Don't take it personally," she begins. "Remember who you are." She also adds: listening without getting angry or emotional; devoting full attention to only one thing at a time; and being focused in the moment and not frazzled everywhere else. Grindell says she has learned to be deliberative, including repeating back what someone has just said to her so that she (and they) both hear the same thing. To ensure that her focus is complete, she never talks to anyone with her fingers near her keyboard or phone. Last, on a personal level, she learned the hard way that her own behavior as director permeates the organization. One morning after something personal and nonwork related had happened, Grindell discovered staff had taken her emotional temperature and attributed whatever was wrong to something at the museum. Now, she says, no matter what is going on personally, when she is asked how she is, she says everything is fine. She also invests a lot in listening to her staff, especially how they couch things. She references President Clinton and his formidable ability to contextualize a problem. "I try to keep the bigger picture in mind. It's about inclusion, remembering everyone's needs, and treating them with respect," Grindell says. And she adds, "To bring a moral compass."

Like many others interviewed for this book, Grindell says that she is a different leader now than she was a decade ago. "Ten years ago I was just stepping into the Associate Director's position," she explains. Today, she says that the lessons of the last few years mean she is less interested in making everyone happy. "It isn't always possible, but being straightforward most people understand," Grindell says, adding that budget cuts, for example, can't be collaborative. "They can't be open, and they're not fun," Grindell notes.

She has worked hard as a mentor, consciously engaging younger staff. "I listen, discuss all the options, help figure out core values," she says, emphasizing how important it is not just to do something because it is expedient. "The thing I say most often is this institution has a history of long-tenured employment. The path is set; the goals are set, but we're the past, you are the future." She counsels her younger employees that they need to be actively involved in decision making. "I tell them the time to create YOUR institution is NOW," she says, emphasizing the *your* and the *now*. Grindell is open about the fact that she is not an entrepreneur. "I follow the rules and change them when I can," she says.

While she is a natural mentor, Grindell is not a natural networker. Her most important network is a group made up of about twenty-five directors of art, science, and history organizations in the Tucson region. "It's been a great way to get to know others," she says. "The members are honest with one another, and the rapport is good."

The biggest impact moving into the director's office had for Grindell personally is its impact on her volunteer work. A former court-appointed special advocate, she has given that up because of its numerous daytime appointments. Of her free time she says, "I am really a hermit-ish person; I need time to myself, to nest build." She has no rules about email, although she tries to leave it alone when the weekend rolls around except to communicate with those above her on the university food chain. "I tend to work longer days in the winter," she says, explaining that January and February are Tucson's busiest months.

As she looks to the future, Grindell sees big challenges for college and university museums, particularly in development. "My mentor," she says, "a former director here, simply asked the university for money." Grindell's world is more complex, and she expects her successor's will be even more complicated. She is currently working with a new development advisory board and a newly employed development person to reach out to the community, emphasizing that it is a whole new world out there. Currently, she is working alongside her parent organization to strengthen the museum's identity and create a base of support. Asked about her own legacy, Grindell laughs. "Some people have suggested that I will be remembered as the first person in forty years to get the building painted," she says. More seriously she adds, "I hope I'm remembered for opening up the conversation."

Lynne M. Ireland, Deputy Director, Nebraska State Historical Society, Lincoln, Nebraska

- MA, American Folk Culture, History Museum Studies, Cooperstown Graduate Program, 1981
- Museum Management Institute, J. Paul Getty Trust and University of California, 1991
- Ireland is an adjunct professor and coauthor of *Museum Administration: An Introduction.*
- Quote: "Leadership is in evidence when others are empowered."

Still recovering from a flulike illness that stayed with her throughout the winter, Lynne Ireland describes her 2013 so far as a long haul. But it is early days yet. The deputy director of the Nebraska Historical Society (NHS), Ireland says she had no idea she wanted to be a leader. "If that means I wanted to grow up to be a museum director, I would say no," she says firmly. Ireland has now been at the Nebraska Historical Society for thirty-two years. "I admire people who are willing to take a risk," she says, reflecting on the times she could have moved. She did think about leaving when she was a few years into her work at NHS, but she says now that the idea literally seemed scary. "I'm pretty attached to place," she confesses.

Like many interviewed for this book, Ireland was also profoundly influenced by her father. A Methodist minister, she describes him as someone who not only excelled as a leader but also as someone who was very good at the teachable moment. Ireland remembers the dinner table as a place where discussions of the higher good were commonplace. It was there she learned that everyone can make change happen; that leadership involves action and moving things forward so others can realize their destinies.

Ireland went to a small liberal arts college, where luckily she was encouraged to use her imagination. For her that meant freedom to risk—to gather up decrepit blacksmith tools and use them—if that is what she wanted to do. "Cooperstown was the same way," she says, referring to her alma mater, the Cooperstown Graduate Program. "There was no place to hide." In addition to her graduate degree, Ireland also attended the Museum Management Institute, now known as the Getty Leadership Institute. "I learned to do more," Ireland says about her experience. "I was almost duty bound to shoot my mouth off."

Not surprisingly, Ireland says that teaching as an adjunct faculty member at the University of Nebraska clarified her thinking about leadership. In addition, having stayed in one place for so long, she has now had the pleasure of watching her students become staff. "It's pretty damning to say," she begins, "but one of the things I feel positive about is the number of people now at NHS because they started at University of Nebraska." She adds that the satisfaction has not been just in giving people jobs, but in watching her former students grow into them. "What we were trying to impart in graduate training," she explains. "We had no idea how effective this would be." Some of her former student-colleagues have gone on to positions in the region. "I don't take credit for their current situations, but I do take a degree of ownership in building skill sets."

As an administrator for the last twenty years, Ireland said that her successes and her failures tend to be process oriented. For example, she recently led a multidisciplinary team through the installation of a large, permanent exhibit. With hindsight, Ireland feels that throughout the process she could have been more directive. Despite all that's been written about leading from the front row rather than the front of the room, this is one case where Ireland is convinced the exhibit could have been better had it had one voice behind it. She takes full credit for that.

It's no surprise that after thirty years of climbing the museum ladder, Ireland has a leadership mantra. It is brief: keep breathing. "So many people get hyperreactive," she explains, adding that she believes leaders are effective when they are relaxed, so she reminds herself to breathe and to respond, not react. She says there are sometimes when she wants to say "no," that whatever it is she has been asked about needs to cease immediately, but, she says, a leader needs to refrain—to sit with the energy and respond instead to where she wants to be, not where she is.

If you are looking for something more philosophical and less Zen, Ireland offers up, "Leadership is in evidence when others are empowered," adding, "You need to create situations where others have responsibility and authority, and they do things efficiently and effectively."

Ask Ireland about someone she admires and she mentions her thirty-year-old daughter who teaches kindergarten in New York City's Bushwick neighborhood. "She teaches twenty-five five-year-olds by herself," Ireland says. It's her passion that Ireland finds awesome. "She's a loyal supporter of the public schools and a great believer that things can change," she says. Others on Ireland's list of admirable people include: Nigerian writer Chimamanda Ngozi Adichie, whose work Ireland says should be required reading for anyone trying to understand human culture; Diane Ravitch, a former Bush appointee who reversed her position on No Child Left Behind and is now a passionate supporter of public schools; and her colleague Hugh Genoways, professor in museum studies at the University of Nebraska.

Ireland says she is not very good at balancing work and the rest of her life. "Curiously, it is more of a challenge without the ready imperative of [having] a family at home who have to be attended to," she says. "For a couple of sixty-year-old people at home, does a postdinner email matter?" she asks. Ireland credits her partner, a landscape photographer, with helping her literally let go. "We have gone to some pretty remote places," she explains. "Hauling camera gear up to eleven thousand feet and hoping lightning doesn't hit the metal tripod puts work in perspective," she adds.

Ireland claims that her imagination is too lame to conceive of where museums are going, especially with the rapidly growing world of technology. But there is one thing she is certain about. "I still believe human beings experience the material world and objects in ways that don't happen with any other being," she muses. And she remains convinced that there is a fundamental difference between seeing an object or a painting online and being in the presence of the real thing. "There is a physical interaction in the presence of an object," Ireland says. When you ask Ireland what she would like her own legacy in the field to be, she says, "I would like to think I created systems and places where a full range of human experience could be examined and celebrated." Ireland says that twelve thousand years of human history, an increasingly diverse population, along with the issue of who we are and how we figure the future out is a conversation she wants to be part of.

Robert A. Kret, Director, Georgia O'Keeffe Museum, Santa Fe, New Mexico

- MA, History Museum Studies, Cooperstown Graduate Program, 1987
- Learned about leadership and inspiration as the coxswain of a rowing crew
- Quote: "When you join the museum profession you stand on the shoulders of those who came before you. My job is to make the place better for the next person."

Rob Kret's museum career has taken him to a range of institutional disciplines, but it began with history. "I was interested in history and the humanities, and I was attracted to the academic subject matter," he says. "I saw myself being a high school history teacher and crew coach." He spent an undergrad summer as an interpreter in the education department at The Henry Ford, and that's where he first understood a museum's capacity to educate. Back in college, he took a class on the history of technology and immediately made correlations between the academic side and the collections at the museum. It was the power of the object to teach, to gain perspective on a part of history, that opened his eyes to the possibilities of collections and to his future in the field.

His first job after receiving a masters degree from the Cooperstown Graduate Program was at the Society for the Preservation of New England Antiquities (SPNEA), now known as Historic New England. Although buildings and architecture are a common theme in his career, it was when he moved to the Midwest and became director of the Ella Sharp Museum in Jackson, Michigan, that he became interested in the visual arts. The Ella Sharp Museum taught him that the visual arts are another way to open up the world to visitors. He's stayed with visual arts museums ever since, building a career and reputation for collaboration that brought him to the Georgia O'Keeffe Museum in 2009. His current position melds art, artifacts, two historic properties, conservation activities, a library, and archive. As far as collections go, Kret kind of has it all.

Kret knew from the beginning that he wanted to be a leader. "I always had positions of leadership, even as a kid!" he says, recalling that he was small enough to be a coxswain, which was exciting. He learned from his coach that a really good coxswain can make a mediocre crew a great one. His time in the boat taught him how to inspire others, lessons that have stayed with him, fueling his desire to be both teacher and museum director. "I was not excited about being a registrar or a curator," he admits.

Nancy R. Coolidge, director at SPNEA during Kret's tenure there, gave him the opportunity to be Director of Museums, overseeing a staff of fifty. "Her expectation of me was to give me enough rope to run as far as I could go. If I fell, I was to get right back up." She taught him to treat employees as if they were your children—but not *like* children—by providing clear expectations, holding them accountable, praising them for jobs well done, and helping them when they needed it. "I wanted to live up to Nancy's faith in me."

Kret recalls his Chattanooga experience, where as director of the Hunter Museum of American Art he worked diligently to weave the institution into the fabric of the community. "The Hunter was physically cut off from the community, and art museums have a tough enough time being seen as accessible," he recalls. He followed a director with a twenty-one-year tenure, so the board saw the transition as an opportunity for the Hunter to become a vital part of Chattanooga. "They were hungry for it," Kret remembers.

There were several elements in place in Chattanooga that led to collaboration between its cultural institutions. First, there was an agreement that collaboration benefits the visitor experience. The Convention and Visitors Bureau and Chamber of Commerce were dedicated to this. There was a new mayor who also supported the idea, money to revitalize the downtown, and a population used to actively participating in conversations about their city.

What began with the museum outsourcing its HR, finance, and IT functions to the aquarium led to joint purchasing, marketing, and exhibitions, capped by a joint capital campaign that Kret describes as very powerful and innovative. Fueled by a government bond issue that provided big money, the project moved forward. In a matter of months, the collaborating organizations raised millions of dollars, allowing Kret to develop an interpretive master plan and involve the community in the conversation. "It was a meaningful process," he says. The good news is the Chattanooga collaboration continues. Kret knows how important working as a team is for himself and for the field. "I learned at the Cooperstown Graduate Program that when you join the museum profession you stand on the shoulders of those who came before you. My job is to make the place better for the next person."

His desire to see this type of collaboration replicated in Santa Fe is still a work in progress. The chemistry that created success in Chattanooga is not currently present in Santa Fe. "I continue to believe that a rising tide lifts all boats," says Kret. "We'll approach collaborations differently here. We'll be more deliberate in choosing partners and projects in order to build momentum."

"Art museums, and museums in general, haven't done a good enough job of telling our stories," Kret believes. By way of explanation, he cites the rising imposition of PILOTS (payments in lieu of taxes) that many struggling municipalities are levying on their nonprofits. "That's the fallout of taking ourselves for granted. We need to talk about our impact. Economic impact, yes, but we need to make the quality-of-life case. Otherwise, we're vulnerable to things like PILOTS."

"We have a responsibility to make a difference in the lives of the people who live in our communities." Kret talks about how museums must become more visitor centered, citing two examples where that's happening: 1) the Detroit Institute of the Arts (DIA), where because of visitor input and master planning, the community voted to increase property taxes for ten years to provide an infusion of funds to the DIA; and 2) the Dallas Museum of Art, where a strong visitor-centered approach, fueled by visitor studies, has tripled visitation.

Kret believes that what prepared him most for a leadership position was due to a great extent to his upbringing and on-the-job learning, furthered by his mentors (which include a variety of peers, Nancy Coolidge, board members, scholars, and his Association of Art Museum Directors colleagues).

"A place like CGP provided a strong foundation, but the reality is you can't learn it all in a two-year course of study," he notes. "You must learn by real-life experience."

Without skipping a beat Kret says lack of training in human resources has been a source of frustration. "There's an assumption that just because you're the director, you know how to deal with people," Kret says. "Bad or no HR can really hurt an institution. A good HR program can propel an organization forward."

He muses that there are many disciplines within the museum field that are solitary—historians, curators, and conservators, for example, study, research, write, and work in isolation. "The field is programmed to not be collaborative." What's needed is training in managing people. "We have to move toward academic qualifications not being as important as team commitment and an understanding of the twenty-first-century museum," he concludes.

As he reflects on how his leadership has changed over time, Kret thinks that being a parent has had a big impact on whom he is as a human being and as a leader. He understands the importance of team, collaboration, and working with governance. He sees the value of engagement and connection with the board of trustees.

When he thinks about how he aligns work, family, community, and self, he says that being a husband and a dad are most important to him, so family is number one on his list. Work takes the second slot, because it's personally rewarding and he can grow from it. Community comes in third, since he sees it as an extension of what he does professionally. As an example of combining work and community he talks about a public sculpture garden project, which engaged the community in dialogue about how to make art publicly accessible. Dead last is self, which he admits has always taken a back seat. The demands of being a director make it tough to balance his time, although he offers that he has found some time to improve his golf game.

As far as the future of museum leadership is concerned, Kret says that it needs to be more flexible and more open to understanding and articulating a museum's role in the community. Leaders must be willing to build community in ways that are meaningful to the audiences and to deliver in ways museums aren't delivering now. "Adopting a visitor-centered approach is a long-term development strategy," he says. He thinks the university museum model is one worth looking at more closely.

There's fruitful collaborative ground in research and development, Kret thinks, especially in conservation, that could result in new revenue streams. He cites the collaboration between the University of Texas El Paso and the Getty Conservation Institute on a light filter that was first tested at the Georgia O'Keeffe Museum and is now known as the O'Keeffe Light Filter.

"We need to make more layers of information about collections accessible to the public—technology will play a big part in that—which means museum leaders will need to become comfortable with giving up some control over the interpretation and use of this information."

Kret's advice for aspiring leaders includes being flexible and smart, with one eye on today and the other on the museum's needs in the future. He encourages all leaders to have a vision and set priorities to meet it. And he echoes the lesson he learned as a graduate student: "Always remember that someone will follow you. You want to leave behind your very best work. Ensure that the organization is better for you having been there."

Burt Logan, Executive Director and CEO, Ohio Historical Society, Columbus, Ohio

- MA, History Museum Studies, Cooperstown Graduate Program, 1983
- Received the General of the Army Omar Nelson Bradley Award for Excellence in Historical Research while at West Point
- Quote: "Every person regardless of capacity can be a leader."

Burt Logan has always been a museum director. He has held four executive directorships in his museum career, including his current one, so it seems likely that he set his sights on leadership from the beginning. "I did, even as far back as graduate school," Logan recalls. While most of his classmates at the Cooperstown Graduate Program wanted to be curators, Logan was more interested in learning about museum operations and how and why they tick. He wanted to learn enough to be able to talk intelligently with experts in the field.

Before he could even get to that point, he first had to complete a five-year obligation in the army after graduation from West Point. "Being a career officer was not a path I wanted to pursue," Logan says. Instead, he was fascinated by museums, finding them to be unique learning centers for civic engagement. He always liked American history, and he had a penchant for wanting to move organizations forward. It was a combination guaranteed to bring him to a museum studies graduate program.

Looking back over his career, Logan admits that he sought some leadership opportunities, but others came to him. "I know I was preparing myself for leadership," he says, "but I was also open to opportunities." Acknowledging there was no predetermined sequence of events, his goal was to do the best he could wherever he was and to be ready if a new opportunity came along.

His preparation for his current position as executive director and CEO of the Ohio Historical Society is an amalgam of his previous experiences. "Each step of my career is built upon the previous positions," he muses. "There's been no watershed event, no epiphany. It's an accretion of experience and knowledge and reflecting on that, the lessons learned." As far as Logan is concerned, every experience has been an opportunity to learn. Nothing has been a waste of time.

Logan readily admits that he's a different leader now than when he first started out. When he looks back on his early career, he cringes when he thinks about his lack of experience, his lack of balance and perspective. There were times when he was overly ambitious and wanted so much to succeed. "I have a broader perspective now," he reflects. "I know when to let something play out."

Early on he saw himself as needing to know all the answers. Now he believes the leader really has to know how to frame and formulate the questions. He considers himself to be a more probing person today, posing questions that lead toward useful answers. He's still directing the conversation, but he tries not to manipulate it. He thinks this approach empowers staff and creates a process for unity and cohesion.

The Ohio Historical Society has a staff of a little over two hundred full-time and part-time employees. His direct reports form a leadership team (he prefers the term *leadership team* rather than *management team*), saying, "Every person regardless of capacity can be a leader." Logan hopes he's more adept now at helping individuals build on their strengths, recognizing he couldn't help an organization achieve without all the people around him. "I didn't always grasp that concept," he admits.

Yes, there are things he'd like to do over again, but not necessarily to make them right or better. Rather, his desire would be to recapture the euphoria he got from doing them the first time around.

Logan's resume states that he transformed the USS *Constitution* Museum in Boston from accepting the status quo, and he's advancing similar organizational change at the Historical Society. When asked how he identifies the need for change, he replies it doesn't take great insight to identify because so often the signs and signals are all there. Successful organizational change occurs on multiple tracks—some tactical, some strategic. Leaders need to deal with lingering issues while determining the larger challenges and opportunities. "First, you must assess the situation—you gather insights by listening and by hearing," says Logan. "Then, it's a matter of sifting through the real priorities and the real ideas that have an impact to transform."

That reminds him of a search committee member who told him during his interview that the Ohio Historical Society wasn't going to be around in five years. That might have been true if the organization stayed on its current path. "But we are much stronger now for having made change," Logan declares. As a leader, he tries to help organizations realize there can be a better future. "When you look at a glass half empty," he says, "it's harder to get where you want to go. We must have a sense, tempered with reality, of a better future."

Logan believes change is generated from within an organization. "An organization is not going to respond to leadership until it realizes that it's better off with you than without you," Logan states. "You figure out what needs to be changed when. . . . it depends on constantly asking what the organization needs." It's his job to knit it all together.

Logan approaches the alignment of work, family, and self in the same sort of organized fashion, making each a priority in its own way. When he comes to work it's to do his best, and he expects this of his staff, also. When he's with his family, his work cell phone is turned off and only answered if there's an emergency. Again, he wants staff to do the same. As for himself, he says it took him a while to discover his personal passion: furniture making. "And I still have all my fingers!" he laughs. Although Logan is plugged into technology, using Facebook and a Droid at work, he finds that his creativity level increases when he's unplugged. "Value and wisdom come in times of quiet," he says.

Logan characterizes his role models as a series of mental snapshots of people he's interacted with over the years, many of which stem from deeply etched teachable moments. For example, at West Point, a fellow cadet was found guilty of an honor violation. Because of a technicality, the decision as to whether the cadet would stay or go was on the fence. The superintendent called the cadets together to make the point that his choice was ultimately between the organization and the individual. Organizations, he told the cadets, outlast the people associated with them. Organizations are resilient. Individuals are much more fragile; one mistake can be ruinous for a lifetime. His decision, then, was made in favor of the cadet. The superintendent is one of Logan's snapshots, resulting in a life lesson about second chances that is as clear today as it was nearly forty years ago.

When musing about how museum leadership is changing, Logan is quick to point out that the field is experiencing the retirements of many veteran leaders, a fact brought home to him at a recent American Alliance of Museums' meeting, where he didn't see the usual faces of long-tenured directors.

"Effective leadership mirrors society. As we look for more transparency and involvement (think user-generated content, Wikis, etc.), a leader has to recognize changes and embrace them and use them for the good of the organization, remaining true to values, but helping organizations be as nimble as possible and not succumb to the whims of society. Be in sync with society." How does a leader be nimble? "Recognize that the leader doesn't know everything. Be open and accessible; listen and be receptive. Doing so will show you where to be nimble."

"I'm always learning as a leader, and the organization is always evolving." He left three previous positions when he felt he had contributed what he could. He needed a new challenge, and the organization needed a fresh pair of eyes. "Knowing what you know and don't know, and when to push and not push, are key," he advises.

His advice for the next generation of museum leaders? Find balance among work, family, community, and self. View each position or task as an opportunity to prepare for the next challenge that comes along. Focus on things you can do as an individual to prepare for leadership. The more responsibility you have, the more it will depend upon being able to work with people and think strategically. These are the intangibles rather than the mastery of content.

Are leaders born or made? Leadership is a combination of personality (you're born with that) and behavior (you make that). "I'm a product of behavior," Logan concludes. "I've enjoyed leadership because I always wanted to be a leader. I've enjoyed the opportunities I've had, but I've had to work for them."

Logan takes a moment to ponder the evolution of museums from cabinets of curiosity to today's teaching and learning institutions. "Museums are just as vibrant as they always were," he says. "Each generation will have the opportunity to decide what role museums have in society—they don't have to be content with what has been."

Andrew E. Masich, President and CEO, Senator John Heinz History Center, Pittsburgh, Pennsylvania

- MA, History/Museum Administration, University of Arizona, 1984
- MA, History, Carnegie Mellon University, 2011
- PhD, History (in progress, all coursework completed), Carnegie Mellon University
- Started his own museum at age ten
- Quote: "I truly believe that our institutions and audiences, with whom our lives/careers become intertwined, are our most enduring legacies."

You could say Andy Masich's museum career began in his Yonkers's bedroom. When he was ten years old, he discovered a Minie ball, the ubiquitous bullet of Civil War fame, in his grandfather's attic. The rest is history. He used earnings from mowing lawns to build his collection. He even persuaded his mother to buy him black powder at the local ammo shop so he could do "research." Andy was a driven boy-collector and curator.

His office today at the Senator John Heinz History Center in Pittsburgh is considerably more dignified than his childhood bedroom with one notable exception—it has its share of personal collections. Scanning the room, Masich catalogs what he sees: "On one wall there are family images spanning 250 years. When I came to Pittsburgh, I discovered I had family roots here. I think it's important for history museum directors to have roots in their communities," he says. There's also a bookshelf with a treasure trove of hats and books. "I'm a hat guy; I guess you could say that hats are a metaphor for my life and career," Masich muses. The books are mostly about American and Western Pennsylvania history, and the Civil War. Several are ones he wrote; others were written and signed by David McCullough, a Pittsburgher, who traditionally unveils his latest book at the Heinz Center.

While Masich held leadership positions in several museums right out of college, he wasn't intent on leadership. "I hadn't thought about it. I wanted to be a history educator," Masich declares. No surprise coming from the guy whose childhood museum was complete with neatly labeled artifacts and a brochure awaiting visitors at the door.

He dropped out of grad school to become curator at Fort Lowell and the Fremont House, sites operated by the Arizona Historical Society in Tucson. Within the year, he was appointed director of Century House Museum and Garden, another Arizona Historical Society site in Yuma. "You had to make things happen by yourself," he recalls of his time there. "I was a dirty fingernails leader." He did research, created exhibits, raised money, cleaned toilets, and, yes, even the aviary's cages. By the time he left, the staff of three had grown to twelve. "You don't have to move to grow," he says. "You can build your organization around you."

Masich's career and leadership opportunities have largely been strategic. He believes the museum you lead should be *the* historical organization in your community. In order to solidify that reputation, leaders need to seek community activities and responsibilities that help them be better directors by leveraging their work and extending their reach. "Any good museum director needs to become an integral part of their community," Masich states. In his case, he serves on the Pennsylvania Historical and Museum Commission, and he's active in both the American Association for State and Local History and the American Alliance of Museums. He's always sought to be on the preservation commissions in the cities where he's worked, too.

When a headhunter approached Masich to apply for the position at the Historical Society of Western Pennsylvania (HSWP), it was ready for change, but Masich wasn't looking for a job. He was in Colorado at the state historical society, where his eight years included serving as interim director. The HSWP wanted a person with a grand vision. When he finally interviewed, Masich was impressed with the passion and dedication he found on the board. He was especially impressed with the board chairman, and he felt there would be the right kind of support from the board for the right kind of leader.

During Masich's tenure in Pittsburgh, the historical society became the Senator John Heinz History Center, a big tent for a growing number of specific collections and sites. Now home of the Western Pennsylvania Sports

Museum, the Fort Pitt Museum, a library and archives, and a living history village with a significant archeological site, the Center is the state's largest history museum.

Masich reckons that the best preparation for his current position came during his tenure in Yuma, where he was detached from the Arizona Historical Society "mother ship," as he calls it, and built the organization by himself. Though the scale of his current museum is vastly different from his Arizona days, he feels having a basic sensitivity to audience is key to the success of a museum, no matter its size. "We're educational institutions with a mission—not just a collection or a building," he says.

When asked what prepared him least for his current position, he says only half jokingly, "Any class I took at a university or college. On-the-job was where I learned." Because Masich took opportunities to try a variety of positions in a variety of institutions, he encourages people to volunteer and try out different museum jobs, particularly in small museums so that they can understand all the functions of a museum. "As a director," he says, "you can defer to expert staff, but your own deep functional knowledge helps you hold your own with the experts and comes in tremendously handy with donors and funders."

"I hope I am a different leader now than when I first started," he says. "The one thing I hope I've retained is passion for the subject matter and the importance of history." He believes he's better at reading and understanding people, too. His secret for success: try to help people feel good about themselves. Good communication is key, adding that you need to let people do things because doing everything yourself won't grow an organization.

As far as success in the bricks and mortar department, the History Center recently acquired a big building nearby as a collection storage and conservation center. "It makes me feel proud to look up and see a thirty-foot-tall neon sign of our logo. You can see it from space!" On a personal level, it's Masich's writing that gives him great satisfaction. His publications are the tangible evidence of his love for history and storytelling.

Aligning family, self, community, and career are seemingly easy for him. His personal and career interests are inseparable. "Friends become donors and board members; my interests in travel and writing are linked to my work and career," he says. This work requires a merging of life and career, but it's no different than what the heads of major corporations do.

Masich admits that burnout is the downside, but he feels that can be offset by the meaning of the work. "We [history museum folks] have altruistic aims. Giving to the community has rewards that for-profit CEOs don't have. We're here for the greater good—that's what helps keep us sane."

In 1982, I participated in the Seminar for Historical Administration, then hosted by Colonial Williamsburg, and spent a month with senior museum leaders and eighteen young museum directors from around the country; we discussed the all-consuming nature of our jobs and the problem of burn-out. I clearly remember being advised to make room in my work plan to do what you love, what you're passionate about, what made you get into history museums in the first place. I was working seventy-hour weeks then (I still probably average sixty today) and it made a big impression on me. So, since then, I've always tried to carve out time (probably less than 5% of my work week) to do historical research and writing. The important thing is that I don't feel guilty about this. It's not an official part of my job description (though it could be) but my boards have always been supportive of this and seem to share my pride in publishing. Sometimes the history books that I've written have related directly to my museum's mission and sometimes not, but they give me a sense of pride and accomplishment apart from my work as a museum director.

Noting that he simply can't do justice to all the people who have influenced him, Masich does reserve a primary and reverential spot on his list for his mother, whom he says, "[She] was probably the most important influence on me, giving me self-confidence and aiding and abetting my boyish interest in the Civil War." She talked to him about leadership, simple but enduring, advice such as not following the pack.

Masich knows the leader has to make the final decisions sometimes. "You have to go with your gut in relating to people, in how a project or a program will be received," he says. "You consult with others, but sometimes you need to make the decision for the betterment of the institution." He says he's seen leaders who can't do that; who rely too much on others' input. Take strategic planning, for example: it's important to have a lot of input and buy-in from the community, but the director must guide strategic vision.

In thinking about the future of museum leadership, Masich acknowledges the strides women have made at all levels. While he sees more women leaders, he hopes that men won't leave the ranks of museum education. The leaders of the future will be better educated, with more advanced degrees and solid theoretical training. "This will help to professionalize our field even more," he believes. The downside could be too much specialization and less broad grounding in the breadth of what museums do and the impact they can make.

"Get a broad grounding," Masich advises the next generation of museum leaders. "And know your audiences, but don't pander to them." Take the five minutes at the beginning of a conversation to learn whom you're talking to, be it staff, donors, visitors, board members, or the community at large. "As I see it, there are two paths one could take," he says. "You can make money and have history as an avocation or you can make your passion for history your career." He chose the latter, but he recognizes that it isn't for everyone.

"I highly recommend a midcareer training program like AASLH's Seminar for Historical Administration—for the knowledge gained from mentors to the camaraderie and network of colleagues, it's well worth the investment in time and effort (though it will seem impossible to tear yourself away from the day-to-day commitments of family and work at the time) and can be a life-changing experience." Spoken like a true alum.

Anne Grimes Rand, President, USS *Constitution* Museum, Boston, Massachusetts

- MA, American Civilization, Brown University, 1996
- Avid sailor; won her ocean racing crew division in Bermuda in 2006
- Quote: "Asking for help can become a group success."

When Anne Grimes Rand joined the USS *Constitution* Museum in 1987, she thought she would stay just three years, master what she needed to know and do, get a bit bored with it all, and move on. Now as she contemplates her career of twenty-six years at the museum, she's both surprised—and perhaps a little amused—but certainly not bored. She is doing what she loves.

"I love to sail and I'm an interdisciplinary learner," she says. "Those two things led me into maritime history." During college, she went to Mystic Seaport as an intern and first saw the possibility of having a job in the museum field. She came to the USS *Constitution* as an assistant curator in a one-person department where she did everything. Once she was named curator, she spent twelve years in that position, taking responsibility for creating new exhibits as well as collections care. The promotion to deputy director gave her responsibility for content by making her responsible for the visitor experience, a component to which Rand is passionately and vocally committed.

Rand was not one of those people who wanted to run a museum. She figured that it wouldn't engage her for very long. What energized her was learning more about the historical narrative and developing content, which she views as internal processes. She saw the director's role as an outward process. She didn't want to be awake at night worrying about money or figuring out how to survive. But a couple of stints as acting director helped her think about the possibility of being the director at some point. When her predecessor, Burt Logan, left the museum, she was named acting director again. Ultimately, Rand figured she might as well accept the position rather than work for someone else who might not share the same institutional values that she helped develop.

She feels that her consistent influence on shaping the museum, combined with a variety of experiences leading teams in strategic planning and accreditation, as well as education program and exhibition development, gave her solid preparation for taking on the institution's top job. And then there is her sailing background, which requires many similar, if not the same, skills as leading institutions: control and handling of the boat in all types of weather, navigation theory and practice, mastery of strategy and tactics for successful racing, and coalescing a crew into a well-oiled machine. It's a relatively easy jump from sea to land in the leadership development department.

However, it did take courage to take on the acting director's job that first time. "There's always fear of failure. You offset it by doing your best, constantly explaining to others what you're doing and why you're doing it, and starting from common ground. This is key," she advises.

Rand doesn't think of her role in the abstract. She's practical about leadership, thinking of it as a means to address specific institutional issues. One example of that analytical, pragmatic leadership approach resulted in the museum's successful Family Learning Project, a multiyear, IMLS-funded revisioning of the museum's exhibitions and programs that now provides the strategic framework from which all operations flow. Armed with research and informed by outside expertise and extensive formative evaluation, Rand and her staff worked tirelessly to create an institutionwide paradigm shift that put family audiences first. "It was a revolutionary experience," she says. Nine years into the Family Learning Project, Rand feels there are still opportunities out there to deliver a great product to visitors. And you can bet she'll be the first one to champion them.

No fan of siloing individuals or departments, Rand's natural inclination is to use her leadership to pull people together and harness their knowledge and creativity. The staff is organized into interdepartmental teams for cross-pollination of ideas and to encourage risk taking. Rand and her staff constantly tweak and test everything from revenue-generation ideas to signage. She raises the comfort level for change by couching decisions as "tests" (as in, "this is only a test"). This approach helps to encourage risk taking, and if something doesn't work, it's changed again. Rand's bottom line for experimentation begins with everyone agreeing on big goals or ideas. (For the USS *Constitution* Museum, it is all about the visitor experience.) It's a useful evaluative tool, and "it also becomes easier to set egos aside," she says.

Not having worked at other museums is somewhat of a drawback, but Rand feels that is more than made up for by the fact that she has tremendous depth of understanding and experience in one organization. Where her skills are weak, she has people who are strong, she says, citing her accounting staff. Development has all been "on the job training"; while she's had lots of grant writing experience, personal donor relations are a part of her learning curve. Again, she has staff to help fill in her gaps.

With two years in the top spot under her belt, Rand admits she's more confident now. She learned early to ask for help if she needed it, and she found aid forthcoming if others saw her as working hard and knew she needed help. "Asking for help can become a group success," she says.

She's also learned to be a delegator. She spends more time on grant applications now, but she doesn't have to stay until midnight finishing exhibitions. And she understands fund-raising isn't about asking for money, it's about supporting a cause.

Networking is important for Rand. Her networks have evolved over the course of her career. For example, the maritime community was her first "family"; then came the New England Museum Association as an important professional connection. Most recently the IMLS-funded Family Learning Project put her in touch with what she terms "smart people who helped me broaden my horizons." She concludes, "Networks can help you navigate which road you're walking down."

When thinking about how museum leadership is changing, Rand wonders how technology is changing leadership. "Or is it the other way around?" she asks. (She's not overly wired herself and considers the museum to be on the trailing edge of technology.) One thing that's not changing is the focus on fund-raising. "Museum leadership is like running an academic institution," she reflects, "but it's the content that is the engine for funding."

For a person who thought she'd leave the USS *Constitution* Museum in three years, Anne Rand is building quite a legacy. She is the first to say there's still more to do. What has her deeply engaged right now is thinking how to integrate STEM education into the museum's educational and family programming, which she says is already a great product. Another goal is to get the museum on a strong financial footing if she can.

Rand's advice for the next generation of museum leaders: "Try to make it fun." That's part of her museum's strategy. In terms of leadership, "People should feel valued, listened to, creative, respected at work." To that, we'll add one of Rand's favorite expressions: "Huzzah!"

Ellen Rosenthal, President and CEO, Conner Prairie Interactive History Park, Fishers, Indiana

- MA, Early American Culture, University of Delaware, H. F. DuPont Winterthur Program, 1978
- Master in Public Management, Carnegie-Mellon University, Pittsburgh, 1984
- Has a special interest in how people learn in museums in addition to organizational behavior, entrepreneurship, and why organizations work the way they do

- Quote: "By bringing visitors into the conversation, we found a tremendous difference in how families engaged."

Ellen Rosenthal has a corner office. That is what comes to you after thirty years in the museum business. She is the president and CEO of Conner Prairie, where she has been a staff member since 1999 and CEO since 2005. Located about twenty-five miles north of Indianapolis, Conner Prairie describes itself as "an interactive history park." A Jacksonian version of America, Conner Prairie is centered around William Conner's grand house. For museum folk it is also the place that birthed the words *living history museum*. Known for its "first-person interpretation," or more simply having museum interpreters speak to visitors as if they are in the time period they portray, Conner Prairie is a place that asks visitors to do their part: to think and question nineteenth-century politics, clothing, family, jobs, and just about everything as they tour the 1,200-acre site. That is the world at Rosenthal's back. She looks outside when she has the time.

Asked if she had glanced out the window the day of her interview, the answer was a sigh, followed by a no. Surrounded by her big wooden desk, an oversized monitor, credenza, sofa, and a lamp made to look like a balloon model, Rosenthal declares the place neat, but adds, "Not in my mother's sense of tidy." Nonetheless, it is hers, and when she has the time, the view of the sheep out the window is glorious.

Rosenthal is one of those people who knew what she wanted to do early on, so her career plan required only minor tweaking to make it work. "I grew up outside of New York City," she explains, "and my interests were art history and history." She went to Barnard College, believing her world would be one of research and curatorial victories.

She began thinking about leadership, three jobs into her career. She had been a reference assistant at the Frick Art Reference Library and a Sotheby's cataloguer when she was hired by the American History Workshop in Boston. "That gave me a chance to see the flaws and the broader perspective," she says of a job that kept her moving and learning as she progressed from one project to another.

Immediately after leaving History Workshop, she enrolled in a masters degree program at Carnegie-Mellon University in Public Management. She already had an MA from the Winterthur Program at the University of Delaware, the gold standard for curators in the mid-1970s. But the second masters started her thinking about things like organizational behavior, entrepreneurship, and why organizations work the way they do, things she still thinks about. "The management degree built on the strategic planning I did as a consultant," she recalls.

She arrived at Conner Prairie with her masters in public management in hand, having spent thirteen years first as curator and ultimately chief curator at the Senator John Heinz Pittsburgh Regional History Center. Although she had spent a lot of her career thinking about stuff, Conner Prairie allowed her to think about people. She had even started auditing a doctoral program in learning in museums. Using that research remains one of her greatest personal and professional successes. "You can't mandate change," Rosenthal says, adding that when museum teaching is ingrained and didactic, to make change means commitment and stakeholders. She ended up taping visitors in the exhibits, listening as they listened to Conner Prairie's interpretive staff. Ultimately she partnered with a sociolinguist from Ball State University to understand how adults with children learned at Conner Prairie. "By bringing visitors into the conversation, we found a tremendous difference in how families engaged," she says. "And the staff has embraced it," she says about the organization's interpretive changes. "It's changed the mission; it's like a snowball," she says, adding that while she is proud of the change, she was not in control, she was only the catalyst.

When you ask Rosenthal about failure, it's more a "do-over" she is hungry for. A lot of her management ideas and vision were cemented during her years as a graduate student/stay-at-home mom. With hindsight, she says, she wishes she had known more about engaging the donor community. "I didn't have an intuitive sense of engaging that community," she says, "or an understanding that they are their own separate audience group."

Rosenthal says she learned about leadership from her father. "It's corny, I know," she says, describing a dad who managed the research and development arm of a major drug company. "He was a boss for 250 and always inspired and empowered and managed to see talent and try to develop it. He never resorted to recrimination or blame." Rosenthal remembers her father as someone who tended to praise quietly. "He would pull you aside," she says, "and if something was wrong, he would ask why you took this approach." He was, she sums up, someone who made things happen both at work where he registered 250 patents, at home, and in town, where he ran the local community center and guided community planning. "More than anything, he's my leadership model," Rosenthal concludes, adding that her father is who she thinks about when she struggles with workplace issues.

Despite the excellent role model her father continues to provide, Rosenthal is adamant that courage is a necessary ingredient for leadership. "It's really hard to be a risk taker and make change," she says, acknowledging that it can be stomach churning and lonely. "You have to distance your feelings," she says. As to loneliness, a supportive husband helps, but she acknowledges that it is hard to "keep your mouth shut and not discuss things with staff."

"You have to consciously look for people to talk with," Rosenthal says. She has used variously a professional coach and board members. She says that finding someone to download to is a goal of hers. "You can get lost in your own perspective," she says. And as for mentoring, Rosenthal says it has begun to feel more difficult recently. "I talk to young people all the time, and I love looking for talent and encouraging them to speak in front of the board or the staff." Her biggest successes happen when staff she's nurtured make the leap and leave the nest. "It's fun when that happens," she says.

Work/life balance elicits another sigh from Rosenthal, who starts by suggesting women's lives—at least their professional lives—aren't straight lines. They zig and zag. "I finished a second masters," she remembers, "but then I had children." The kids, three boys in eleven years with a physician/researcher husband meant a full-time job at home as well as at work. "When I came to Conner Prairie to be vice president, it was a better job, but I was still the primary parent." Rosenthal became Conner Prairie's CEO after a governance dispute that left her as interim director. At the end of the interim period, she threw her hat in the ring. "I'm now an empty nester, and the kids have survived," she says. "I regret that I didn't have that experience [of leading an organization] earlier in my career. Most women seemed taxed to the limit." After a pause, she adds, "Guys always have someone at home with the dinner."

Ask Rosenthal about the future of museum leadership and she says that for her, it is coming closer to for-profit leadership. Recently she took a weeklong class at Wharton in leadership. "There were only three of us from nonprofits in the class," she explains, "and there was no separation in how we approach leadership." Rosenthal remembers a fellow student who commented that when she spoke, he heard passion, reflecting that he had not really understood what being passionate about work was like. Whatever happens next for Rosenthal, being passionate is hardly a negative.

SUMMARY: LESSONS LEARNED

Lesson one: Authentic leaders are map makers.

Let us begin with self-direction. These folks, indeed all of the leaders interviewed for this book, did not wait for an organization to give them road maps for their lives; instead, they are the map makers. Take Anne Cathcart, whose experience in the history museum field is relatively brief but who has created an email network of young professionals that puts her squarely in the center of an active, committed professional world. Recall her advice to her peers: Take initiative; don't fear making a wrong move. She adds, "Our parents are known as the helicopter generation and we're shaped by that. Many of us are not particularly resourceful, yet there are tons of resources available." And once again there is a spillover effect. Individuals who take control of their own lives are also decision makers, experimenters, and innovators, the kind of behavior that benefits any organization. Last, remember Pam Green's (her story is in "The Courageous Leader" section) immortal remark: "If you've chosen to be an executive director, you have chosen to find the best for the organization. That's not the organization's responsibility."

Lesson two: Authentic leaders are also fiercely self-disciplined.

Beth Grindell, whose rise to leadership was swift, used a personal counselor and a job coach to help with her transition and recruited two members of the museum's staff to serve as a backup team, signaling to everyone how seriously she took what would ultimately be a temporary position. Grindell also found she had to put her volunteer life on hold, something she wasn't happy about, but again, something the job required. And then there is Rosenthal, who, in raising two children, balancing her career with her physician husband, completing two graduate degrees, and running a major history organization, is a model of self-discipline.

Lesson three: Authentic leaders nurture close relationships and are compassionate.

It is clear that all our interviewees have close relationships. Cathcart's is not limited to her peers via email. She is extremely close to her family and to her professional (and older) mentors who act as sounding boards as her career unfolds. At the other end of a long career, Rosenthal reminds us, "You have to consciously look for people to talk with," adding that finding someone to download to is a goal. "You can get lost in your own perspective."

In understanding their own narratives, authentic leaders are more understanding of the challenges facing followers both at work and in the rest of their lives. Rosenthal has thought a lot about women in the workplace, particularly women in museums, and she is quick to acknowledge that women's lives have more zigs than zags, especially when children enter the mix. "Most women seem taxed to the limit," she says, adding, "Guys always have someone at home with the dinner." Being understanding and being a leader aren't mutually exclusive. And like most traits in this section, compassion sends out its own ripples. Acknowledging the ghastly effects of a sleepless night with a sick toddler doesn't give an employee a free pass, but it does say, I understand.

NOTES

1. Sally Helgesen, "A Journey to Authentic Leadership," in *Learn Like a Leader: Today's Top Leaders Share Their Learning Journeys*, ed. Marshall Goldsmith et al. (Boston: Nicholas Brealey Publishing, 2010), 17.

2. From an interview with Christy Coleman that aired on WTVR, CBS 6, Richmond, December 10, 2012, http://wtvr.com/2012/12/10/virginia-this-morning-christy-coleman/.

Chapter Seven

The Courageous Leader

Courage is about conveying vision and having the strength to sell something even when it doesn't make any sense.
—Pamela E. Green, executive director, Weeksville Heritage Center, Brooklyn

The third attribute we believe is critical to twenty-first-century history and cultural heritage museum leadership is courage. Aristotle wrote, "Courage is the first of the human qualities because it is the one that guarantees all others." True in ancient Greece and still true today, even in a history or cultural heritage museum where in many instances courage is the catalyst, without courage there is no vision, and without vision there is no action. Too often we associate courage with something physical: Navy SEALs executing a daring rescue; the D-Day landings; a triathlete's victory. But courage in this instance is ethical and, sometimes, moral. It is not doing things correctly but in doing the right thing. [1]

In times when it seems to make better sense for an institution to hunker down to ride out a rough patch or hold back in the face of the unknown, the courageous leader has an innate understanding of when change or innovation will work and when it won't. The courageous leader knows that by taking a counterintuitive approach outside the proverbial comfort zone, it is possible to succeed even in challenging times.

These leaders hold deep convictions about the nature and impact of their work. They know when to pull back, but they also champion barrier-breaking programming. Courage allows leaders to give staff the authority and responsibility they need to flourish both personally and professionally. Courageous leaders think differently about communication inside and outside the organization, challenging outdated rituals or confronting uncomfortable situations. They work toward inclusion. They're entrepreneurial, too, seeking results that equal more than the sum of their parts.

Courageous leaders sometimes serve as an institutional moral compass, educating boards of trustees and volunteers in particular, but sometimes staff as well, who are ignorant about professional museum standards. Just think of the curators and directors who must challenge well-meaning trustees who see selling collections as a way to raise operating dollars. Or turn the mission inside out precisely to chase new, but dubious, forms of funding.

A leader can't lead in moments like these unless she is sure about her own beliefs.

She may find her choices and gut instincts make her a majority of one, facing resistance from staff or board. When that happens, leaders need the confidence to stand alone if need be. In his *Fast Company* article about the five characteristics of great leaders, Bill McBean writes, "Having the courage to stand alone, the tenacity to not succumb to pressure, and the patience to keep fighting until you win the day—and sometimes being able to do all three at the same time—is something you will have to develop if you want to be a true and successful leader."[2]

The leaders we chose for this section all push the boundaries of what history museums can and should be; they have confidence to "navigate the jungle" as Kippen de Alba Chu puts it. They are independent seekers and thinkers, and straight-talking influencers. And they would likely all agree with David Young, who says, "People need to see museums as places where community needs are met."

Hope Alswang, Executive Director/CEO, Norton Museum of Art, West Palm Beach, Florida

- BA, American History, Goddard College, Plainfield, Vermont
- Feels too many history museum staff are in retreat from the modern world
- Quote: "You've got to be courageous. It's the number-one issue."

Hope Alswang's office is not what you'd expect. "I figured after thirty years in the business, I'd earned the right to paint my office the color I wanted," she says. She chose pink, which is fitting given that she is currently director of the Norton Museum of Art in Palm Beach, Florida. There are two paintings on the walls: one by Louise Nevelson and one by Milton Avery. She describes the furniture as pretend Ikea. And there's her dog, Pip, a six-month old wire-haired dachshund who comes to work with her.

Alswang's route from her original position at the Brooklyn Museum where she worked in the Decorative Arts department was all history until recently. She served as director of both the New Jersey Historical Society in

Newark and the Shelburne Museum in Vermont, before moving to the Rhode Island School of Design, and most recently to the Norton. She likes art, but she misses history. And what she loves is material culture. "I like what people live with and the way they live," she says. But while she misses the subject matter, she does not miss working in a history museum. "Honestly, I couldn't stand the history museum field," she says. By way of explanation, she says that if she asked her current staff about an article in the *New York Review of Books*, about 80 percent of them will have read it. She does not feel that's true of the average midsized history museum staff, and she is adamant that individuals charged with interpreting culture should be as invested in the present as the past. She feels too many history museum staff retreat from the modern world, and they are ultimately unable to make connections between today's world and the one they are charged with interpreting, something that she feels is important to visitors.

She still visits history museums, though. And if you ask which ones she's impressed with, Colonial Williamsburg makes the list, along with New York City's Jewish Museum. "It's probably the single institution I admire the most," she says. "It just understands its public." In the world of smaller history museums, Alswang is a fan of the quirky and the unusual. Tucker Castle, a Historic New England site in Maine, comes to mind, as does the Edward Gorey Museum on Cape Cod. Despite her professional proclivity for relevancy, she's drawn to places that give her a sense of time stopping.

Making those kinds of connections and helping visitors understand that even the recent past is history is something Alswang fought for. While director in Newark, New Jersey, she and her staff created an exhibit called *Teenage New Jersey, 1945–1971*. "It was the crucible for teenage-ness," she declares about the state now home to Chris Christie and Snookie, but also the birthplace of Frankie Valli, Bruce Springsteen, bikinis, and the boardwalk. Ultimately, the exhibit won awards from both the American Alliance of Museums and the American Association for State and Local History.

Years earlier Alswang, while curator at the Society for the Preservation of Long Island Antiquities, lobbied for a Levittown exhibit, a battle she lost, although later she created a 1950s house at the Shelburne. Opened as a temporary exhibit, the house, filled with Lincoln Logs, dial telephones, a black-and-white television, and a record player, was so popular with visitors that it remained open for several years. "And we did it all for $35,000," she says, adding that absolutely everything in the house was purchased at tag sales and thrift shops, often by staff so young they had no idea what they were looking for. "I showed them pictures," Alswang explains, laughing. "Nobody but me and five other people would think a 1950 house would work," she adds, and yet creating a place where everything could be touched on a forty-five-acre site where nothing was touchable was a stroke of genius.

Ask her if she knew she wanted to be a leader when fresh from school and looking for work and Alswang shakes her head. "In 1974 there were no women directors that I knew of," she says. What she wanted, she thought, was a position at one of the big, interactive museums like Sturbridge or Williamsburg that in the early 1970s were tackling complex problems of interpreting not just furniture or decorative arts, but all of life, food, work, and family. "I wanted to do something more innovative," she says.

Her training ground for leadership came later when she became head of the New York State Council on the Arts Museum Program. With a staff of 3.5, Alswang supervised grant giving, both general operating support and project support for New York's 1,500 museums and historical societies, something she describes as a remarkable training ground for a wannabe director. "It was a million case studies every day," she says. "And an amazing view of more than two hundred museums a year."

In addition, she had the opportunity to learn not only about the importance of public funding but also she quickly realized the program was a leadership laboratory. Furthermore, it wasn't about places, but people. "We were funding leaders, not organizations," she says. "It's about the people, not about the site."

Ask Alswang about failure, and when she answers it is more about regret. And worry. When she thinks about previous positions, she can't help but wonder whether what she did was enough. "When you leave, you're always concerned about whether an organization is stable enough to sustain itself," she says. That circles back to her idea that leadership rests with people, not places; remove the individual and not every organization can sustain itself, although she suggests that the time between a leader leaving and total collapse may be shorter in smaller museums than huge ones. "If the Met [Metropolitan Museum] lost its director today, it would probably be thirty years before anything happened," she quips.

One thing Alswang is sure of: leadership demands courage. "You've got to be courageous," she says, especially in a history museum. "It's the number-one issue." She continues, adding that history museums have to know what they are saying about culture, and further to know why. She also thinks museum directors need thick skins. "If you have thin skin, this isn't the job for you," she says. "You're in the middle between the board and the staff with no place to step back. You want to protect the board from the staff and vice versa, but there is nowhere for *you* to go." Being trapped in the black hole of no close friendships at work means that mentors, friends, and advisors are important. Alswang has had a cohort of friends—among them Gretchen Sorin, now director of the Cooperstown Graduate Program, and David Kahn, director of the Adirondack Museum—but she says the need for the network isn't so acute these days. And when it comes her way, she loves mentoring. "I'm very interested in young people. I like that stuff a lot," she says.

When you ask Alswang about work/life balance she says she doesn't buy it. She loves her life. "I have the most privileged life you can imagine," she says. "I have a great husband, I raised two kids," she continues, before asking rhetorically, "Was it hard?" Then she answers, "Only in a society as rich as ours would people pay us to do what we do. It's incredible." On a more serious note, she points out that many if not all of the first generation of female history museum leaders were childless, underscoring that the path breakers, whatever their faults, may have made sacrifices to push through to the top.

And the history museums of the future? Alswang sees a world of worry on the financial side. "It's changed dramatically," she says, comparing the mid-1970s to the present. For her there are two great cultural revolutions, the first from the robber barons of the late nineteenth century to the Depression and then from the 1970s to 2008. Today, Alswang sees history museums entering a world where there are fewer and fewer resources. "On the art side though," she says, "the rich are still rich."

One thing that Alswang sees as endemic at many museums, art and history, is a culture of perfection. "It's the enemy of progress," she says, describing staffs mired in process and fearful of action. She notes that working a program or exhibit to death in the name of perfection is another way to suck the life out of it. "Be creative, take risks," she exclaims, which is maybe just another plea for courage.

Trevor Beemon, Creative Services Coordinator, Atlanta History Center, Atlanta, Georgia

- BA, American History with a Certificate in Public History, Kennesaw State University, 2007
- Doesn't think of himself as a leader, but rather an influencer and an instigator
- Quote: "Don't ever feel limited by what you have access to or what's been done in the past."

"It's been a journey being in the right place at the right time," Trevor Beemon states as he reflects on his nearly decade-old museum career. Two overarching factors in Beemon's career story are that his dream started young, and he's been in dogged pursuit of it ever since.

Beemon's journey to the Atlanta History Center (AHC) began when he visited as part of a first grade school trip. He was hooked. Most of us might have tucked that memory away until college or graduate school. Not Beemon. He was so fired up about it he started volunteering at age twelve in museums in Marietta, his hometown.

As a kid, he thought he might want to be a curator, but a Boy Scout project changed his thinking. He created a panel exhibit only to find out that he really enjoyed the graphics part of it (interestingly, graphics are now a large part of the work he does now). When he got to college, he majored in American history and worked on a variety of projects at a couple of museums near school doing graphic design, educational programming, exhibit development—you name it. "There's a lot to be said for working in a small museum," he says. "You get a range of experience."

It wasn't until college that he got to go back to the Atlanta History Center to work, first as creative services director and now as manager of digital communications. He's a one-man operation who reports to the vice president of marketing, a "great leader." Social media, graphic design, video production, photography, and the website are all his responsibility and require him to work with every department in the institution to create content.

That means Beemon has had to encourage and educate people across the institution to help them get over their fear of social media and using the Web to advance the mission. "Pretty much everyone is on board now," he concludes. It's also his job to create the balance between offering great information to the public along with a bit of goofiness that social media requires. "We are a little bit irreverent," he acknowledges. He's pleased that other institutions have emulated what AHC does.

Beemon has had to do some education and trust building with his boss, the vice president, too, to get the free reign he needs to keep social media activities timely and fun. "Because the time frames for social media are so compressed," he observes, "what you want to say can't be held up in red tape for hours or days. We try to stay one step ahead of what's hot out there so that AHC's social media ties into what else is going on."

Since social media is twenty-four hours a day, you can find him doing a chunk of that work in the evening when people are online. "I'm lucky that history is my wife's passion, too," he says. "She likes to tag along with me."

He doesn't think of himself as a leader, but rather as an influencer and an instigator. "I try to make friends with everybody," he says. When he reflects on what helped him prepare to be a successful influencer, he ticks off a list that includes:

- Knew exactly what he wanted to do from a very young age
- Started volunteering at age twelve—helped him be comfortable with adults
- He took adult art classes as a kid

- Sought encouragement and wants to exceed expectations (it surprises people), and it gets him pumped
- Able to focus attention on one goal
- Worked in a smaller institution, which helped him respect the positions of others and helped him figure out what he wanted to do.

His bottom line, however, is that he's done his own thing no matter how circuitous it may seem to others.

What's next for him? "The Atlanta History Center is like the Holy Grail for me, and I have a strong attachment to it," he says. Someday, though, he'd like to lead a marketing department and maybe work in a large institution with a global reach. "I would love to stay in social media," he admits.

When he muses about where museum communications are going, he immediately says the biggest changes are in the technologies—mobile tours, apps, and touch-screen displays in exhibitions and into places where you don't want a kiosk. "Leaders need to embrace technology in order to keep museums relevant and to engage generations who learn differently. They need to be fluid about it, too, because technology changes so fast."

His advice for aspiring museums professionals comes from deep within his personal experience: "Be creative"—push the boundaries; don't ever feel limited by what you have access to or what's been done in the past. "Passionate people will experiment and try new things."

Robert Burns, Director, Mattatuck Museum, Waterbury, Connecticut

- MFA, Theatre Performance, University of South Carolina, 1989
- Chair for the New York State Council on the Arts Museum Program peer review grant panel
- Quote: "I want people to feel like they have a voice."

From his office overlooking Waterbury's "green," surrounded by the superb architecture of this once-moneyed city, the newly appointed director of the city's Mattatuck Museum radiates energy. Burns arrived in Waterbury in 2012. Asked if he entered the field knowing he wanted to lead, Burns's answer is a succinct "no."

"Does anyone say yes?" he says. "I came from a different path," he adds, tracing a career that took him through eleven years of nonprofit development work before landing him at The Olana Partnership, the not-for-profit arm of one of New York State's preeminent historic sites, and from there to his first directorship at the Mattatuck Museum.

While he may not have intended to be a museum director, Burns is sure about what prepared him for leadership. First, he attributes it to his large family. He is one of eight children with a grandfather who raised beef cattle. "In order to get anything, I had to learn to be outspoken," Burns says. With a mother who worked outside of the home, Burns and his siblings spent weekends, vacations, and every summer on the farm. "All the boys were born into servitude," Burns says, smiling. He learned a great deal though, watching his father and grandfather interact with the world. And it paid off. Of the eight children, six are in leadership positions.

Burns also credits his theatre major with a piece of his leadership success. "Theatre taught me to work with a group making sure it's done right," he says, adding that, in addition, it taught him to speak with authority. As a young film actor his attention to detail catapulted him to a position of leadership because he was one of the few who took the time to read the union rules, quickly finding himself the go-to person about what was and was not allowed on set.

Like most actors, he had a series of temporary jobs that paid the bills. Three weeks into one of those positions, Burns's boss fired the entire staff, except him. "I went from the lowest-paid person to the only person," he remembers. "I *had* to do a good job." That position was in development. The rest, as they say, is history. He moved swiftly from a New York City nonprofit to the State University at New Paltz, and eventually to The Olana Partnership.

Of his current position, Burns says he wasn't the search committee's first choice. As he tells it, the committee kept dropping his resume, but the firm handling the search kept putting it back in the pile, believing that the museum needed Burns's fund-raising skills more than it needed someone with a more traditional background in American history or museum studies. "I can learn the script," Burns says. "That's why we have curators."

Maybe it's the sibling thing, but Burns takes his role as a leader seriously and enjoys being a mentor. "Early on in my career I made the decision to encourage my staff to look for better jobs," he says. It's something he's regretted every time a capable staff member leaves, but he believes it is important nonetheless. "That's the only way we grow," he says. One memorable time, when he pushed a staff member to leave, she asked him why he wanted her to go. His answer: there was no way for her to move up and he believed her heart was somewhere else. It was. She just finished her PhD in poetry. "She blames her life on me," he says smiling, adding, "It's a really important role we all play, and the pushing is good."

Burns may be a mentor, but he is not a micromanager. "Here's what I say when I'm hiring someone," he explains. "I'll work with you to set up the end goals and to get you on the path, and if you can't get there, I'll help." But in between, Burns expects staff to work independently. "My door is always open," he says, but it's clear he is a cut-to-the-chase manager. "I won't waste your time so don't waste mine," he concludes. In a perfect world Burns would like a litmus test that would predict an employee's ability to act independently. During the interview process he has been known to present potential employees with a crisis scenario to see how they prioritize. "Some people need to be pushed," he sighs.

Asked how his leadership skills have changed over time, Burns responds that he is better at dealing with other people's issues. "We all have problems," he says. "I try to be fair, but we can't have too much personal time at work." That's the present-day Burns. Earlier in his career, he says, he spent too much time enabling and coddling. That doesn't mean it is easy. The hardest part Burns says about leadership is that it isn't a place where one can share one's fears and frustrations. That's where his colleagues come in and his partner, Gary Shiro, director of the Hudson Opera House in Hudson, New York. But he's careful about letting problems at work poison home life. When the two used to commute together, they limited time discussing work issues to the moment when they passed the Stewarts Ice Cream shop. For the rest of the drive the conversation had to be about something other than work.

"I want people to have a good time because that makes them more productive," Burns says about work at the Mattatuck. "That's entirely appropriate, of course, but that's another difference from twenty years ago: having a good time." He continues, "I want people to feel like they have a voice." He confesses he doesn't change his mind often, but he wants to listen. "There's a sort of lightness now," he says about work at the Mattatuck, and these days he comes to work eager to get things done.

Burns has mentors himself. Among the people he admires are his oldest sister, who he characterizes as his hero, and Shiro. "He sees the best in everyone and gets people to go there with him," Burns says. "I don't know how he knows what he knows, but he makes it seem easy." In his new state of Connecticut, Burns has already discovered a group of colleagues. A member of the pilot class of cultural entrepreneurs at Cooperstown's Graduate Program in Museum Studies, Burns reached out to the four Connecticut alumni on his arrival in Waterbury. All responded and they, plus a growing group of Connecticut museum directors, have proved to be welcome sounding boards.

And the future? As a relative newcomer to the history museum field, where does Burns see it going? "Is younger a fair word?" he asks. "I think it has to be geared toward a younger audience to survive." For him the days of the don't-touch and be-quiet museum are long over. "Museums will change. The art won't go, but there will be new ways to engage and make it easier and more accessible so it doesn't feel boring and tired."

It hasn't all been a wild ride to the corner office. Burns is forthright about his mistakes, and one in particular still rankles. In his former position a wealthy donor tried to endear himself to the community by donating to a variety of nonprofits. His goal: to pepper the city with gifts in the hopes of getting what his business needed when the time came. Eventually he approached Burns's organization with a large, but anonymous, gift. Burns decided to accept. His boss felt otherwise, telling Burns to refuse the gift on the grounds that when the community found out it would do more damage than good. Ultimately, Burns refused the gift, but not before telling the donor why and what his boss's role in the decision was. With hindsight, he says, "I should have found a way to work with my boss and return the gift without blaming her." While he stayed on, he says the interaction became the elephant present in every room. The lesson learned? "Always have the mission in front of me. Take the time and ask whether something is about me or whether it's best for the institution." He adds, "That's a hard lesson to learn: mission-driven leadership."

Kippen de Alba Chu, Executive Director, Iolani Palace, Honolulu, Hawaii

- Bachelor of International Business Administration, The American University, Paris, 1988
- Named one of the 20 Emerging Leaders for the Next 20 Years by *Hawaii Business Magazine*, 2010
- Quote: "Failures are where you learn the most."

Although it is midafternoon on the east coast, it is 8:00 a.m. in Honolulu, Hawaii, where Kippen de Alba Chu is already in his office. He is the executive director of Iolani Palace, Honolulu's 1882 Italianate building once home to Hawaiian royalty. A native Hawaiian, de Alba Chu has a friendly voice and a warm laugh. Although he has been director of the Palace for almost seven years, he still seems surprised that he is there at all, much less as director. After studying business in Europe, working for the Insurers Council, and serving as Chief of Staff for State Representative Bertha Kawakami, de Alba Chu seemed an unlikely choice for the Iolani Palace's search team who sought him out. "I had concerns about being outside the field," de Alba Chu remembers. "I had no experience." The board responded, however, that he brought other skills to the table, skills they could not teach. "They said they could teach me about museums," he recalls.

de Alba Chu believes his time in the Hawaii legislature was the best preparation for leadership he could have asked for. "I learned about procedures, especially human resource legislation," he explains, adding that the legislature is sometimes guilty of not following its own laws. "Being head of a museum," de Alba Chu says, "is like herding cats." For him, both the decision to take the Iolani Palace position and his success in the museum field probably go back to a much earlier fork in the road when he chose not to pursue a career in the visitor services industry. "I don't think I'd be in the place I am today if I had," he muses.

Ask de Alba Chu about his career successes and failures and he responds, "Failures are where you learn the most." He is frank about a failure, which happened while he was still in the legislature and went into business with a family member. The short version is it did not work out. In the end de Alba Chu filed for bankruptcy, but he learned something. Watching his own capital as well as that of investors flow in the wrong direction gave him a crash course in cash flow, budgeting, and spreadsheets—something he says has been very important since 2008.

When he speaks about successes, though, his first thoughts are about a disaster, more particularly, Hawaii's 1992 hurricane. He describes the event as an important learning experience. He was working in the legislature when the storm hit Kauai, his boss's home district. "There was complete devastation," remembers de Alba Chu, who flew in three days later. Tasked with working on the recovery, his role was to assess, make decisions, and offer support, not unlike the role of many leaders. In retrospect, he describes the experience as a great training ground, a kind of decision-making-at-the-point-of-transaction on steroids.

Because de Alba Chu's museum is the former home of Hawaii's royalty, he also deals on a regular basis with issues of activism and civil disobedience. In fact, he recalls being at a museum conference on the mainland and speaking about "a takeover." He was asked if his museum was being taken over by another agency, and he had to say no, what he meant was a takeover by protesters, many of whom see the palace as symbolic, and who come to Iolani for acts of civil disobedience. Prior to de Alba Chu's tenure, the palace refused entrance to protesters. Under de Alba Chu that has changed, and so has the frequency and volatility of the protests.

Ask de Alba Chu about courage, and he replies that for him it is more about confidence than courage—the courage that a leader needs to stand behind his or her decisions. In his case the palace is a symbol of the sovereignty movement, and the decisions he makes reflect on the palace. Twenty years ago, at the beginning of his career, he says he was not confident, and, he says, he was inexperienced. The Iolani Palace position came at the perfect time, however, allowing him to bring experience from outside the museum field to the palace.

As for work/life balance, de Alba Chu attributes the fact that he has it—and he says he does—to his wife. "She keeps me on my toes and helps me separate work and home," he says, adding that she has on occasion threatened to remove his cell phone battery if he could not put it down. "Physical activity is also important," he says. Not surprisingly, he likes water sports. And while more traditional beach sports are part of his repertoire, there is something else he has learned to love since coming to the palace. "I love to water the grass," he confesses. "You stand on the grounds; you are there, but it is separate; and it is destressing."

As for people de Alba Chu admires, it is no surprise that his wife is at the top of the list. "She moved from Mexico to Michigan at sixteen," he explains. "It was the coldest winter in a century. She got her GED; got a job at Wendy's, and built a life on her own. That takes courage." The other person de Alba Chu mentions is Irene Hirano, former CEO and founder of the Japanese American National Museum in Los Angeles, and currently president of the Ford Foundation. "I know her personally," he says, adding that he admires her a great deal, both what she has done and what she continues to do. He credits Hirano, a former chair of the American Alliance of Museums board, with helping him make the transition from the legislature to the museum world, and with the fact that he is now a member of AAM's board himself. Looking back on his career, de Alba Chu says there was a moment when he was working for the Insurance Council and he realized, "Going to help the insurance industry doesn't get you going every morning." He feels differently about Hawaiian history and his work at the Iolani Palace.

de Alba Chu is a great believer in networking, something that he says comes from his years in the State Legislature. "It's definitely from my political background," he explains. "It's all based on strategy, on how you navigate the jungle." After joining the Hawaiian Museum Board, he became the liaison to the Western Museums Conference, which led to him lobbying the group to come to Hawaii for its annual meeting, which was a wowing success. Currently in an MBA program at the University of Hawaii, de Alba Chu sees his graduate program as another valuable form of networking. He also sees it as critical for twenty-first-century museum directors. "Unless you have an unlimited endowment, museums need to run as businesses," he says. "You need to create new revenue and become more efficient."

He believes you can learn to be a leader if you are careful with the mentors you choose. And he uses his business school connections frequently. "When you learn leadership in a group," he explains, "you learn from everyone else's mistakes." He is, however, still stunned by how lonely the top position can be. "You can't talk to the rest of the staff," he says, explaining that not only is it inappropriate to talk with staff about a variety of problems at the museum but he also feels staff also need their own form of networking, which might or might not include their director.

When he thinks of the future, de Alba Chu thinks of two things. On the personal side, he and his wife await the adoption of a child in the new year, an opportunity to give back in a new way that he views as very important. On the professional side, he says, "I really want the Palace to have a new reputation as being open and inclusive." He continues, "Before I came [here], it looked closed and uninviting. It had a siege mentality, almost as if it were a bunker." He describes the museum as a place that was not big on outreach, which welcomed visitors a bit grudgingly. All that has changed, however. "I would feel satisfied if the Palace became a 'must see,' a place where community groups don't have to protest," he says.

Pamela E. Green, Executive Director, Weeksville Heritage Center, Brooklyn, New York

- MBA, Finance, University of Chicago
- Was two weeks on the job at Weeksville when September 11 happened
- Quote: "My door is always open. Anyone can ask me anything, and they do."

If you listen, you can hear Pam Green's Mississippi roots. On the telephone from the Weeksville Heritage Center in Brooklyn where she is executive director, Green has just returned from a vacation seeing family in Gulfport, Mississippi. Returning just ahead of Hurricane Isaac, Green is back at the helm of the Heritage Center, a position she's held since 2001. Weeksville is the only historic site in the five boroughs dedicated to a community of free blacks. The site includes three nineteenth-century houses that portray Weeksville life from 1860 to 1930.

Ask Green about the trajectory of her museum career and she chuckles. "Quick and dirty," she says, referring to her hiring at Weeksville, her only museum job. A former vice president at the Sesame Workshop for the Children's Educational Television Network, her first encounter with a nonprofit, Green had never worked for a museum. The closest she had gotten was as a consumer. "The whole process was a blind date," she recalls. "A consultant suggested I send in my resume." From there, she remembers, it was an investigative process on both sides.

Asked if she has a mantra that guides her at work, Green says, no. "What I believe is that you have to have an understanding of how people work and how they are motivated," she continues. "It's something you are learning all the time." Pressed, she says that leaders must engender trust, hopefully centered around a vision agreed upon by the trustees and the director. "I guess being accessible," she concludes. "There's no one place to get answers, and nobody's 100 percent correct."

And her desk? Green describes it as pretty nasty, although since she just returned from vacation it contains only two piles. "They're important," she explains, laughing. Describing herself as not too tech savvy, she says, "I learn what I have to know." She uses a cell phone and texts, and she reminds her interviewer that once upon a time she was a programmer back when computers were the size of trailers. She likes Excel but loathes having things in her ears. "I may take forever to get through the Museum of Modern Art because I don't want one of those headphones."

Ask Green about mentoring, and she verbally shrugs, saying that there is not one particular person there at the other end of a landline to talk through her problems. She does, however, have a mental telephone book of individuals, some from city government, some from foundations, even one from her current board of trustees. Each, she says, has special skills that she has come to appreciate. "They give me guidance if I'm having a moment," she says. As for mentoring others, Green says she is open to providing assistance to anyone interested, but as far as a formal mentor/mentee relationship, not yet. "I like to think I project as someone approachable," she says. "My door is always open. Anyone can ask me anything, and they do."

Green recalls one individual who told her she was a candidate for an executive director's job. Green's response was to tell her she did not think she was ready. Describing the individual as smart, enthusiastic, and full of integrity, Green felt as a candidate, this person lacked personal and life experience, something Green sees as an important arrow in any director's quiver. "You're young and you think everything's life or death, and you don't understand how many boards are not well configured and well managed."

On a roll, Green continues, "There's a whole lot of things no one can tell you. You can't be an executive director right out of college. You can be a founding director, but not an executive director," she says, implying that the too-good-to-be-true first job–first directorship right out of graduate school might be just that: a recipe for trouble. Green has an MBA, not a degree in nonprofit management. She credits it with certain things, including her equanimity around spreadsheets and budgets. Her business degree and her long record as a nonprofit consultant are two things she feels are important. Consulting, she says, means you see the same things happen again and again, so when they finally happen to you, it's not such a surprise.

Ask Green who she admires and she immediately says her mother. Now ninety-six, Green's mother has been on her own since 1970. "She raised three children and sent them to college," Green says, describing a parent who ran her own kindergarten before anybody had heard of early childhood education. "Because it's a small town, almost everyone went to her school. She enriched and enhanced the lives of hundreds of people." Apart from her mother, Green says she is filled with admiration when she meets someone with a disability, particularly if she is having a whiney moment herself. "Can you imagine navigating the subway as a blind person?" she asks. "And [yet] whatever is supposed to hold them back, just doesn't."

For Green, though, work/life balance is a conundrum. Circling back to her mother, who worked until she was close to seventy, Green says, "You just get it done." Warming to her subject, she asks, "What does having it all mean? Does that mean you're worn out at the end of the day?" she asks before waiting a beat and answering, "Well, then don't have kids." Green admits that everyone's life needs a bit of balance, especially those in long-term relationships, but she says, "If you've chosen to be an executive director, you have chosen to find the best for the organization. That's not the organization's responsibility."

Describing Weeksville as a pretty flexible place, Green explains that there are fundamental things you want to do to keep employees who are producing happy. Some of her employees work from home to accommodate family situations, for example. That said, Green still believes that it is an individual decision to make the kind of commitment some organizations demand. "If being an integral part of a family is important to you, you may have difficulty when your workplace interferes with that," she says.

Green underscores that she's only talking about house museums like Weeksville in part because her museum experience, at least as a director, is deep but not broad. That said, she believes that anyone entering the field needs to be clear about why they want to be part of it and whether their expectations are real. She believes that individuals seeking the director's path come with different expectations that influence the choices they make; that a curator who becomes a director brings different expectations to the director's chair than an interpretive programmer.

Regardless of the baggage brought on board, she still feels historic house directors have two roles: be true to history and serve the community. "I think it is important that just because there's a piece of history does not make it relevant; you have to work to constantly stay relevant."

The battle for relevancy and reinvention brings Green to courage. "In the historic house field, and maybe it's the case for all museums, if you're the director of a small to medium [sized] organization, you absolutely need courage." Why? Because Green says "you're always trying to sell things that are a little bit different from the way they really are." At the end of the day, she says, it is the director, no matter what anyone says, who is likely to be thrown under the bus.

"People don't fire boards," she quips.

For Green it is the executive director who is on the front line. "It's the executive director who has to say 'We can no longer do this.'" And it is the executive director who has to take chances; the executive director who says now we have to raise money this way or we have been telling the story this way, how about being authentic and correcting it this time around?

Courage she says, comes in many forms, but frequently it is about conveying vision and having the strength to sell something even when it doesn't make any sense.

"I believe in strategic planning," Green says, "but the plan I really believe in is getting it done." She believes directors have to be flexible. "If you're the kind of person that needs a structured environment to survive, I don't think you can be a [successful] director," she says. "There are some control freaks who are directors and they make it work. I'm not. Control freaks want people to work a certain way. I believe in understanding outcome, and staff members are responsible for working out how to get there." She pauses before adding, "If you scare easily, you can't be an executive director."

Asked about how leadership in the museum field is changing, Green responded, "Leadership is changing, and I think it may need to change." She continues, "If museums are going to continue to thrive in a changing world—and I'm not just talking about technology—people are going to have to look at an organizational structure that is easier to move and be more forward and progressive." Green believes history museum directors must be open to thinking about their institutions in a variety of ways. "Leadership must be almost radical in what the organization can do," she says, adding, "We don't consider anything we're doing outside of mission. We ought to be able to wake up and say historic houses do XYZ and not lose sight of their history."

Her parting words: "It's the story you're projecting and the use of that story in terms of your community."

Christopher J. Taylor, Diversity Outreach Program Manager, Minnesota Historical Society, St. Paul, Minnesota

- MA, Museum Education, Cooperstown Graduate Program, 2005
- Tries to pay it forward every day
- Quote: "I'm in a unique position to make a difference, and that is most meaningful."

There are those among us who would characterize their education as a lifesaver. Chris Taylor is one. Being chosen for a Coca-Cola Foundation Museum Fellowship followed by a masters from the Cooperstown Graduate Program changed Taylor's career trajectory in a big way. Headed for a social studies teaching career, Taylor had little idea that he could do that in a history museum setting. Like hundreds of thousands of people of color, he didn't see the museum environment as a place for him. "Museums aren't on the career radar for diverse populations," he states. "There's no foundation for working in museums." And then he got into the Fellows Program and he's rarely looked back. It was, as he says, an epiphany.

While the Coca-Cola fellowship headed him in a new career direction, the Cooperstown Graduate Program has had the biggest and most long-lasting influence over his life. Because of its generalist thrust, he is able to continually draw from it for his work, particularly with college students. Add a healthy dose of mentors ranging from professors, who opened his eyes to the worlds beyond the traditional historical narrative, to African American museum leaders who became his role models, Taylor readily acknowledges that who he is now is made up of pieces of everything in his past. He returns to this understanding again and again.

Chris Taylor is a guy who tries to pay it forward every day. For those of us who associate Minnesota with Norwegian bachelor farmers, potlucks in the Lutheran Church basement, and eyeball-deep snow, the word *diversity* in any ramification may not immediately spring to mind. The fact is, 30 percent of the Twin Cities is made up of minority populations, and there are more than sixty thousand Native Americans across the state. Since 2006, the Minnesota Historical Society (MHS) has been diligently focused on busting the myths, exploring the hidden narratives of life in this state, and raising diversity awareness among schoolchildren, visitors, and the society's staff in the process.

This is the tip of the iceberg for Chris Taylor, whose job is as diverse as his title. The diversity program at MHS began with Taylor, where he was a "one-man show" and the first African American staffer. "It's exciting, but anxiety making because we're breaking new ground all the way," he admits. Taylor's program is housed in MHS's education department, which encompasses all education programs from grade six to college. He tries to make kids aware of the broader historical narrative; to go beyond the stories of great white men, which are still a big part of social studies curricula in the American classroom; and to look for hidden or marginal voices.

Mirroring his own experience, he's also responsible for recruiting diverse undergraduate and graduate students as interns to introduce them to the museum and public history fields with the goal of encouraging their pursuit of museum careers. He also helps them find jobs. The program is a partnership with the University of Minnesota and includes coursework and an internship. He's continuing to develop and expand his work by creating a similar internship for Native Americans. He also wants to develop immersion programs for high school students to get them comfortable with the idea of going to college, and perhaps pursuing careers in history and museum studies.

Because he's an African American male, he feels he has a responsibility to bring different perspectives and community relationships to the table, and he makes it a point to be vocal about it. He is charged with helping people think differently about race and diversity generally, and he wears a lot of hats—facilitator, idea generator, door opener—to accomplish that. In this regard, he considers himself an entrepreneur.

As an advocate for diversity within the ranks of MHS, he works closely with all departments. His mode of teaching diversity is often through story-telling, where the lesson comes from a variety of viewpoints, including his own. When he speaks about his sensitivities around diversity, people listen. He especially loves when he can connect his co-workers with overarching meaning.

"I never really thought about being a leader, but I did know I wanted to move up the ladder." He echoes what so many entry-level staffers admit: "When I was just starting out, I was just trying to hold on. I'd say, tell me what my job is and I'll do it!" When he left graduate school he didn't feel like a professional, he just felt lucky to have a job. Now, he is self-aware; he is a professional and understands he is pretty good at it.

When asked if he would like to be the director of a museum, Taylor quickly says no—"too many hats!"—along with too much politics and public scrutiny for him. Then, he takes a reflective step back and considers that he could probably do it in another ten to fifteen years at a smaller museum. For right now, though, he's satisfied where he is and how he has gotten there. His big goal, however, is to create a lasting legacy at MHS for his work.

For Taylor, work, community, and self blend together, thanks to a job that he regularly reinvents and a supportive family. His typical workweek is forty to fifty hours, but he finds he works constantly, especially when he's out in the community meeting people. "I have lots of opportunities to engage communities," he says. As an example, he cites his child's championship baseball game where he ran into a person who could help him with one of his programs. Rather than let the opportunity slip because it was outside the confines of the office, he used it to begin the conversation. Having said that, he adds emphatically, "Work will never take priority over family."

He knows the work and his program have been successful, but he never thought of himself as being a national leader. "I'm fortunate to work in a place with a lot of support and resources," he says modestly. "I'm in a unique position to make a difference, and that is most meaningful."

His advice to aspiring leaders is also the recipe for his own success: "Make sure you're passionate about what you do. The museum field is a big umbrella. Figure out where you want to focus and define what success means for you. Get on top of the vision-making thing. There's something to learn in almost every experience, nothing is wasted."

"I've got the greatest job in the world," he says, "I'm happy to go to work everyday."

David W. Young, Executive Director, Cliveden, Philadelphia, Pennsylvania

- PhD, History, Ohio State University
- Collects pencils from other museums and historic sites
- Quote: "I love the young talent at work. I love mentoring."

It's July midway through the 2012 drought and even in leafy Germantown, Pennsylvania, the heat has become something palpable. For David W. Young, the executive director of Cliveden, a National Trust Historic site, it's also the summer his home air conditioners were stolen, an almost understandable theft given July's brutal temperatures. Young lives within walking distance of Cliveden, and listening to him talk about his job is also listening to him talk about his neighborhood.

Ask Young why he became a museum director and he will tell you it was accidental. He moved from a part-time staff position to junior department head to his first directorship at the speed of light, a journey he says he made in order to make change. Why? "There were some issues in the field," he says. "The preponderance of organizations needed work. They were busier defining their own position than in problem solving." Then there were the simplistic historical explanations that Young saw masking hugely nuanced narratives.

He planned to be a teacher. In fact, he continues to teach at the University of Pennsylvania's Graduate Program in Historic Preservation. An undergraduate major in German studies, the recipient of a Fulbright that took him to Europe for a year, Young was on track to wear tweed, teach history, and push the next generation to question the narrative at Philadelphia's house museums. Then before he finished his doctorate he took the fork in the road marked public history. Ultimately he finished his PhD, but not the way he started. Instead, he wrote about his Germantown neighborhood in a dissertation titled, "The Battles of Germantown: Preservation and Memory in America's Most Historic Neighborhood."

"I'm a generalist and an explainer," Young says, adding that he sees administrating as another form of teaching. Recently, he's pushed the bounds of leadership beyond his position at Cliveden, becoming the point person for a fifteen-member project funded by the Pew Center for Arts and Heritage that redefined the neighborhood's historic sites. "You *can* change the narrative," Young says, adding, "We've been in the nostalgia business a long time. Now there's a new narrative of hope and progress." It was a lengthy, complex project that threw open doors and brought local residents inside. It created intergenerational dialog, as high school students interviewed grandparents about the community's public transit strike, a moment when Franklin Delano Roosevelt sent soldiers to guard the neighborhood's black bus drivers. The dialog helped everyone understand they were part of a single story. There wasn't one "important" narrative of Revolutionary War incidents, wealthy homeowners, and fancy homes; there were also jazz clubs, the arrival of crack, and new immigrants. "Cliveden is a slave owner's mansion," Young says. "And people were eager to talk about oppression and poverty."

It isn't always easy though. "I have bags under my eyes," Young says. "It's hard to be an overly sensitive agent of change," he quips. When asked if he could have a "do-over" of any leadership decision, Young pauses before answering, "I think I would have assessed earlier if I had the right people on the bus." He's made some difficult decisions and lost friends in the process, and recently the huge grant-funded projects Cliveden has been involved with gave it the appearance of a well-funded organization. "Lots of money means everyone saw us as an ATM, and that attracted people with an agenda," Young says. He concludes, "A bit like producing Ben Hur while driving the chariot."

Asked whether he thinks most history museum directors are prepared for the myriad personnel decisions they end up making, Young says no one is given those skills. "What graduate school teaches you how to evaluate what shape a board [of trustees] is in?" he asks. He goes on to say that perhaps when a curator, for example, is elevated to an administrative position, that person's narrow specificity can get in the way of the good of an organization. For his own part, even after six years in the driver's seat, Young remains shocked by how lonely the director's job can be.

So what mantras does he live by? "It's not a hospital," he answers quickly, adding, "If we don't get it right children won't die." And a corollary to that: Keep it all in perspective. "I'd like to say that carries over into the rest of my life," he says. "If I've learned anything, you can't overpersonalize. You can't become agenda-driven rather than what's good for the organization."

Young describes his desk as creative. "It gets blown off periodically," he says, adding that every piece of paper, every sticky note represents a decision waiting to be made. So it's full of piles, from the large and needy to slimmer, less acute-looking stacks, and . . . pencils. Yes, Young is a collector, but at work at least, only pencils from other museums and historic sites, each one a memory of a visit, a family outing, a talk, a panel discussion. And is he tech savvy? Not really. He credits the Cliveden staff for making him look more knowledgeable than he is, especially when it comes to social media. At home, he takes one day off to detox with no email. "I had to learn that the hard way," he notes. And the whole work/life balance thing? "I have a wonderful wife, a teenage son." Young says. He loves to travel, to ride his bike, to cook, and to eat, the former hopefully working to counteract the latter. "I love the young talent at work. I love mentoring."

Ask Young about his own mentors and he immediately mentions George McDaniel, a fellow National Trust director (Drayton Hall). "He's a member of the National Trust family," Young says. "He has a curiosity for all things; he's generous in a meeting, asking the kinds of questions that others benefit from." Young also credits Stephen Haugue, the director who prepared the groundbreaking work in Germantown. "There's no one who doesn't like him," Young says. "I aspire to be him." As for networking, Young sees it in its most catholic sense, believing it underpins much of what he does: a walk through the neighborhood; participating in the Germantown business district; testifying before City Council. On a personal level he believes networking director-to-director is crucially important, sharing problem solving and best practices. "It's one of the things that's benefitted me the most: lending perspective."

And the history museum field? Young sees more change coming in the next five years than he's seen in the last twenty-five. "At Cliveden we have staff and volunteers from [age] eighteen to ninety-five working together. How do you communicate across the generations?" he asks. He goes on to describe the role of IT in learning and in the way visitors learn. "We know now that museums are more than just venues for intelligent learning, but places for emotional and even spiritual learning," he says. "We need to meet the visitor there."

"Organizations need to change to meet the needs of communities whether that's films or coat drives or a warm place to be," he says. "People need to see museums as places where community needs are met."

Asked about his own legacy, Young is quiet momentarily. Then he says, "That passion is important, but it's equally important to learn new tricks. There's a difference between passion and adrenaline." Directors, Young believes, need to be willing to learn from their mistakes and possess a certain amount of courage. "What's exciting about the Cliveden project," he says, is that people come in like missionaries. "Museums can be verbs," he adds. "The downside is living up to it." Leadership, Young explains, isn't a birthright. He believes it's condition specific and environment specific. On a roll, Young continues, "Most historic sites would be sustainable, they just lack will or leadership. What could they be if they worked together?" In short, Young believes leadership isn't so much about an individual, but an institutional choice, concluding, "A lot of organizations have to allow leadership. It has to be needed and wanted."

SUMMARY: LESSONS LEARNED

These seven leaders represent courage in all its guises. They are all self-aware, a quality discussed in chapter 5.

Lesson one: Know thyself.

To reach way outside of the museum field, when the *New York Times* interviewed G. J. Hart, the CEO of California Pizza Kitchen, he was asked about leadership and self-awareness. He said, "The first step is to be the very best that you can be, because you can't lead anybody if you can't lead yourself. So you have to be honest with yourself about your good qualities, your bad qualities and the things you need to work on."[3] Pam Green, Trevor Beemon, and Robert Burns know who they are. They are unafraid to chart their own course. Beemon describes himself as someone who has known where he wants to go almost from the beginning, someone who did not need the affirmation of a group to make it happen. His museum world resides in the parallel universe of IT and social media, and he is passionate and understanding about melding the faster-than-the-speed-of-light nature of his work with the more staid world of history museums. He knows that leaders need courage to stand behind what they believe, but he understands that the constantly changing nature of things means that control is impossible. That is something Pam Green emphasizes as well. Courage is necessary when confronting the unstable, changing nature of things. Remember, it was Green who said, "If you've chosen to be an executive director, you have chosen to find the best for the organization. That's not the organization's responsibility." Robert Burns, on the other hand, finds courage in independence, his own and his staff members. Burns wants employees to have their own courage, not look to him as the parent of some museum family. Burns is so concerned about this he has sometimes required potential employees to describe how they respond to a hypothetical crisis.

Lesson two: Be willing to walk alternate and sometimes unpopular paths.

de Alba Chu, David Young, and Hope Alswang present us with another view of courage. They are leaders whose courage allows them to embrace the unpopular choice. De Alba Chu was the first director of Iolani Palace to welcome protesters rather than refusing them entrance. The result was an easing of conflict, a growing chink in the armor of an institution that looked embattled even as it yearned for visitors. Young and Alswang have each walked alternate and occasionally frankly unpopular interpretive roads, sometimes dragging organizations steeped in nostalgia toward something like intellectual freedom. Alswang's career is hallmarked by transformational exhibits that originate in ideas as much as in things, while Young's is marked by a dedication to collaboration that is atypical among history museums. Both see history as an ongoing narrative, not something bound by the four walls of an historic building or the dates of a collection.

Can the courage exemplified by these seven leaders be learned? First, understand that courage isn't fearlessness. Ask these leaders about fear and they will describe the fear of acting on their beliefs, the isolation of decision making, or the fear of taking a stand, but in reality they are describing the ability to act in spite of what scares them. Being courageous isn't about banishing fear. Next, followers need courageous leaders. And as we learned from Robert Burns, a leader's courage empowers employees to find their own decision-making moments. Courage like this also has a moral honesty. Staff reacts differently to leaders who act with integrity and who are willing and able to apologize. A courageous leader isn't one who hides her mistakes. She owns them and moves on. Remember, courageous leaders have courageous followers.

Lesson three: Invest in the 2 percent.

Last, we know from Alswang and Young that courage also demands innovation and the faith to know when to experiment. Don't forget that 98 percent of our ideas are mediocre. Be prepared to take a risk; invest in the 2 percent.

NOTES

1. Colonel Eric Kail, "Leadership Character: The Role of Courage," April 4, 2011, www.washingtonpost.com blogs/guest-insights/post/leadership-character-the-role-of-courage/2011/04/04/AGvfAohH_blog.html.

2. Bill McBean, "The 5 Characteristics of Great Leaders," *Fast Company*, January 23, 2013, accessed January 25, 2013, http://www.fastcompany.com/3004914/5-characteristics-great-leaders.

3. Adam Bryant, "The Six Steps of Leadership (Plus Courage)," *New York Times*, January 5, 2013, http://www.nytimes.com/2013/01/06/business/california-pizza-kitchens-chief-on-6-steps-to-leadership.html.

Chapter Eight

The Visionary Leader

If you can dream it, you can do it!
—Walt Disney

Where would we be as a society without JFK's call to put a man on the moon? Without Elizabeth Cady Stanton's provocative *Woman's Bible*? Without Martin Luther King's "I Have a Dream" speech? Where would we be without people who see something millions of others do not?

Every one of the leaders interviewed for this book has a vision for their institution and themselves. They could all be in this category just as most, if not all, fall into the other leadership categories we've chosen to highlight. However, it seems appropriate to limit the profiles in this section to underscore the fact that few people are real visionaries. All the rest of us are simply happy to follow them.

It is almost impossible to be a leader without some sense of what an organization can be and what impact it might ultimately have. Organizational vision is about possibilities; it is not about maintaining the status quo. When was the last time you heard a museum leader say, "Let's stay as good as we are right now!"? Not particularly far-sighted or aspirational, right? If you want the same-old-same-old, the tried and true, the safe and secure, then visionary leadership is not for you.

Visionary leaders not only see possibilities, they articulate them in such real and compelling terms that their followers see them, too. They create what Chip and Dan Heath talk about in their book, *Switch*—"destination postcards," vivid and highly detailed pictures of the future. Capturing in words or pictures what the future looks like, much like an architect's rendering of a building or restoration project, is an absolutely critical step in advancing the vision, the idea, the dream. [1]

149

Once the dream is articulated, the visionary leader creates pathways to make it real. These definitive, decisive steps are what set true visionary leaders apart from dreamers, who never quite make their ideas come true. With no ability to bring others along and no follow through, dreamers and big talkers lack authenticity, and they ultimately fail to command respect from their staffs or peers. True visionary leaders, on the other hand, may be loved or hated, but they're almost always respected.

Organizational founders have visions. Something or someone pushed them to fill a need, to right an injustice, to move humanity one step closer to being human. Take Sally Roesch Wagner, for instance. As the founding director of the Matilda Joslyn Gage Foundation, Roesch Wagner integrated a lifetime of women's equality work, teaching, and writing about Gage (the suffrage movement's lesser-known visionary) by making a place for social discourse at Gage's upstate New York home. She'll tell you her original vision didn't include a museum until later, but once it emerged she knew she was the catalyst to bring it to reality. Just as with a wind-up toy, founders have the wonderful job of cranking the organizational key and setting it in motion. At the same time, they, along with their boards and staff, have an obligation to make sure the organization doesn't dissipate its energy by running amok and getting stuck under the couch. True to that analogy, in recent years Roesch Wagner has focused her attention on succession, ensuring that the vision she set in motion will continue long after she's gone.

Change agents are also visionaries. In Fort Worth, Texas, former Disney executive Van Romans puts Walt's dream-it-do-it philosophy to work every day at the Museum of Science and History, where he serves as president. One reporter described Romans talking this way, "[He] is cutting through the air in front of him with this hands. 'This place is about (Slice!) learning, (Slice!) learning and (Chop! Chop! Chop!) learning!' he says."[2] This is classic Romans, creating destination postcards amid a flourish of gesticulations that exude palpable energy and vitality. Romans's career advice could just as easily be his everyday mantra: "Never say no to an opportunity."

Experimenters and inventors are also visionaries; in fact, experimentation fuels vision. Even though Nina Simon wrote her destination postcards well before she led a museum, her experience as a consultant, working with many different institutions around the globe, informed her thinking about what museums can mean to communities. In fact, she was on the verge of opening her own beer bar/gallery to try out ideas on her own turf before she became director of the Santa Cruz Museum of Art & History. If you know Simon primarily through her blog, you know she percolates and tests ideas there on a regular basis, despite or because of her full-time museum laboratory.

Integrative thinkers are also visionaries. If you cast a wide net as you go through life, it stands to reason there are many points where ideas and information intersect in purposeful, random, or exciting ways. By her own admission, Tonya Matthews's vision is a big one. She believes her institution, the Cincinnati Museum Center where she serves as Vice President of Museums, should serve everyone. Period. Like Van Romans, she's equally comfortable with right- and left-brain thinking thanks to her education in science and engineering; a slew of teaching and consulting opportunities in cultural and ethnic studies, urban policy, and museums; and a stint at the Getty Executive Leadership Institute. Her broad educational and experiential platform means Matthews integrates opportunities from a variety of disciplines when tackling big or complicated projects.

Tonya Matthews, Vice President of Museums, Cincinnati Science Center, Cincinnati, Ohio

- PhD, Biomedical Engineering, The Johns Hopkins University, 2005
- A published poet with three volumes to her credit
- Quote: "You can't deny leadership, and I discovered what propels me is vision."

Tonya Matthews is an unlikely museum professional. Her background is so diametrically opposed it makes you wonder how her brain wraps itself around the yin and the yang of her. She has a bachelors degree in science and engineering with a certificate in African American Studies from Duke University; she followed that with a PhD in biomedical engineering from Johns Hopkins University, and she is the author of three books of poetry. Matthews is currently the Vice President of Museums at the Cincinnati Museum Center. The second in command, she is responsible for everything from education, to community engagement, to vision and direction for a site with three museums and two research facilities that serves almost two million children and their families annually.

To put it bluntly, Matthews is very lucky. She describes her selection as vice president as one of her boss's classic bold moves. Young, black, and female, she replaced a longtime, retiring vice president. "Once you have the title," she says, "you can't deny leadership, and I discovered what propels me is vision." Her vision is a big one, but it does not trouble her. "I believe we can reach everyone," she says. And after a lifetime of balancing the rational and the artistic, Matthews is not as surprised by her art/science background as someone meeting her for the first time. "The engineering side asks what is the problem and tries to fix it," she explains. "The creative side never looks at anything in a vacuum; it's not one child, it's all children. That side resists leaving things out."

Describing herself as an artist and poet at heart, Matthews says she was more than content as a trench worker, happy on the biology and biotechnology floor at the Maryland Science Center in Baltimore. "My male mentors have a hard time understanding I didn't want to be in charge," Matthews recalls, but she says sometimes you recognize you are on a ship going in the wrong direction. "I've come to grips with captaining my own ship," she says, adding, "Leadership takes you out of the trenches. It keeps me grounded."

Listening to Matthews talk, it is no surprise that work/life balance is an issue for her. "A female mentor told me to give myself the gift of returning to the trenches," she says. "You can't forget what learning and not knowing is like." So periodically, she returns to the floor of the museum and spends the day teaching. She has also discovered that she needs a moment of full stop. Recently she took what she described as a breather. She had done this before, but this one was different. "This was a personal retreat to think about what my endgame is," Matthews recounts. It was, she says, an opportunity to find some balance and transition, to disconnect and reconnect with what inspires.

Matthews says she has to be almost rigid with herself in terms of work. She arrives at the office at 7 a.m. and leaves at 5 p.m. "That's ten hours," she says. "I have to tell myself there's nothing you can do spending eleven or twelve hours." She has also added some things to slow herself down, like a monthly massage that's prescheduled so there is no avoiding it, and vacations. And by vacation, Matthews means time without family. Of these last two, Matthews says, "They make a world of difference. They make you more sane and more productive. It really does work."

Ask Matthews whether her leadership style has changed and she will tell you about her unusual tenure at the Cincinnati Museum Center. Like many new to the leadership business, she learned a great deal through on-the-job training. "Some things I've learned by direct intervention," she says, explaining that she has been the beneficiary of some wonderful executive coaches provided by her boss. "That was relatively new for the museum," she says. "It goes along with things new leaders need, integrating into a new community and a new workplace." She describes her first four years as developing herself and her second four years as learning how her staff sees her. She is acutely self-aware. "Perception wins if you need to get something done," she quips. "If you are perceived as indecisive, it makes a difference in whether you are allowed to make a decision." She has also worried about whether staff perceived her as authentic or not, realizing that some situations might challenge her value system because they felt inauthentic. She has also learned to slow down, she says, and listen. "There is a difference between someone believing I don't respect them and me slowing down to make them understand [me]; then I felt more authentic."

Matthews says a fly on the wall at her museum might wonder how the leadership team gets along. "We're different and we don't fit the mold," she says. But she says the team works to make things happen. The result, Matthews believes, is that everyone's skill set is stronger because they work on such a diverse team. She credits her CEO with skillful management of the museum's leadership group and with mentoring her. "I spend most of the money," she quips. "He watches it." Sometimes that means her initiatives go through the CEO's office, but she believes that increases her skill set. "I learned to quantify mission," she says.

There are three people Matthews admires: Dr. Martin Luther King, the Dalai Lama, and Michelle Obama. "There are no surprises really," she says. She loves King's abilities as an orator, his ability to deliver a message in context, and the fact that he was a major figure in the antipoverty movement. About the Dalai Lama, she says it is his contentment that draws her. "He looks so damn happy all the time," she says. "He looks at peace." Describing herself as Christian as they come, Matthews says there is a centeredness about the Dalai Lama that she admires. "I take everything on. I need to figure out how to be committed, but sleep soundly at night." And then there is Michelle Obama, who Matthews views as a kind of quintessential black woman, a role model for African American female leadership.

When Matthews thinks about the museum world of the future, she worries about succession, specifically the age gap between those ready to retire and those ready to step up. "There is a real shift in demographics," she says. "Gen X, which I'm part of, we're not necessarily the generation that stays in place for ten to twenty years." She continues that she sees her generation as slightly less attached to tradition than baby boomers. Gen Xers, she says, are children of a truly diverse world. A younger cohort with a shorter tenure, she predicts, could have implications for instability resulting in change over the long haul. "It removes a barrier to museums being nimble and drives change."

Matthews also sees museums as a field overrun by women, the dominant players especially in the history museum field. "The male workforce may have gone to more ambitious pastures," she muses, "and women in high levels of leadership tend toward ruthlessness and outcomes." And what about her own legacy, as a player in this field of women? "This crazy tree hugger streak [in me] just wants to make a difference." She was strategic when choosing her current position, and she likes to believe she is a change agent. She has made the museum a player in the city of Cincinnati's STEM (Science/Technology/Engineering/Mathematics) program. "We have gone from play space to partner," she says. "Now we're working on relating to parents."

The other thing Matthews would like people to remember about her is her contribution to diversifying the workplace. Once again, she compliments her boss, who hired her in the first place, and who, according to Matthews, welcomes diversity and champions inclusion. "Championing inclusion isn't easy," she says. "But it is important to me and I've talked about it." She is hopeful that her effort at transparency and honesty about hiring people of color has succeeded in a way that setting a hiring quota might not have. As the person who took over—at least in part—for John Flemming, who Matthews describes as a legend in black museums, she says, "The bridges he built, at least I didn't let them fall down. And getting the floor staff that looks like the community it serves is important. At least I didn't mess that up." She pauses and then says about her staff and other museum staff of color, "If you're not in charge, you still have to be empowered."

Van A. Romans, President, Fort Worth Museum of Science and History, Fort Worth, Texas

- Master of Fine Arts, USC
- Spent more than twenty-five years with The Walt Disney Company, including the creative design and development arm of the company, Walt Disney Imagineering
- Quote: "Museum leadership is changing toward a business model with a creative edge."

Van Romans was already retired when he joined the museum field. Romans had a long and successful career at The Walt Disney Company before he was tapped to head the Fort Worth Museum of Science and History. It wasn't as wrenching as one might think to move from the corporate sector to a nonprofit since he had already worked with and championed many museums at Disney Imagineering, where he facilitated exhibitions in Disney's parks and resorts. In a way, his move to a museum was a natural extension of who he is rather than a radical departure from what he was.

Romans's business experience gives him a unique vantage point from which to assess the two sectors, corporate and nonprofit. He sees some similarities and some marked differences between them. In a corporate environment, he explains, the response time and the work ethic is much more pressured. The culture is different in a not-for-profit, he posits. It's not the dog-eat-dog of profit and loss; it's more humane because most not-for-profit missions are about societal improvement. As a result, he thinks people who gravitate to these jobs are not driven so much by money or convinced they need to work seventy hours a week. Is that good or bad? He thinks it can be detrimental to the not-for-profit if there's no internal sense of urgency to make an impact. He's observed that what often happens is that an external stakeholder—a funder or a board member—has that sense of urgency, and they pressure museum leaders to make things happen.

Musing about his career, Romans notes that leadership usually seeks him out. "It's kind of embarrassing," he admits. "I've never really looked for a job. I'm not sure I'd know how to do it." Citing timing and luck, Romans describes a career journey that began at age twenty-eight with his first real job. It was a college teaching position that he landed with one of the few interviews he's ever done. As a result of that interview, he taught design for thirty years, working for Disney for twenty-seven years at the same time. Describing his life then as on the edges of the "Hollywood thing," he says he had no desire to go anyplace else. He reported to CEO Michael Eisner and long-time Disney executive Martin Sklar, the International Ambassador for Walt Disney Imagineering, a subsidiary that designs and constructs the Disney theme parks and resorts around the world. He feels they gave him a job he could do, and those relationships last to this day. "The combination of museums and Hollywood was extraordinary," Romans says.

When working on Epcot thirty years ago, Romans attended his first American Alliance of Museums (AAM) conference. His badge read "Van Romans—Walt Disney," and he recalls how museum professionals backed away once they saw where he worked. "I was not one of them," he said. Fueled by distrust, many museums took an arm's-length approach to what was a relatively new notion for them: the melding of entertainment and education. Romans laughs now, "I'm on the AAM Council now. What goes around, comes around!" He believes that after all these years, museums understand there's something to be learned from the Disney model, and they're benefitting from it.

Romans feels it wasn't so much his tenure at Disney that prepared him for his switch to museum leadership as it was a supportive boss there who taught him about leadership and about having a passion for the culture and for the parks. "He made it very clear that the [Disney] parks were not to be carnivals," Romans remembers. Disney is audience driven, and its corporate philosophy is embodied in three words: show, quality, and standards—SQS for short—something that is drummed into all Disney staff. "It's all about presentation and whether or not it functions as it should," Romans states. "I really understand that." He doesn't think the museum industry focuses on this enough, though. "I don't think most museums know their audiences or what those audiences want."

What surprised him most after his move to the museum world is the slow pace of nonprofit culture. He notes that even education environments (colleges and universities) move faster. "I'm not being derogatory," Romans apologizes, "it's just the way museums are." He's worked hard to change the pace at the Fort Worth Museum of Science and History, and he feels his staff is ready to move quickly.

Is he a different leader than when he first started? "Oh, yeah," he says, remembering that the first time he called Disney executives in to look at Epcot's "Home of the Future" he was soundly rejected for a less-than-stellar presentation. Today, he basks in the glow of a newly constructed museum, a

$95 million, 166,000 square-foot facility dedicated to discovery-based learning that opened in late 2009.

When he thinks about his career trajectory, Romans says it's hard to limit his workplace successes to just one. He points to professors he had who saw his potential to go to graduate school as a success. The Disney opportunity is another personal success story, of course. "I was discovered in a shoe store," he says, conjuring up similar anonymous-to-famous discovery stories that Hollywood dreams are made of. "I was asked to design a shoe store. One day a Disney executive was in the store and asked who the designer was."

That all seamlessly led to Romans's transformation of the Museum of Science and History. "We've gone to a whole other plateau," Romans says, as he ticks off what's been turned around: building, budget, finances, programming. "I love how it all turned out!" How did he identify and manage change? "I don't know!" he exclaims, citing that it was complex, involving different levels of change, but he did provide a peek at what his process looks like: Romans drew visuals—in this case circles—(similar to the *Switch* authors' destination postcards) to envision how the museum board and staff would create a new building. He warns that you have to articulate your program first. Then, he built excitement, and, no doubt, a healthy measure of urgency for the project. Then, he implemented SQS—show, quality, and standards.

He writes in his biography that he's an advocate for project-based learning. "I was an average student. I was always better at doing things than reading about them," he remembers. "My mother was a teacher, and she would give me projects." So Romans knows firsthand how important it is to give young people—all people, really—the opportunity to roll up their shirtsleeves and learn by doing. He fully understands that informal learning is as powerful as formal learning. "That's the core value of this museum," he states. He goes on to talk about the five new innovation studios at the Museum of Science and History, each designed for specific programs. There's the Doodler's Studio that replicates the discovery approach to learning by combining artistic interpretations with natural and physical sciences and history and anthropology. And the Inventor's Studio, which encourages tinkering with technologies. "I was a studio art major and was always making things," he says. He still makes art, which he feels is important to the total person.

As the leader, he's very much aware of the museum's big concepts, while the designer in him looks for the little details. How does Disney's SQS become part of the museum's ongoing conversations? "We talk about quality and quality of work," he replies. The new strategic plan includes quality as part of its imperatives, adding that it becomes a part of the vernacular and a part of the culture. "Everybody just does it; it is part of everyday being," he says. "When I retire, they'll remember that I helped to build the building. What I hope they'll remember is SQS."

Romans admits that his role at the museum means that his home life isn't his own. "We're often out three nights a week, and we have made friends through work," he says, adding, "I really rely on my family, because we are all creative people. When I go home I bounce a lot of things off my wife and she can be objective." Describing his interest in travel and his wife's involvement with Mustang horses, he adds, "We have a varied life that connects back to the mission at the museum, which is about the West and western culture."

And his role models? "Abraham Lincoln was a genius leader who was able to break up the tension of decision making with stories and laughter," Romans says. "I love Lincoln's leadership style." He keeps Donald T. Phillips's book, *Lincoln on Leadership*, with him and refers to it frequently.

Of the leaders at Disney, Romans says he is grateful to Martin Sklar, chairman of Imagineering and the last executive who worked with Walt Disney. Sklar promoted the idea of adding museum exhibitions into the parks, which is what Romans did. "He encouraged me and made every opportunity available to me," Romans says.

"Museum leadership is changing toward a business model with a creative edge. Though I have both an academic and a corporate background, I believe leaders are emerging that are grounded in two areas: creativity and, if they're not MBAs, they have a sense of business needs. This comes out of a necessary 'survival of the fit' attitude of reality that 'guests' to the museum drive business models and create a successful environment for our museums."

"My advice to next-generation leaders is never say no to an opportunity. It's difficult to see what might come your way, but try whatever is in front of you and never say no. Even if you fail, you learn! Always bring creativity to the table, and when there elevate it. It's so easy and yet we seem to relegate story, visuals, and other more creative work to the lowest level of the pile. . . . promote the process and the people doing it (make them quarterbacks, not just receivers), advance it, and praise it, as ultimately, it will be your friend and will bring people to your museum!"

Nina Simon, Executive Director, Santa Cruz Museum of Art & History @ the McPherson Center, Santa Cruz, California

- BS, Electrical Engineering with a minor in Mathematics, Worcester Polytechnic Institute, Worcester, Massachusetts
- Learned about leadership by reading books, playing sports, and talking to her "brilliant entrepreneur husband and executive mom"

> - Quote: "I tell myself and my staff to never rely on what we have within the four walls of this building—always search for partners, seek collaborators, ask for help."

There are few first-time directors who attract attention from around the globe. Then there is Nina Simon. Thanks to a seemingly endless stream of thoughtful and deftly argued observations about the role of the twenty-first-century museum, she's garnered thousands of followers and loyal fans and built a national platform from which to hone ideas and evaluate institutional engagement that now includes the Museum of Art & History in Santa Cruz, California.

With two years under her belt as a first-time director, Simon is frequently asked what her first twelve months were like. She quickly responds, "It's been awesome and very intense; exhausting and challenging. I firmly believe that being engaged is the single source of happiness [for me]." For Simon, being engaged runs the gamut from stemming a tide of red ink, to learning how to be the boss, all while moving the museum squarely toward the center of community life. Not surprisingly, serving her community is a central theme in Simon's own life.

Known for her blog, *Museum 2.0*, and her book, *The Participatory Museum*, Simon's passion flows from her fierce belief that museums hold the potential to bring people together, create an environment of belonging, and energize a sense of place. Her philosophy requires most museums to make fundamental changes in the way they think about people who come through their doors, and those who do not. Her new leadership position allows her to put her philosophy to the test in her very own laboratory, the Santa Cruz Museum of Art & History.

The museum was ripe for change when Simon and her husband arrived in Santa Cruz a few years ago, deciding this friendly, quirky place was home. Simon was ready for a change herself. Weary from the constant travel that comes with being a successful consultant and author, she wanted to put down roots. While continuing to write, speak, and teach, she laid plans for opening a Belgian-beer-bar-cum-exhibition space that she envisioned as a gathering spot for community conversations.

Then the museum called.

It had created a strategic plan, really more of a "strategic pamphlet" as Simon describes it, and it wanted to know if she would be a consultant. Because of the plan's brevity, Simon saw a great deal of flexibility in strategic direction, which she viewed as intriguing and freeing. But it was the vision statement that grabbed her because it underscored her vision of what museums were all about: "a thriving, central gathering place where local residents and visitors have the opportunity to experience art, history, ideas, and culture."

Seeing the intersection (and synergy) between her beliefs and the museum's, she knew she wanted to be more than a consultant. So she asked the museum to hire her. For her interview she wrote a three-year plan based on the pamphlet. She got the job.

"When I started, I wanted to try out my theories. I wanted to reintroduce the museum to the community—that's been the thrust," Simon says. "We are working to become a thriving, central gathering place for our community around art, history, ideas, and culture—a 'museum 2.0,' and it's a cool feeling."

Acknowledging she's a less-stressed director now than when she started, Simon doesn't deny it's tough being the boss. Although there is now a surplus in the bank, and she's found that she enjoys fund-raising, there are a variety of management issues, including delegating authority, that she's still getting comfortable with. But it's the role of change agent that is Simon's biggest challenge.

She's surprised at how quickly the museum has changed, even though she knows everyone is not happy with the results. Change or even the idea of change breeds insecurity that staff and volunteers experience inside and outside the organization, where many were comfortable with the museum as they knew it. In an effort to raise the comfort level, Simon makes it very clear that she's in it for the long haul.

She is also learning to address people's concerns in a straightforward way, in part by educating them about what it means to be a community museum. "We're here because we perform a public service; there's room for everyone," she says. When a patron complains about the sticky notes on the walls of a gallery, she reminds them not all visitors appreciate traditional object labels, which hang there as well. "Can't we all just get along?" she asks, rhetorically.

In thinking about what prepared her for this position, Simon ticks off a list of skills and experiences she feels are particularly important to her directorship: a stint at the Spy Museum taught her about entrepreneurship; her bachelors degree in mathematics helps her be data driven; her international work taught her the importance of experimentation; her blog connects her to colleagues and issues; and her family helps her think about the museum as a business.

Simon says her most important trait is being externally driven. "I tell myself and my staff to never rely on what we have within the four walls of this building," she says. "Always search for partners, seek collaborators; ask for help." She spends a lot of time thinking about what she needs to learn as a museum director and who can help her.

"I entered the field wanting to be an exhibit designer at the Exploratorium in San Francisco; it was my dream job." But she moved to Washington, D.C., and pestered the Spy Museum for a position until she was hired, something she describes as a foundational experience.

A big change in career came because of her blog, *Museum 2.0*, which she started in 2008, as a place to think about museums. The blog's popularity vaulted her into a celebrity she never expected. "It's weird," she confesses. "I'm a shy person, but now there are gaggles of graduate students who want to have their pictures taken with me."

Because of the blog even her mentors aren't typical. Some of the people she regularly relies on came to her first because of what they read at *Museum 2.0*. The blog, with its 8,600-plus following, facilitates a diffuse two-way mentoring, since many of her readers are recognized experts in their own right. As a result, the number of people who build on her posts with their own insights offers a fertile exchange of information, ideas, advice, and learning.

She's quick to point out, though, that she has consciously tapped the field's collective wisdom since she first started going to conferences at age twenty-two. She purposely went alone to force herself to meet new people; given her shyness, she felt she had to push herself that way. As a result, she developed a large network. From her vantage point as a director, she sees value in teams of staff attending professional development opportunities, but she encourages individuals to strike out on their own at conferences, workshops, and seminars to meet new people.

Simon believes that if you love demanding work, why shouldn't it be the centerpiece of your life? Why would you want to say it's not? Embrace it. "Come in early, stay late, and make it happen," she says.

In a small community, it's almost impossible to keep personal and professional lives separate. If a board member or donor sees her playing beach volleyball, she's going to engage them, not ignore them. "Because I'm so much younger, I think my board, donors, and members expect to see me being active and dressing my age; I'm clearly not in their peer group!" She's seen by older people as someone with a lot of energy, which she regards as a plus. She thinks this is tougher for older directors, who may be viewed as peers with the attendant pluses and minuses.

She's developed a few techniques to manage the demands of her job, along with writing, speaking, and traveling. Embracing it all is one. A supporting and loving family and friends are another.

Her advice for aspiring museum directors includes asking what an institution's "hot button" issues are before accepting the job; focusing on what's important instead of what's urgent; and reading the book *The First 90 Days: Critical Success Strategies for New Leaders at All Levels* by Michael Watkins (2003).

She advises boards and search committees to spend a long time thinking about how they advertise positions as well as the search process itself. You're out to locate talent, not a widget.

Sally Roesch Wagner, Executive Director, Matilda Joslyn Gage Foundation, Fayetteville, New York

- PhD, History of Consciousness (Women's Studies), University of California, Santa Cruz, 1978
- Antiwar, pro–women's rights civil disobedient
- Quote: "I'm a leader *with*, not a leader *to*."

Speaking from her home state of South Dakota, Sally Roesch Wagner remarks on the prairie's vastness, the blue bowl of sky, and endless fields of corn. "I can drive for seventy miles without seeing another person," she says. Roesch Wagner is the founder and executive director of the Matilda Joslyn Gage Foundation, which operates the Gage Home in Fayetteville, New York, just outside of Syracuse. When she's not running the Foundation, Wagner, who wrote her doctoral dissertation on Matilda Joslyn Gage, still teaches in Syracuse University's Women's Studies program.

As a founding director, Roesch Wagner's story and the narrative of the Gage Home are intertwined. She says that at the beginning, leadership was the last thing on her mind. "I was thinking about the organization, not about me!" Looking back, she remembers that in the late 1990s in the midst of trying to save Gage's home and launch a new nonprofit dedicated to Gage's life and work, she realized she knew a great deal about Gage but very little about museums and nonprofits. "I came in so dumb, I knew I had so much to learn," she says. "And the only way to do it was to surround myself with people who filled my gaps."

At the time Roesch Wagner began her crusade, she was a distinguished visiting professor at Syracuse University, and the Gage house was a rental property owned by a local teacher. To say Roesch Wagner was besotted with Gage would be a bit of an understatement. She performed as Gage. She spoke about her. Gage appeared in Roesch Wagner's syllabus and in her books and articles. In 1998, Roesch Wagner was the scholar in residence preparing for the 150th anniversary of the women's rights convention, which included two exhibits on Gage. In addition to the exhibits, Roesch Wagner, along with two other scholars, produced a modern reader's edition of Gage's writings that included a brief biography. "Gage suddenly had a presence," Roesch Wagner remembers.

Meanwhile, conversations continued about the future of the Gage house, an unrestored Greek Revival home where Susan B. Anthony once scratched her name on a second-floor window pane. In the end, after a great deal of soul searching on everyone's part, the decision was made to open the house as a museum dedicated to Gage. Roesch Wagner sold her South Dakota house, cashed in her retirement, and resigned from a tenure-track position. More than a few people thought she had lost her mind. "They told me it was academic suicide," she remembers. Laughing, she adds that after a month of counseling, she realized that while the move might not be conventionally "right," it brought her heart and head together. "I had the flexibility to move, and I never looked back," she said.

Asked what prepared her for her current leadership position, Roesch Wagner laughs again. "Probably work in the antiwar movement," she says. "And the women's movement." She describes herself as someone who was very wary of leaders. "During the women's movement, the press always wanted to talk to our leader," Roesch Wagner remembers. "We always answered, 'We're all leaders!'" When the time came to launch the Gage Foundation, she drew on these experiences. "We wanted to create a less hierarchical organization of cooperation," she says. She had a summer intern contact women's organizations nationwide asking to see their bylaws in the hopes of understanding how organizations worked, and thus how to build the Gage Foundation. Roesch Wagner is the first to admit that the clean slate offered by Gage's house meant endless opportunities for innovation and change. Had the house come with ten thousand objects, the project might have had far less appeal.

Roesch Wagner remarks that she had heard scary stories about "founder's syndrome" early on and took them to heart. "I've tried to decentralize myself," she says. She is not shy about her age. "I'm seventy," she exalts. "And I'm proud." Roesch Wagner says that being seventy and male means you can run for president; being seventy and a woman means you dye your hair and get Botoxed. A victim of neither, she says she has never had more energy and more focus. "And I'm able to put the personal stuff aside, which is a skill I didn't have at thirty," she adds. She sees leadership as another form of teaching; in fact, her teaching style is very like her leadership style. "I'm a leader *with*," she says, "not a leader *to*," adding, "My classes are class led." That is a style she reinforces as the semester progresses until the class has enough ownership over the topic and confidence in themselves to carry on by themselves, something she tests occasionally by showing up late.

The same style works for the Foundation. "A good event is one where I don't necessarily have to be there or be part of." When the Gage Foundation received a $100,000 grant, Roesch Wagner and her staff took to the Internet, asking friends, members, and sister organizations to "dream with them" and tell them how they would use $100,000 to further the Gage Foundation's work. "The responses were amazing!" Roesch Wagner remembers. Her staff took the ideas, developed prototypes, and then invited the public to vote on the ones it liked best. The winners are now being turned into exhibits and programs. Of course, there was at least one respondent who couldn't help chastise, arguing that if Roesch Wagner didn't know what to do with $100,000, then she wasn't ready to handle a grant that big. Needless to say, it's hard to imagine Roesch Wagner without an idea, but asking her constituents gave the Gage Foundation an immediate buy in from people who care about the organization the most.

Asked about the important influences in her life, Roesch Wagner deadpans, "Being arrested three times." She is only half kidding. Roesch Wagner believes that every leader has to have a kind of courage. She loves the fact that the International Coalition of Sites of Conscience called the Gage Foundation a gutsy organization. "It means that we're confronting issues of choice, and that creates an ethos and environment of courage," Roesch Wagner says. During the ramp up to the opening of the Gage Home, Roesch Wagner brought her class to the museum. Together they discussed what students did and didn't like about more traditional museums. Roesch Wagner quips that she took her students' list of things they hated to heart. That led to the wall you can write on. Yes, there is one wall at the Gage Home where visitors can write or draw. It took many conversations to initiate, with Roesch Wagner arguing that the wall came from Home Depot and therefore was not original. Ultimately, the Gage received special permission from New York State's historic preservation officer, and it has been a great success.

"We didn't want to create something that just speaks to the choir," Roesch Wagner says. "We want to find creative ways to use Gage's words instead of giving walking lectures." As a result, visitors can choose a tour or not. Museum guides are available to talk or not. "A docent's responsibility is to engage," Roesch Wagner says. Her constituency isn't old school, and neither is her board. "And, we don't have an entrenched story to push against."

As might be expected, Roesch Wagner has many mentors. In no particular order they include Michael Hutchinson, her first grandchild, whom she describes as a warm and wonderful person and a major mentor. He shares the stage with Rachel Maddow, Chris Hayes, and a group of museum folk including Linda Norris, whose blog Roesch Wagner counts on; the Museum Association of New York; and Nina Simon. "*The Participatory Museum* is my bible," Roesch Wagner says. It's no surprise that she is an active mentor to the Gage's interns and to her students. "I tell them you have the experience; trust your instincts."

Roesch Wagner, who is now beginning succession planning for the Gage Foundation, has her office at the top of the stairs on the building's second floor. "It's kind of clean now," she says, noting that she tidied up before leaving for South Dakota, but normally there are big piles of paper and a large mug of tea. She depends on her grandchildren, particularly Michael, as well as the Gage's interns to keep her tech savvy. "They amaze me with their generosity," she says. This fall a group of Syracuse University interns will study the Gage's website and work to bring it a social media presence.

Ask Roesch Wagner about work/life balance and she laughs, admitting that for her it's hard not to work. "Balance is a hard thing," she says, acknowledging that if it weren't for her partner, she might not stop working. In fact, her idea of hell is a beach and one of those sunset-colored drinks with a little umbrella. "When I reach for work," she says, "it's like I'm reaching for the bottle," adding, "It's not funny when you're that driven because the expectations are totally unreal for yourself and for others." But unlike other addictions, Roesch Wagner finds great rewards in work.

SUMMARY: LESSONS LEARNED

The first thing you may have noticed about our four visionary leaders is that none has academic training in museum studies. Two come with serious grounding in science and math; two come from the humanities and the arts. What they have in common is passion, which eventually led them to where they are today. They prove two incredibly important points about visionary leadership: it can come from many quarters, from people who are not consumed by the profession's standards and methodologies, and it is not bound by age.

Lesson one: Creativity enhances and facilitates the visionary leader's ability to see what others cannot.

First and foremost, these four individuals are creative people apart from their museum lives. Matthews, Roesch Wagner, and Simon are writers of prose and poetry on a regular basis. With books, articles, and blogs to their credit, these three women continually synthesize ideas and information, a key ingredient to developing and articulating vision. Van Romans is a visual artist and designer, two lenses that allow him to see things differently and often with great clarity. When mapping his plan for change at the museum, he *drew* it. When Roesch Wagner dons a costume and takes the stage, she *becomes* Matilda Joslyn Gage. She is completely absorbed by her subject and the power of the message. All four are teachers, each charged with opening minds, eyes, and ears of students, colleagues, and the public. They are conceptual thinkers who, through creative communication and probably some brilliant improvisation, are able to make us see what they see.

Lesson two: Visionary leaders are externally driven.

Each of our visionary leaders is squarely focused on audience. They have a finely honed intuition about what audiences—be they students, visitors, staff, or communities—want and need. For them it is the person entering the museum, attending an event or program, or searching the website who is the most important person in the world. As Roesch Wagner said about the programming at the Gage Home, "We didn't want to create something that just speaks to the choir." The external focus brings with it a sense of urgency to make change, to open, to shake up, to throw off hidebound constraints of museum authority that assumes audiences are monolithic and says, "We know it all; we are right; listen to us."

Lesson three: Visionary leaders believe deeply in the power of museums to teach and foster understanding.

When Van Romans talks about the power of informal learning being the core value of his museum, he speaks from personal experience and for many in the field. He's amplified that value through the design of the institution's new interactive studios and exhibits. Roesch Wagner's "Write on Our Walls" project gives visitors the opportunity to lend their voices to ongoing conversations about social issues that challenged Gage in her day and continue to challenge us today. Tonya Matthews periodically leaves her office to return to the museum floor to teach. And Nina Simon constantly experiments with ways to expand and deepen the meaning of the participatory museum.

NOTES

1. Chip Heath and Dan Heath, *Switch: How to Change Things When Change Is Hard* (New York: Crown Business, 2013), 76.

2. Samuel Hudson, "Re-Imagineering," *Fort Worth Weekly*, July 12, 2006, accessed February 7, 2013, http://archive.fwweekly.com/content.asp?article=4056.

Chapter Nine

How Do We Know What We Know?

When you know better, you do better.
—Maya Angelou

Any fool can know. The point is to understand.
—Albert Einstein

We have now met thirty-six successful history museum leaders from across North America. We have read their stories and know a little bit about their lives. In some cases we learned how they came into the field, what motivates them, and what keeps them interested. We know they share certain qualities: courage, vision, authenticity, and self-awareness. And we have learned how those traits can have a positive impact on how leadership is personally and institutionally wielded and acknowledged.

But what else do we know? Let's drill down a bit by beginning with the facts.

FIRST, AGE DOESN'T SEEM TO MATTER.

Our leaders range from the midtwenties Anne Cathcart to septuagenarian Sally Roesch Wagner, who will tell you one of the defining moments of her career was getting arrested during a protest march in the 1960s. And if we weren't convinced earlier, we know leadership can happen anywhere in the room, not just from the podium, but the front row, the back row, and any place in between. Among our sampling there are directors, founding directors, education directors, curators, and one so young she is still trying on a variety of hats. So we know title doesn't confer leadership, behavior does. How individuals, institutions, and the field as a whole can build a culture that sustains leadership is addressed in the last chapter, "The Leadership Agenda for History and Cultural Heritage Museums."

EDUCATION MATTERS.

Almost all of our leaders have graduate degrees. More than a quarter of them spent time teaching either as a first career or as outgrowths of their current museum positions. While the move from classroom to museum is not surprising, it does say something about the intrinsic nature of museums as educational institutions and the ease with which one can slide from being a teaching assistant in a PhD program to a museum staff member. What is also interesting is that more than half of our interviewees—60 percent—did not receive traditional museum studies degrees. Some have degrees in law, business, or subject-based masters in art history or the sciences, for example. Four have bachelors degrees. Not one of our interviewees mentioned the degree as a ticket to his or her career, the way an MD or a JD is a necessity for medicine or law. Most seem to find the graduate school experience valuable, a few in surprising ways. Further, a great many of our leaders have been the beneficiaries of postgraduate leadership training, whether from the Getty Leadership Institute or the American Association of State and Local History's Developing History Leaders @ SHA, formerly known as the Seminar for Historic Administration, or any number of smaller leadership training programs.

And a smaller number still found workplace training opportunities, either through a formal process of coaching or a more informal mentoring situation or a combination of the two. For some employers, hiring a biomedical engineer with two books of poems under her belt to take the second spot in an urban history museum might have been too far outside the box. It was a risk the Cincinnati Museum Center was ready to take when it hired Tonya Matthews. CMC leaders realized, however, that Matthews's move from the world of engineering, science museums, and teaching in the greater Washington, D.C., area to Cincinnati would be a sea change. The museum made sure she had the support she needed, offering job coaching, leadership training, and mentoring. And she, rather than seeing herself as not quite up to snuff, accepted, soaking up lessons like a sponge.

It is also clear that leadership training, whether it comes during graduate school, in the form of an MBA, or in a midcareer break for specialized programs such as Getty or SHA, yields another benefit: a network. Almost every interviewee mentioned groups of individuals from fellow alumni, to program participants, to local colleagues who they contact on a regular basis. Decision makers need reference points, and frequently it is better if those come from outside their institution.

VARIETY AND PERSEVERANCE MATTER.

Our group teaches us the value of experience, and more specifically the value of variety and perseverance when it comes to experience. If you remember Malcolm Gladwell's book *Outliers*, you probably remember his chapter on the ten-thousand-hour rule. In it, Gladwell expounds on research by K. Anders Ericsson, now at the University of Florida, on the differences between concert violinists and pianists. Ericsson and his colleagues were interested in what separated people of similar natural abilities, some becoming gifted amateurs and Sunday pianists, while others took to the concert stage. Ericsson wanted to know why.

It turns out that the professional pianists steadily increased their practice time from roughly three hours a week to more than double that, so that by the time they reached their twenties they had practiced approximately ten thousand hours, thus the chapter title. Ericsson's and subsequently Gladwell's point is that what separates the sheep from the goats among the innately talented is the time devoted to deliberately learning, honing, and practicing increasingly nuanced and difficult skills. Ten thousand hours of rote practice will not make any of us concert pianists. Not unless we already possess the ability to get into Julliard. [1]

What does any of this have to do with museum leadership? We believe it is likely that no matter how talented they are, successful people, including this group of gifted history and cultural heritage museum leaders, need a minimum of ten thousand hours developing and advancing their craft. Think of Nina Simon, who blogged for years about what makes a successful exhibit or community program, or Hope Alswang, who ran the New York State Council on the Arts museum program for five years, evaluating the merits of several hundred applications annually, or Jennifer Kilmer's years as a foundation grants manager before taking her first museum directorship. Remember Kippen de Alba Chu's posthurricane experience in Hawaii, Ted Bosley's years in the cutthroat world of New York advertising, or Bob Burns's time as a wannabe actor. All of these examples required repetitive decision making at the point of transaction.

Even if we quibble with Gladwell and Ericsson, believing ten thousand hours is too arbitrary, each of these disparate scenarios demonstrates something about the path to leadership. Through a combination of luck, diligence, and opportunity, our leaders took advantage of repeated practice recognizing problems, evaluating alternatives, and providing solutions. Their situations offered, to a greater or lesser degree, both authority *and* responsibility. And even if, in reading a basic biography of de Alba Chu, it looks as though disaster management and statehouse politics might not apply to history museum leadership, we know that they do. In fact, what is running a history museum except disaster management and politics writ small?

Although they did not set out to "interleave," many of our interviewees practiced the latest in learning strategies by layering one skill on another. Pioneered by Robert Bjork, a professor of cognitive psychology at the University of California, Los Angeles, interleaving is the method of practicing a variety of skills from under the same umbrella over time. According to Bjork, over time the sum of these small steps is much greater than the sum of the leaps you make if you focus on a single skill.[2] Think of Rebecca Slaughter, who volunteered at her local museum and moved swiftly from cataloging to receptionist to development. Or Jamie Bosket, who directed a tiny, rural historical museum in upstate New York, interned at the Smithsonian, and has been on a fast track in the interpretation and events division at Mount Vernon since starting there in 2007, becoming its head in 2012.

CALCULATED RISK-TAKING MATTERS.

Our interviewees share various characteristics and inclinations. They love what they do. They are not martyrs, however; they do not toil for minimum wage. Their passion and perseverance make them marketable. They take advantage of opportunities and are willing to take risks, not just organizationally, but personally as well. Remember Tim Grove's colleagues telling him that leaving to serve on a National Endowment for the Humanities (NEH) exhibit team, and giving up the golden handcuffs of the Smithsonian, might mean dead-ending his career? Today he is back at the Smithsonian and looks at his NEH experience as one of the best things he ever did. Or think about Melissa Chiu, who was put off by the lack of meaningful opportunities for young curators in her native Australia. She didn't want a life of patched-together part-time jobs, so she began her own organization that, combined with her scholarship, launched a career. And then, of course, there is Sally Roesch Wagner, who at a moment when many folks are thinking about retirement mortgaged everything she owned to start a museum, doing it in such an imaginative way that she is known as much for her methods as her subject matter.

BEING PART OF A WHOLE MATTERS.

In many of our conversations our interviewees offered advice for new or emerging leaders. Out of the thirty-six interviews certain themes stand out. First, these leaders are not lone rangers. Even those who work largely alone or have worked alone see themselves as part of a whole. Remember Melissa Chiu telling us that you can't do it on your own. And while Andy Masich acknowledges that his time as a solo leader shaped his learning curve, providing his ten thousand hours of decision making in Gladwell-speak, Masich also lets us know how important mentors, colleagues, and family are. Jim Enote's work is embedded in his tribe's religion and culture. Colin Campbell, CEO of one of the country's most iconic history organizations, concludes his interview by saying, "In the absence of a collaborative style, you're going nowhere; going it alone is not an option."

BALANCING WORK AND LIFE MATTERS.

While Ted Bosley's story of a lost marriage is perhaps the most dramatic, almost everyone acknowledged the difficulty of devoting oneself full tilt to a job while still having time and energy left for family, friends, and community. Still in the first half of his career, Nathan Richie is quoted as saying, "There is something to be said for making the other things in life an obligation." Many have had to be intentional about friendships, volunteer opportunities, even family; more than a few interviewees have standing dates with a parent or other relatives.

Then there are the women, who if they have children, find the work/life balance more complicated. Women such as Hope Alswang, Ellen Rosenthal, and Christy Coleman know they follow an earlier generation of female museum professionals, many of whom were single because the jobs were too old line and old school to deal with things such as maternity leaves and childcare arrangements. Even with her physician/researcher husband, Rosenthal tells us that during her early career and second masters degree, she was the primary parent, raising three sons, going to graduate school, and working. Coleman and her husband, who are both native Virginians, made the decision to leave Detroit to give their children the opportunity to grow up in a less frenetic environment. Their agreement was whoever was first to get a job the family would follow. Coleman got the job in Richmond.

For the younger female cohort among our interviewees, things have definitely changed, but probably not enough. Again, Melissa Chiu laughingly told us that she was convinced she would go back to work a week after giving birth. After all, she had things to do. But real life intervened. At the close of her riff on work and family life, Chiu tells us, "I would be surprised if anyone with children said it was easy or not foremost in their mind." And it was she, when asked to name someone she admires, who picked her twin sister. Why? Because she chose to give up a career to stay home with her children.

BEING AUTHENTIC MATTERS (A LOT).

All our leaders are authentic, and not just the group of twelve we labeled as authentic. All of them are aware of who they are and the power of their own story and the integrity it breeds. Tim Grove tells us, "Without integrity, there's no respect or trust. A leader must be honest and transparent." Some of our interviewees use their stories with staff, while for others it is a touchstone that keeps them leaning forward. For Gonzalo Casals, the act of immigration—the willingness to change careers from architecture to museum studies—and countries—from Argentina to the United States—is a metaphor that informs who he is.

SO NOW COMES THE BIG QUESTION:

In light of our interviews, is it possible to say whether leadership is accidental or intentional? Yes, it is. And the answer is: both. The leaders profiled here are intentional leaders. They like being leaders, whether it is from the office that looks out on the whole site or from the middle of a team making change. But not one got there on his or her own. In each and every case serendipity played its part, and more importantly, each interviewee was open to change. When opportunity was offered, they took it. How would Chris Taylor's career have been different if he hadn't taken the offer of a Coca-Cola Foundation Museum Fellowship? What if Rob Kret hadn't made the switch from history museums to visual arts museums? Would he have had the opportunity to be a critical part of a major cultural collaboration and funding opportunity as he experienced in Chattanooga? What if Rebecca Slaughter had not been comfortable volunteering at her neighborhood museum when she was between jobs? What would have happened if she stayed at home, blindly applying to entry-level museum positions? How would Hope Alswang's career have changed if she said "no, thank you" to the position at the New York State Council on the Arts, holding out for a museum directorship? Some of our leaders began their career narrative when they were children. Remember Andy Masich and his childhood museum, or Trevor Beemon, who started volunteering at his local museum at the ripe age of twelve, both thinking about history as something people experience before either of them began high school, much less college. Both had the good fortune to learn leadership while learning history.

One of the things we appreciate about Professor Stewart Friedman is his insistence that work and life are intertwined, not separate, and that being authentic at one enriches the other. While allotting time for family, community, *and* work remains an issue for many of our interviewees, most see that their work is linked in very special ways to community, family, and self. For some, such as Chris Taylor and Gonzalo Casals, the circles overlap. Van Romans describes how he and his wife have made many friends through his work: "We have a varied life that connects back to the mission at the museum." For others such as David Young and Burt Logan, it has been a process of giving each sector its due, even when that means turning off their phones and email for part of each weekend or while on vacation.

Friedman suggests that leaders who live solely for work shut off parts of who they are. The result? They are less authentic and less creative, failing to meet challenges. A leader who knows who she is can use her story to reveal aspects of her character. He writes, "It's not manipulation when you tell a story with the intent of increasing the sense of connection; it's leadership, because even though it's about you, it's really about the relationship if you are doing it right."[3] Not all our interviewees balance work, community, family, and self perfectly, but the important thing is that all of them, no matter whether leading from behind the big desk or from the middle of a department, recognize the importance of the spheres in keeping their lives whole. As Friedman writes, leaders who know this "continue learning their whole lives. And they encourage people to learn from their experiences, from trial and error, knowing that this builds strength as well as the resilience to take on new challenges."[4]

NOTES

1. Malcolm Gladwell, *Outliers: The Story of Success* (New York: Little, Brown and Company, 2008), 35.

2. Garth Sundem, "Everything You Thought You Knew about Learning Is Wrong," *Wired*, January 29, 2012, accessed February 1, 2013, http://www.wired.com/geekdad/2012/01/everything-about-learning/.

3. Stewart D. Friedman, *Total Leadership: Be a Better Leader, Have a Richer Life*, (Watertown: Harvard Business School Press, 2008), 191.

4. Friedman, *Total Leadership*, 187.

Chapter Ten

Ten Simple Truths

We began this book with a list of myths about museum leadership, opinions voiced so often they feel like truth. They've shaped our profession generally, and its leadership in particular. They need to be set aside, abandoned, thrown on the trash heap, in favor of a new set of guiding principles that we call "simple truths."

We call them simple truths because they cut through the myths, the prevaricating, and frankly a level of contentedness about leadership. They're basic, easy to remember, and easy to put into practice. None should cause readers to scratch their heads because we believe they make such good, common sense. We didn't make these up; we didn't have to. They come from our interviewees, perhaps not in so many words, but certainly from the spirit of our conversations and most definitely from the way they act.

- **Get invested.** Leaders must know the challenges their communities face, where the obstacles and resources are, and who influences opinions and pocketbooks; they must be willing to place their institutions in the midst of community conversations, and in doing so be ready to ask the unasked questions, weather rejections, and navigate uncharted territories. Because without long-term external impact, what's the point of a museum? Without community interaction we are all Miss Havishams standing guard over a never-changing group of objects.

- **Be a trust builder.** Leaders know that nothing of lasting value is accomplished without trust. After all, history and cultural heritage museums are created by, for, and about people. They succeed or fail on the personalities of people involved in them. When a museum hits a rough patch, it is trust that holds the whole thing together. When a museum celebrates success, it's because people worked together to make something great happen. Museums, as all nonprofits, are enterprises that need everyone pulling in the same direction, devoid of ego, stubborn partisanship, and petty bickering. We have to watch out for each other. Leaders who play personalities and agendas off of one another, who withhold or ignore information because it might make them look incompetent or just plain bad, who treat audiences unequally, and who undermine staff and volunteers to burnish their own reputations sully the understanding of the sacred public trust.

- **Embrace "the greater good."** Leaders know why their museums exist, and they place the public benefit front and center. It gets them out of bed in the morning. Leaders are keepers and protectors of this flame. Leaders are the ethical (and sometimes the moral) compass for their institutions, and sometimes they take heat for it. Ultimately, the only reason museums are in business is for society's benefit, so their leadership answers to a higher authority.

- **Create a candid culture.** What fuels trust is honesty, saying what you know when you know it; saying what you don't know when you don't. Nobody wants anything else—no smoke and mirrors, and no silent treatment. We're museums, after all, not a covert spy agency. So get your motives and your facts straight. The more trust stakeholders have in their leaders, the more honest leaders and followers can be with each other. It's a tough but glorious cycle, when, as the leader, you're lucky enough to attain it.

- **Up your frequency.** In this case it has nothing to do with being an introvert or an extrovert. The fact is that leaders who stay behind closed doors are leaders who know only what they are told. Do you want to build trust and community engagement? Then you need to communicate more, not less. As our friend Aristotle (you remember him from chapter 7) said, "Nature abhors a vacuum." When board, staff, volunteers, and stakeholders don't hear you or see you, they'll assume the worst, going to extra lengths to fill in the blanks you've left for them. [1]

- **Learn and grow together.** As we discussed in earlier chapters, commitment to leadership development by staff and boards varies widely because by and large institutions don't see leadership as integral to running a museum, nor do they place much value on developing it. We know of so many history and cultural heritage museums that shrug their proverbial shoulders, saying they are nothing more than stepping stones for professionals on their way to bigger and better opportunities elsewhere. That sort of small-minded thinking keeps institutions in suspended animation as talented people come and go, and go, and go. Museums that commit to developing their board and staff talent, along with their missions, keep talent longer while making substantive institutional strides. The organization that grows together stays together.

- **Get integrated.** Leadership for the twenty-first century is all about integrating ideas, information, practice, and standards from diverse places and industries (including the museum field) to leap frog your museum forward. It's about habitually thinking across spectrums and pulling common threads together. It's about multidimensionality, abundant thinking, and asking who can add to your institutional narrative. It's about using the wide-angle lens 90 percent of the time, not the jeweler's loupe.

- **Tap your entire network.**[2] When leaders understand their leadership is not about them, but about others, they open themselves and their institutions up to new possibilities they have never seen before. We've just begun the twenty-first-century journey. No one knows where it will lead us, but what we do know is that we're on this journey together. We've got lots of company along the way, so we need to tap into it.

- **Commit to leadership.** Think about it: If institutions poured as much time, energy, and funding into leadership training and development for both boards and staffs as they do into collections management and care, exhibitions, and programs, would they be grappling with as many of the seemingly intractable organizational issues they are today? We wonder.

- **Be accountable.** Set the bar high and work hard to meet or exceed it. If you expect others to do the same, you must do it yourself. Take the heat. Don't play the blame game. You're a leader for a reason.

NOTES

1. Denis Wilson, "Why Year-End Reviews Are a Big Fat Waste of Time," *Fast Company*, December 20, 2012. We have the following article to thank for the language "create a candid culture" and "up your frequency." We used them out of context because they're memorable phrases—ones we hope you'll remember. Accessed January 8, 2013, http://www.fastcompany.com/3004111/why-year-end-reviews-are-big-fat-waste-time?utm_source=dlvr.it&utm_medium=linkedin.

2. Jesse Lyn Stoner, "8 Things Collaborative Leaders Know," *Jesse Lyn Stoner—My Blog*, November 16, 2012, accessed November 16, 2012, www.seapointcenter.com/what-collaborative-leader-know.

Chapter Eleven

Turn, Turn, Turn: The Changing Nature of Leadership—Advice for Aspiring Leaders

The best leaders understand the present is nothing more than a platform for the envisioning of, and positioning for, the future. If you want to lead more effectively, shorten the distance between the future and the present.
—Mike Myatt, managing director and chief strategy officer, N2growth.com

If you've made it this far, you know by now that none of the leaders profiled here are at a loss for words, ideas, or advice. In the course of most of our interviews we asked two related questions: How did interviewees see museum leadership changing, and what advice did they have for aspiring leaders? The two questions are related because the next generation of museum leaders will enter an environment different from today and most certainly different from their predecessors a generation ago. While their answers to these questions are included in their profiles, we thought it would be useful to examine them more closely here, to try to shorten the distance between future and present.

Several of our leaders remarked on how much the field has changed in the last five years, or is changing as we speak, or will change significantly five years from now. If David Young at Cliveden is an accurate predictor of the future, the field is about to experience more change by 2018 than in the last quarter century. Melissa Chiu agreed, predicting a sea change, although she wonders if it is happening quickly enough. What's clear to us is the *pace* of change quickens each year, so if you procrastinate, struggling with multidimensionality and agility—two key twenty-first-century leadership fundamentals—you will likely be overtaken by expectations of forward-leaning boards, staff, and audiences.

We found that our interviewees' observations on the changing nature of leadership fell into five broad categories. Here they are:

DEMOGRAPHIC SHIFTS

After years of speculation about when the baby boomer retirement wave would begin, a generational leadership shift is finally underway. While not in full bloom, the field's demographics are beginning to change, a thought echoed by Dina Bailey, who muses, "I hope to see a younger generation of leaders; I hope leaders will bring younger people in." Kent Whitworth believes hiring younger is better, saying, "We're not playing a nostalgic game. History museums need new, forward-looking perspectives." In spite of this, Nathan Richie admits he hasn't seen much leadership succession take place yet, but he's building skill sets and is ready to take the challenge. He's not alone.

But some suggest a younger, more professionally mobile cohort might destabilize institutions as leaders move in and out every few years. Rebecca Slaughter wonders whether or not museums can stay strategically agile with a revolving door of leaders. "We're definitely seeing the end of the director keeping a job for forty years," she says, but she also acknowledges that there are many who still want to keep the status quo.

Shifting demographics mean some workplaces have three, or maybe four, generations working side by side. David Young remarks, "At Cliveden we have staff and volunteers from [age] eighteen to ninety-five working together. How do you communicate across the generations?"

From a gender standpoint, more women enter an already female-dominated history and cultural heritage museum field every year. Women fill the ranks at all levels in small- to middle-sized museums, often in the director's chair, while among the forty-eight state historical society directorships, twenty-nine are held by men and nineteen by women. Andrew Masich believes the field will see more women leaders, but Melissa Chiu points out, "While there has been a great shift in numbers, the larger museums are still thought of as positions for men."

When it comes to diversity of the museum workforce and its boardrooms, staffs and board members rarely reflect the racial, ethnic, and cultural diversity of their communities. Chris Taylor and Tonya Matthews are two of our leaders who are deeply engaged in diversifying the field; however, today's workforce and graduate programs remain stubbornly homogeneous. As a result, there is a crying need for the field to address diversity in a coordinated manner involving institutions, professional associations, and academic programs (including tweens and teens), with individuals and funders working together to create pathways to attract and retain diverse talent. And let's not fool ourselves—diversifying a profession requires both a bold stroke and a concerted long-term effort, along with a deep pool of resources to make it happen.

We'll leave the last word here to Burt Logan: "Museums are just as vibrant as they always were," he says. "Each generation will have the opportunity to decide what role museums have in society. They don't have to be content with what has been." *Don't be content with what has been*—remember that.

LEADERS: CHANGING SKILLS

It perhaps is no surprise that when describing how museum leadership is changing our leaders emphasized the same four fundamentals and four personal qualities we write about. First of all, museum leadership *is* changing, in large part because many in the field *want* it to change. But the pressure for change is coming from outside as well. Van Romans responds, "Museum leadership is changing toward a business model with a creative edge." This is due in large measure to a competitive external environment forcing history and cultural heritage museums to adapt to survive. Christy Coleman recognized the business model/creative edge duality as well, telling us, "Strong leaders must be entrepreneurs—venturists, really—as well as risk takers—it's a different mind-set. It's more than simply being business minded." Ellen Rosenthal's Wharton experience opened her eyes to the fact that museum leadership is now closer to for-profit leadership. "There were only three of us from nonprofits in the class," she explains, "and there was no separation in how we approach leadership."

Gonzalo Casals thinks leadership is changing precisely because more museums see themselves as community institutions—mission driven, relevant, and ingenious—remarking, "Museums have become the human center—the public living room for the community." Rob Kret advises, "Leaders must be willing to build community in ways that are meaningful to their audiences and to deliver in ways museums aren't delivering now." Janet Carding agrees: "Museum leaders need to be more like leaders of NGOs and some educational institutions. They must be able to talk about relevance and relationship building—these are becoming more important." Burt Logan adds, "Effective leadership mirrors society. As we look for more transparency and involvement, a leader has to recognize changes, embrace them and use them for the good of the organization, remaining true to values, but helping organizations be as nimble as possible and not succumb to the whims of society."

Trevor Beemon, whose focus at the Atlanta History Center is technology and social media, suggests, "Leaders need to embrace technology in order to keep museums relevant and to engage generations who learn differently. They need to be fluid about it, too, because technology changes so fast." Kippen de Alba Chu adds networking to the twenty-first-century museum director's list of critical skills.

Andrew Masich thinks the leaders of the future will be better educated, with more advanced degrees and solid theoretical training. "This will help to professionalize our field even more," he says. He sees a downside, too, asking if specialization and less grounding in what museums do and the impact they make will be a detriment.

Dina Bailey gets the last word, reminding us, "Museums need innovators at higher staff levels and at the board level."

RESOURCES

Financial resources for history and cultural heritage museums remain one of the field's biggest challenges, one that goes hand-in-hand with leadership. "For me, that is a question between how museums deliver on their missions and how they put together their support to meet their missions," Janet Carding says.

Hope Alswang sees history museums entering a world where resources are scarce. Anne Grimes Rand notes that one thing that is not changing is the emphasis on fund-raising. "Unless you have an unlimited endowment, museums need to run as businesses." Kippen de Alba Chu reminds us, "You need to create new revenue and become more efficient." Rand sees a parallel between museums and higher education leadership, saying that both require constant fund-raising. The fund-raising question makes Ilene Frank wonder who among her cohorts will want the director's role. So far, few of her former graduate school classmates have accepted the challenge of leading resource-starved institutions. While Colin Campbell notes that museums are not the only institutions under stress, he underscores that all types of cultural institutions are. "It's quite clear that more can't be sustained," he says.

ORGANIZATIONAL STRUCTURE, CULTURE, AND FOCUS

Robert Burns believes history and cultural heritage museums must adapt to the needs of younger audiences in order to survive. To do that, an institution must stay relevant. "If museums are going to continue to thrive in a changing world—and I'm not just talking about technology," Pam Green says, "people are going to have to look at an organizational structure that is easier to move and be more forward and progressive." That's agility.

"Leadership must be almost radical in what the organization can do," Green says. Alswang concurs, noting that the culture of perfection at so many museums suffocates progress. "Be creative, take risks!" she exclaims.

Open up to collaboration, Colin Campbell advises. "In the absence of a collaborative style," he says, "you're going nowhere; going it alone is not an option."

RELEVANCE AND CONNECTIVITY

The bottom line for twenty-first-century history and cultural heritage museums is engagement. "We know now that museums are more than just venues for intelligent learning, but places for emotional and even spiritual learning," David Young says. "We need to meet the visitor there. People need to see museums as places where community needs are met." Kent Whitworth believes: "The field is very different now even from four to five years ago. If we're not meeting real needs, our game is over. It's incumbent upon us to figure out those needs and let the rest go." Jennifer Kilmer agrees: "I think we're having to fight harder and harder to get people to understand our value," she says. "The day when it was a given that museums were important is over." Rob Kret adds that museums need to adopt a visitor-centered approach as a long-term development strategy.

Jamie Bosket agrees, adding, "Museums need to be far more willing to be flexible; far more open to nontraditional audiences and to technologies," he says. "Objects stay the same but connectivity with audiences changes." Robert Burns continues: "The art won't go, but there will be new ways to engage, and make it easier and more accessible so it doesn't feel boring and tired." One thing Lynne Ireland is sure of is that there will always be the need for the human-object interaction. It's where magic happens. "I still believe human beings experience the material world and objects in ways that don't happen with any other being," she says.

"I really hope that we're getting past the idea that museums are just great repositories," Ryan Spencer says. "Museums can be causes for good, but they must be relevant in order to do good. We can't get stuck in the 'good enough' mentality."

ADVICE FOR ASPIRING LEADERS

It is likely advice is one of the reasons you are reading this book. Once again, we've left advice giving to our leaders, but we've grouped it into some familiar overarching categories that we think will be helpful.

Be Self-Aware

Dina Bailey: Keep pushing yourself and your institution. Recognize your sphere of authority and learn when to push and when to pause, that way the system is less frustrating. Have a sense of experimentation and encouragement. Learn to be aware of yourself and your environment, and where you came from. This is critical in dealing effectively with the people you work with.

Jamie Bosket: Constantly search for ideas and people who will develop *you*. Seek out mentors and people to help (young and old); constantly collect other perspectives; be open to techniques. Find ways to assert yourself to receive opportunities.

Janet Carding: Use all channels available—online, social, print, and broadcast—to look externally for information to bring to bear on your current situation. Pay attention to trends in economics, politics, and technology and look for disruptive trends, too. It's critical to gain input from outside the organization, too.

Burt Logan: Find balance among work, family, community, and self. View each position or task as an opportunity to prepare for the next challenge. Focus on things you can do to prepare for leadership. The more responsibility you have the more you will need to be able to work with people and think strategically. This means understanding the intangibles, not just mastering content.

Andrew Masich: I highly recommend a midcareer training program like AASLH's Seminar for Historical Administration—for the knowledge gained from mentors to the camaraderie and network of colleagues, it's well worth the investment in time and effort (though it will seem impossible to tear yourself away from the day-to-day commitments of family and work at the time) and can be a life-changing experience.

Nathan Richie: I learned what I know from observation, trial, error, consultation, gut instinct, improvisation, action, and recalibration. Diversify your skill set; be a sponge out there.

Ryan Spencer: Be willing to learn and to keep your eyes open. Remind yourself about the magic that got you interested in the profession, because if it ever becomes just another job, there are more lucrative businesses to get into. Make time to reflect and know that we're here to inspire.

Christopher Taylor: Make sure you're passionate about what you do. The museum field is a big umbrella. Figure out where you want to focus and define what success means for you. Get on top of the vision-making thing. There's something to learn in almost every experience; nothing is wasted.

Be Authentic

Catherine Charlebois: Do what you love, truly believe in yourself and what you can do, be true to yourself. "You're the only guardian of your personal integrity," have fun, and enjoy the present moment.

Jim Enote: In order to truly be able to represent the community and the issues that affect it, work as close to home as possible. Where you are grounded, you are good. Constantly work at building and maintaining relationships. And know that the all-nighters don't end with youth. "If you see something that needs to be done, do it."

Rob Kret: Be flexible and smart, with one eye on today and the other on the museum's needs in the future. All leaders have to have a vision and set priorities to meet it. "Always remember that someone will follow you. You want to leave behind your very best work. Ensure that the organization is better for you having been there."

Andrew Masich: "Get a broad grounding. And know your audiences, but don't pander to them." He adds that all leaders should take the five minutes at the beginning of a conversation to learn whom they're talking to, be it staff, donors, visitors, board members, or the community at large.

Anne Grimes Rand: "Try to make it fun." In terms of leadership she says, "People should feel valued, listened to, creative, respected at work."

Nina Simon: Ask what your institution's "hot button" issues are before you get into the job; have a plan to focus regular amounts of time on what's important instead of always focusing on what's urgent; and read the book *The First 90 Days: Critical Success Strategies for New Leaders at All Levels* by Michael Watkins (2003).

Be Courageous

Edward Bosley: "You talk with anyone who will listen and you assume everyone is capable of writing a million-dollar check."

Anne Cathcart: Take initiative; don't fear making a wrong move. "Our parents are known as the helicopter generation and we're shaped by that. Many of us are not particularly resourceful, yet there are tons of resources available."

Van Romans: "My advice to next-generation leaders is never say no to an opportunity. It's difficult to see what might come your way, but try whatever is in front of you and never say no. Even if you fail, you learn!"

Be Visionary

Trevor Beemon: Be creative—push the boundaries; don't ever feel limited by what you have access to or what's been done in the past. "Passionate people will experiment and try new things."

Van Romans: Always bring creativity to the table and while there elevate it. It's so easy and yet we seem to relegate story, visuals, and other more creative work to the lowest level of the pile. . . . promote the process and the people doing it (make them quarterbacks, not just receivers), advance it, and praise it, as ultimately, it will be your friend and will bring people to your museum!

Chapter Twelve

This One's for You: (More Than) a Few Words of Advice about Leadership for Boards of Trustees

An individual leader can make a lot of noise and raise the bar on expectations, but collective leadership binds leaders at all levels of the organization to shared and sustainable actions.
—Dave Ulrich and Norm Smallwood, *Leadership Sustainability*

MODELING LEADERSHIP STARTS AT THE TOP

Don't think for one minute that this book is only about individual leadership. It's also about collective leadership. And nowhere does that apply more than in the history and cultural heritage museum boardroom, where the twenty-first-century organizational fundamentals of convergence, multidimensionality, agility, and in touch/in tune join the leadership qualities of self-awareness, authenticity, courage, and vision. Certainly, the ten myths cited in chapter 1 are just as often perpetuated by unknowing, disengaged, or bellicose boards as they are by external stakeholders. On the other hand, if boards adopted chapter 10's simple truths as part of their operating charters, it could make a world of difference in how history museums are led and governed.

While the focus of board leadership and staff leadership is different (although finely dovetailed), the principles of leadership are the same. Creating environments that value, develop, recognize, and share leadership across an organization are essential for history and cultural heritage museums to thrive at any time, but particularly in a landscape with too few resources. We believe that if history and cultural heritage museums were to invest as much in leadership training and development for boards and staff as they do in collection management and care, programming, and management techniques, they might weather the boom-bust-glut-scarcity scenario more resiliently and creatively.

Investing in leadership can happen in many ways, and it does not necessarily require tons of money. It does, however, require an organizational culture open to self-assessment, individual and group learning, and the willingness to practice techniques that strengthen decision making and communication. Boardroom cultures range from tightly controlled hierarchies wedded to rigorous rules of order to wildly creative free-for-alls. Wherever your board falls on this spectrum, know that it is there because someone steered it there, whether by conscious decision or benign neglect. Know, too, that a board's place on the spectrum can be changed for good or ill.[1] While there is no one-size-fits-all approach to the way boards work, embracing and nurturing healthy collective leadership is a critical element of twenty-first-century governance.

The point is that if it is to lead effectively, a board must build its own learning culture.

The fact is no one is born knowing how to be a board member. It is a learned skill usually accomplished on the fly while in the board seat. Depending on who you learned from, coupled with your own leadership talents, you may hit or miss the mark or struggle to find middle ground. Just as with staff leadership, board leadership is the all-important combination of *knowing* and *doing*. Before assuming their governing roles, the overwhelming majority of board members receive nothing similar to the basic leadership training offered to professional staff in graduate school or postgraduate programs. The result is *doing* without necessarily *knowing*. These are the shoals that ensnare many an institution's reputation, directorship, or trust with a donor.

THE SELF-AWARE AND AUTHENTIC BOARD

Knowing the board's role, learning the expectations of the institution and its supporters and its regulators, and understanding that the museum is part of a professional community with standards and networks is a continuous process that begins with new trustee orientation and lasts throughout a member's term. As much as an institution is responsible for providing information and discussion around issues and expectations, it is also an individual trustee's role to understand governance and its institutional impact, internally and externally. That said, the board as a whole must encourage learning and discourse as a way to develop skills conducive to group decision making— skills such as trust building; generative, integrative, and abundant thinking;

listening and reflection; and self-discipline and compassion. This is conscious governance; this is the hallmark of the self-aware and authentic board.

The most self-aware and authentic boards we know value and shape a culture of learning about how and why they govern. They make time for learning when their members are together, and they encourage learning and reflection to continue when members are apart. They build it into meeting agendas and create special gatherings solely for learning. They seek context for their work, apply external information to their deliberations, measure and compare performance with cohort institutions, listen to their stakeholders, and constantly ask questions of themselves and their staffs. They pinpoint fulcrums that can lead to change.

They figure out how to help their leaders lead well, creating space for emerging leaders to learn the ropes, to experiment, and to develop skills. As Barbara Miller and Jeanne Bergman write:

> There is a tendency to think of leadership in terms of hierarchy, with the board chair playing the strongest leadership role. It is certainly true that an effective board chair contributes enormously to the board's productivity, and that a poor board chair can be a significant obstacle to performance. Every board member, however, has a leadership role to play.[2]

Self-aware and authentic boards, therefore, encourage leadership around the board table, not just from the chairman's seat. (Convergence of leadership happens in the boardroom, too; in fact, it is essential to group decision making.) These boards are on the lookout for opportunities to adopt or adapt new ideas and ways of doing board work. In doing so, these boards ultimately deepen board members' ownership in the museum enterprise. And they recruit board members who support and extend this ethos.

Far too many board members disengage because decision-making power seems to be in the hands of a few. We have seen board members more engaged with their handhelds and tablets than with the agenda or the discussion at hand. Absenteeism creeps up, quorums go unmet, meetings begin late or end late or seem as though they'll never end at all. And we've seen board work become staff work when the staff is unwilling, unable, or simply unavailable. We've also seen the pendulum swing the other way, where staff does the board's work, shoring up weak governance. In other words, we've seen a lot of square pegs trying like crazy to fit into round holes. Collectively, we have to understand board service is not for everyone and act accordingly.

Perhaps it's the "hole" that needs reenvisioning. Aaron Hurst, president & CEO at the Taproot Foundation, writes:

> The governance and board model has been largely static for decades while the sector and our society [have] gone through radical shifts. This has in many

ways held the sector back from realizing its critical role in society. The modern day board is anything but modern. It was designed in a different era, a time when: white men were the only Americans who could vote; the only "office professions" were lawyers and accountants (no marketing, HR, IT, etc.); nonprofits worked almost exclusively domestically; and there was not only no Internet, but also no television.[3]

This model is designed for hierarchical, not convergent, leadership. It focuses on past activity as the sole predictor of the future; it is tightly bound by too little integrative and too much internally focused thinking, misunderstood analysis, or poorly executed procedural rules. Self-aware and authentic boards reshape board work to better meet the needs of their evolving organizations. They understand that governance must evolve, too.

We know of boards that begin every meeting by going around the table asking each member to share a piece of information that has come his or her way that could have some relevance to the museum—perhaps it's talk of a new charter school or the unveiling of an updated streetscape plan. We know of organizations using "blue sky" committees to stay current with evolving issues and professional practices or to generate new or refocused institutional responses or directions to emergent trends and investigate their feasibility. We see the widening use of strategic meeting agendas, where board discussion is focused on forward thinking and integration instead of numbing reports of past activity. We're seeing more boards use parts of their regular meetings and special retreats as opportunities to delve deeply into a topic, to plan for the future, and to learn new governance skills.

SUSTAINING GREAT LEADERSHIP FOR THE LONG TERM

The selection of the institution's staff leader is one of a board's top responsibilities, yet it is many a board's Achilles' heel. This responsibility cannot be shirked by passing it off to the board president, a major donor, the outgoing director, or even a professional search firm. Think about this: If a board is not clear about its own leadership needs, how could it possibly be clear about what it needs in chief executive leadership? How else to explain boards that hire for convenience rather than talent and persuade themselves there isn't a difference? Or boards that don't provide skill development for an inexperienced leader? Or boards that fail to understand they have a responsibility to shape a leader? Or boards that fail to recognize that all staff comprise an organization's *talent*, and that talent is worthy of investment?

Matt Monge, a blogger who focuses on the importance of workplace culture and leadership, writes:

From an organizational perspective, we ought to be looking for the folks who are leading change, initiating things, and pushing us all to be what we could become. It's those people who are undoubtedly some of our organization's greatest assets. Frankly, the future of your organization just might depend on them doing their thing. So encourage the catalysts. Give them room. If you empower them in meaningful ways it's far more likely they'll do meaningful work.[4]

The selection of the institution's governing leadership is another of a board's essential responsibilities if forward momentum is to be maintained and institutional vision met. To be successful, the board and its nominating or board development committee must have a deep understanding of where the institution is going and the kinds of talent its leaders must have in order to reach the destination. Learning organizations know not just how to connect these dots—they've carefully chosen and defined the dots that need to be connected. It makes us wonder why so many boards relegate this activity to the bottom of their to-do lists. Why is there a predictable mad scramble at so many museums to assemble a slate of "warm bodies" right before board elections? Why don't more institutions see the board recruitment process as a fulcrum for change and/or long-term success?

Boards must see themselves as key players in building the next generation of history museum board and staff leaders, a role that will grow as veteran leadership retirements quicken in the next ten to fifteen years. With this in mind, it's time to add what the authors of *Leadership Sustainability* term *new human capital developers* to the job descriptions of museum boards.[5]

Part of this is about planning for leadership succession, and part is about making systemic behavioral change to allow for succession, development, and training that will stand the museum in good stead over the long haul. We know from our research that too few history and cultural heritage museums have a delineated plan for developing leadership, much less passing it to a new generation. When we wrote the white paper, "Report to the Field: The Status of Succession Planning in New York State Museums" for the Museum Association of New York in 2008, we found that 91 percent of reporting museums in the state had no succession plan, written or otherwise. We believe New York State museums are not alone and, further, we are certain that not much has changed since 2008, precisely because boards and staff leaders haven't made leadership health a priority.

Putting human capital first and investing in staff—whether directors, middle management or those just beginning their careers—will make individual organizations and the field as a whole more competitive in a world where the pool of potential employees is growing smaller and competition more cutthroat. Failing to invest in staff limits the museum field's diversity when talented individuals are lost to higher paying jobs elsewhere. And it does not take a rocket scientist to understand the museum field is overwhelmingly white and female. While that alone is not a bad thing, it may be emblematic of the field's slowness to change and adapt. And what is succession planning if not change on both a personal and an institutional level?[6]

PUTTING LEADERSHIP FIRST

For leadership training, development, and succession planning to be institutionalized, basic organizational behaviors must change. It is one thing to raise awareness about intentional leadership and offer sporadic training and development opportunities to leaders, but it is quite another to make leadership the core of a museum's values. Putting leadership first must become second nature. Dave Ulrich and Norm Smallwood, the authors of *Leadership Sustainability*, write, "Developing leadership capability (the capability to build future leaders) matters even more than developing individual competence."[7] When you think about it, what's the point of investing in leadership training, development, and succession if the museum simply doesn't have the ability to carry it forward from administration to administration?

Ulrich and Smallwood offer up seven behavioral disciplines an organization needs to embrace if it is serious about keeping leadership a priority. Of them, we think the following have particular importance for changing history and cultural heritage museum behavior: time, accountability, tracking, resources, and adopting a mind-set of continual learning (what Ulrich and Smallwood call melioration).[8]

Time: Simply put, boards and staff must work to allow enough time for a new or more robust leadership ethos and its attendant behaviors to take root and flourish. Too often, we look for the quick fix. We retreat or allow ourselves to get sidetracked when we find the changes we need to make are too difficult to overcome. We give up too soon.

> For leaders who want to sustain their desires and make change happen, *time* means that the future is not bound by the past and that behavioral cycles can be consciously modified. Time becomes a key discipline for sustainability because leaders who want to demonstrate a new behavior or create a new pattern of behaviors can do so only by being intentional about their use of time. Time is both a fixed asset (we all have the same amount of time) and a variable asset (we conceive of and use our time differently).[9]

Accountability and Tracking: Aspirations left unsaid and unmeasured are aspirations unmet. Once the commitment is made to make leadership an institutional priority, board and staff leaders must hold themselves accountable for making it happen. Boards must openly declare their intentions to make change precisely to prevent them from straying, and they must develop plans for change and ways to track their progress. So write a leadership plan and work it together. Transparency and evaluation are critical to success, or as Ulrich and Smallwood write, "Leadership is sustainable when the leader's agenda becomes the personal agenda of others."[10] We love that.

Resources: We've said that it doesn't take a fortune to make leadership a top priority, but it does require work. Ulrich and Smallwood call them intangibles, the things "that leaders enlist to support their desired changes and build an infrastructure of sustainability."[11] For boards, these may include group coaching, individual mentoring, one-on-one evaluation, or simply making time in an agenda for topic-specific learning or for some wide-ranging integrative thinking. To sustain staff leadership development, boards may need to support the realignment of a human resources department or rethink the traditional chief executive's evaluation. What might happen if a board and staff shook up the organization chart, moving those little boxes around to reflect a desired way of working together? Once again, it's more about mind-set than money.

Adopting a Mind-Set of Continual Learning: Organizational change or growth is sustained by continual improvement—the conscious effort to learn from one's missteps, apply lessons learned, and move on. Learning organizations understand that the inherent risks of experimentation, innovation, and improvisation are greatly mitigated when the core infrastructure is sound, and, thus, elastic enough to accept failure as well as success. Continual learning is one of the most important and cost-effective tools an organization can use to meet the leadership challenges of the twenty-first century. It requires intentional commitment from board and staff leadership, beginning with conversations around what it can help accomplish and how it can become a natural part of the institution's ethos and daily rhythm.

Great acts of leadership play out everyday in the museum community, yet why are they so seemingly isolated or sporadic? We run like lemmings from success story to success story hungry for new ideas and solutions—the magic bullet—to intractable, long-standing problems. Perhaps the problem morphed into something else. Too often history museums let routine mask a dearth of ideas, resources, and courage.

> News Flash—innovation, growth and development cannot occur by pretending we live in a world that has long since passed us by. Leading in the 21st Century affords no safe haven for 20th Century thinkers. Old, static, institutionalized thinking will gate the pace of forward progress faster than just about anything. If you want to expose yourself as an out of touch, dated leader, keep trying to address today's issues and opportunities with yesterday's thinking.[12]

It's time for every board to pick up the mantle of leadership and say: ideas start here; resources start here; and courage starts here. This is about leadership first.

NOTES

1. We like Nathan Garber's discussion of various governing board models. Find it here: http://garberconsulting.com/governance%20models%20what's%20right.htm, accessed January 10, 2013.

2. Barbara Miller and Jeanne Bergman, "Developing Leadership on Boards of Directors," *Journal for Nonprofit Management* 12, no. 1 (2008): 4, accessed January 12, 2013, http://supportcenteronline.org/wp-content/uploads/2013/04/scnm_journal_2008.pdf.

3. Aaron Hurst, "Is the Tide Turning for the Nonprofit Board Model?" *Taproot Foundation Blog*, December 7, 2012, accessed April 28, 2013, http://www.taprootfoundation.org/about-probono/blog/tide-turning-nonprofit-board-model.

4. Matt Monge, "Are You Encouraging the Change Leaders?" October 24, 2012, accessed January 18, 2013, http://themojocompany.com/2012/10/are-you-encouraging-change-leaders/.

5. Dave Ulrich and Norm Smallwood, *Leadership Sustainability: Seven Disciplines to Achieve the Changes Great Leaders Know They Must Make* (New York: McGraw Hill, 2013), 15.

6. Joan H. Baldwin, "Report to the Field: The Status of Succession Planning in New York State Museums," Museum Association of New York, 2008, 3–4, accessed January 18, 2013, http://manyonline.org/wp-content/uploads/2010/06/NYSMuseumsSuccessionPlanningStatus.pdf.

7. Dave Ulrich and Norm Smallwood, "Leadership Sustainability," *Leadership Excellence* 30, no. 1 (January 2013): 3, http://rblip.s3.amazonaws.com/Articles/Leadership%20Sustainability%20in%20LE.pdf.

8. Ulrich and Smallwood, *Leadership Sustainability*, ix.

9. Ulrich and Smallwood, *Leadership*, 51.

10. Ulrich and Smallwood, "Leadership Sustainability," 3.

11. Ulrich and Smallwood, "Leadership Sustainability," 3.

12. Mike Myatt, "10 Things Every Leader Should Challenge," Forbes.com, March 7, 2013, accessed March 24, 2013, http://www.forbes.com/sites/mikemyatt/2013/03/07/10-things-every-leader-should-challenge.

Chapter Thirteen

There Be Dragons Here

Mercer: [Dutchman is headed toward the Maelstrom] Steer out!
Davy Jones: She'll not harm us! Full bore and into the abyss!
Mercer: Are you mad?
Davy Jones: HA! You 'fraid to get wet?
—*Pirates of the Caribbean: At World's End*, 2007

As the history and cultural heritage museum field moves inexorably into the twenty-first century, how *will* it grapple with leadership and governance? Will anything change? Will we steer out or move full bore into the abyss? Will these twin issues be as important as collections and interpretation were forty years ago when the United States approached its bicentennial? We think they should be.

We asserted throughout this book that the history museum field has not placed enough emphasis on the individual and institutional value of leadership training and development; that it lacks understanding of who benefits from leadership training and development, and why it is important to keeping pace with the field's changing needs; and that its ability to address issues of leadership training and development is hampered by the glacial pace of competency articulation and leadership definition key to nurturing outstanding leaders. We think the museum field, but particularly history museums, historic homes, and heritage organizations, needs to put leadership at the top of the to-do list. Why? Because by now we hope you believe, as we do, that intentional, forward-leaning leadership is the key to moving history and cultural heritage museums beyond the doldrums in which so many find themselves. There's not enough wind in the sails now, so since we're drifting into uncharted territory, why not risk getting a little wet?

The personal leadership journeys found here give readers a snapshot of our leaders' museum careers. In doing so, we get a glimpse of how leadership manifests itself individually. But you may still ask, "How do leaders structure organizations to capture convergence, multidimensionality, agility, *and* be in tune/in touch?"

ARTICULATING UNIQUE VALUE

A great deal has been written and talked about how history and cultural heritage museums must understand, interpret, and articulate their value to themselves and their stakeholders, so it is puzzling that so few actually do it. Faced with the prospect of being permanently sidelined, the field as a whole rarely states its value with one clear voice. Could missing the boat regarding value be the result of poor leadership that misunderstands or misdirects institutional priorities?

Failing to be clear about value creates a climate where history and cultural heritage museums cease to have a place at the table in any discussion about national history education, social studies, civic education, or more broadly, humanities education; we are a field benched during community planning, nor are we seen as ready collaborators for tourism or economic development. Could the history museum field be overlooked because its current leadership does not lead outward?

MAKING A DIFFERENCE

Since the publication of *Excellence and Equity* in 1992, many of the profession's leading figures have asked museums of all types to step out of their insular bubbles and interact with communities on issues of wide-ranging relevancy. Harold Skramstad's 1999 article, "An Agenda for American Museums in the Twenty-First Century," was one of the first to peer into the crystal ball, calling for museums to be model community institutions offering high-value educational programs and experiences. He offered a recipe for success built on shared authority, connectedness, and trustworthiness,[1] one that sounds painfully familiar fifteen years hence.

Skramstad's voice was just one in a chorus of thoughtful leaders that continues to this day. From western Canada, Robert R. Janes joins the "value" chorus, reminding us that museums' continued inattentiveness to social issues will be their undoing, especially in a world of too many museums and too little resources. Janes urges the field to accelerate social interaction, not retreat from it. History and cultural heritage museums are not seen as community problem solvers or cultural innovators for a reason: current museum leadership reverts too quickly to small-bore thinking.[2]

There is no question that an awesome handful of today's history and cultural heritage museums make a difference in their communities, but since

Skramstad's agenda was published (which seems like a lifetime ago), there are nowhere near enough. As we head toward the quarter century mark, when will we be able to say that history and cultural heritage museums have finally turned the high value/high impact corner? When will the field define its leadership in high value/high impact terms? When will the field universally acknowledge leadership competencies that support high value/high impact outcomes?

INVESTING IN LEADERSHIP

So what should happen? First, the field needs to embrace and understand the importance of individual leadership training. When leadership takes hold, we know good things happen at the admission desk, in collections storage, and in the boardroom. And we know organizations benefit when they empower individuals to act, entrusting them with not only responsibility but also authority. History organizations—like Zappos, the online shoe emporium—need to support staff decision making at the moment of transaction, no matter where it happens.

History museums and cultural heritage organizations need to realize that investing in leadership training, whether it is through the local chamber of commerce—as with interviewee Ilene Frank—an online course, or one of the traditional programs like the Getty's is as important as good collections care. A strong leader will figure out how to care for collections, or more importantly, raise money to hire someone who will. Remember what interviewee Jennifer Kilmer said, "I look at myself as an administrator. I rely on curators and staff to provide me with guidance [about collections]." This from the director of the Washington State Historical Society whose first history job—also a directorship—found her leading an $11.7 million capital campaign.

Which is worse: A historic house with beautifully organized and cared for collections but no visitors, or that same historic house filled with laughter, argument, lively discussion, and plenty of people? No, we are not suggesting collections are not important. They are. For most organizations they are the catalysts that spawn the ideas. But too many history organizations and their staffs are mired in process to the detriment of leadership. Their leaders manage, but they do not lead.

We know that what we've witnessed in our interviews is just the tip of the leadership iceberg. What we've left largely unexplored here is how history and cultural heritage museums can effectively embrace leadership training and development and make them their own. Nor have we addressed what the long-term impact would be for history museums if leadership training and development for boards and staffs became a sustained priority, going well beyond what is currently available, including AASLH's Standards and Excellence Program (StEPS) and AAM's Museum Assessment and Accreditation program.

COMMITTING TO LEADERSHIP PERSONALLY

We've introduced you to a group of museum leaders who we believe are self-aware, authentic, courageous, and visionary. They ask the hard questions. Institutions can't lose when staff is active and intentional about their work. We know individuals influence and shape organizations, and *vice versa.* Leaders who model courageous and visionary behavior lead organizational change. History and cultural heritage museums with this kind of leader are subtly transformed. As Peter Senge writes in his book *The Fifth Discipline,* "Organizations learn only through individuals who learn. Individual learning does not guarantee organizational learning. But without it no organizational learning occurs."[3] So we believe there needs to be an investment in individual leadership on the part of history and cultural heritage museum professionals (for themselves and all the institutions they will work for), on the part of boards of trustees (for themselves and the leaders they hire), and on the part of graduate programs (for the leaders they are molding).

Almost all of our interviewees have been given, and more importantly, taken opportunities to expand skills, building confidence in leading. Your growth as a leader is yours and yours alone. Networking and mentoring is an obvious first step. We know it occurs informally throughout the field. The question for us is, "When an individual wants to pursue leadership development, are there enough opportunities available? And will his or her organization be supportive?"

CHANGING GRADUATE SCHOOL CURRICULUM

And let us pause here to say a word about graduate programs. Almost all of our interviewees have graduate degrees. But many have degrees that once upon a time would have been considered "outside the field." Frankly, it doesn't seem to have held them back.

We would like to suggest that general museum studies programs not currently offering separate courses in leadership should intentionally weave them into their existing programs, or create new leadership courses in partnership with business programs on their campuses or professional associations off campus. We suggest this not just because some students may someday be offered directorships, but because it is important that all members of the history museum field be good leaders, no matter what position they occupy. We can't underscore this too strongly: no matter where you are on the organizational ladder, the qualities of authenticity, self-awareness, courage, and vision are important. It would also not be a bad idea if newly minted graduate students were comfortable with facilitating meetings, pitching funding and project proposals, and thinking like an entrepreneur. The world is moving too quickly to send students into the job market without helping them understand that leadership isn't about job description, it is about behavior.

INVESTING IN ORGANIZATIONAL LEADERSHIP

Committing to leadership begins when a board and staff understand the power and possibility of their institutions. Without that understanding, coupled with the belief that museums have a critical role to play in society, there is little need to champion strong leadership over plain vanilla good management.

Boards must hold themselves accountable for identifying, recruiting, and effectively using members who are willing and capable to experiment with governance models to facilitate change. Granting agencies need to look for it, providing funding for organizations that want good governance.

Boards need to build leadership training into their overhead and hiring costs. Until tiny, underfunded historical societies realize that having board members take a board training course or a new director take leadership training through the local chamber of commerce, college, or university is important, the culture won't change. Organizations will worry about how to fund a program when they have no idea why they matter to the community.

We believe there is a crying need for leadership training and development within institutions not touched by existing programs. How could existing training programs work with the consortia of museums and/or the field's professional associations to create a coordinated network expressly for training and development of history museum leaders?

As a field we are in perilous waters. We acknowledge these are extremely fragile times for nonprofits in general and history organizations in particular. If we were seventeenth-century mapmakers, this is the place where we would write, "There be dragons here." The Internet pulls us closer, but it creates a series of cookie-cutter experiences available at the click of a mouse. History organizations need strong leaders who are articulate about their organization's uniqueness; who can persuade a community they shouldn't stay home and look at exhibits online from the comfort of their sofa. That takes people with passion, entrepreneurial spirit, and the ability to size up problems, make decisions, and take risks. That's why leadership matters.

NOTES

1. Harold Skramstad, "An Agenda for American Museums in the Twenty-First Century," *Daedalus* 128, no. 3 (Summer 2009): 109–28.

2. Robert R. Janes has written extensively about museums and social relevancy. His most recent books include *Looking Reality in the Eye: Museums and Social Responsibility* (with Gerald T. Conaty) and *Museums in a Troubled World*. He is the editor-in-chief of the journal *Museum Management and Curatorship*.

3. Peter Senge, *The Fifth Discipline: The Art & Practice of The Learning Organization* (New York: Doubleday, 1990), 139.

Chapter Fourteen

The Leadership Agenda for History and Cultural Heritage Museums

Through me. By me. This has become a mantra I have adopted and acts as a leadership moral compass. Anything that needs to be accomplished has two ways for that to happen. I can facilitate it happening by empowering and supporting others to do it, or I can do it myself. Quality leaders definitely understand that there needs to be a healthy blend of these two approaches in order to be fully effective.

—William Powell, *The Leadership Advisor*

We hope this book will spark a leadership revolution among our history museum colleagues. In order for that to happen, personal commitment is required, and a road map might be useful.

There is no question in our minds that in order for leadership training and development to become a widespread priority in the history and cultural heritage field, it must be addressed in a coordinated way on a variety of fronts, through you and by you. If history and cultural heritage museums are to thrive, not merely survive, now is the fragile, vulnerable moment when the field's emphasis on leadership must become *as* important, if not *more* important, than the issues of collection care, building preservation, and educational and public programming. Without forward-leaning, mission-driven, and intentionally entrepreneurial leadership, no amount of collections care, building preservation, or programming will be enough to secure a museum's future.

As we hope we have illustrated, the art and act of leadership is both deeply personal and necessarily public, involving an institution's board and staff leaders, as well as those charged with training and developing the field and those with the capacity to fund the advancement of the cultural sector.

The following agenda is an amalgam of directives from our previous research for the Museum Association of New York on leadership and succession planning and from our current research for this project.

For Individuals	Recognize your leadership development needs and articulate them to those who can help you meet them.
	Seek opportunities now to take leadership responsibility in order to grow and expand skills. Practice new learning whenever you can. Prepare for serendipity.
	Advocate for leadership training and development at your institution.
	Assist with or take responsibility for leadership training and development activities for your team, your department, your volunteers, or if you're the lone professional, for yourself.
	Mentor others in need of leadership skill development.
	Encourage your graduate programs to offer leadership training and mentoring opportunities to alumni and/or to communities of practice in the field.
	Encourage your professional associations to offer leadership training, mentoring, and development opportunities.
For Institutions	Realize that it is not your job to maintain the status quo. The job of institutions and their leaders is to make a difference.
	Encourage institutional commitment to developing *all* human capital—staff, board, and volunteers. Have high expectations of those charged with developing leadership.
	Consciously and consistently nurture leadership within boards and staff by creating and implementing written individual development plans and succession plans and making space for leadership to take root and flourish.
	Support cross-functional experimentation and learning within and among institutions for board and staff to learn and expand leadership skills.
	Develop boards that support leadership training and development at all levels in the institution, that understand the particular professional development needs of the emerging

Table 14.1 Leadership Revolution Agenda

	Use board development committees to regularly assess collective and individual leadership training and development needs at the board level, and to develop boards that represent broad knowledge and are committed to forward-leaning leadership overall (convergent, multi-dimensional, agile, and in-tune/in-touch).
	Ensure equality in hiring, promotion, access to leadership opportunities, and compensation.
	Insist upon institutional support of the emerging leader and lone professional, and the diversification of governing boards.
	Make allocation of resources for leadership training and development for staff and board a priority.
	Make safe and sizeable spaces for practice and failure.
	Understand that perfection impedes progress.
For Professional Associations	Heighten awareness of the need for leadership training, standards, and development by emphasizing it in existing professional development programs and in institutional assessment programs.
	Focus on leadership training and development as a key ingredient in building healthy history and cultural heritage museums.
	Expand commitment to leadership and succession planning education for boards.
	Develop, facilitate, and/or promote leadership training and development opportunities for boards and staff in collaboration with graduate programs, independent training organizations, and/or nonprofit consortia.
	Promote equality in hiring, promotion, access to leadership opportunities, and compensation through collaboration with graduate programs, allied associations, collection and dissemination of research, and training.
	Insist upon competitive pay, institutional support of the emerging leader and lone professional, and the diversification of governing boards.

Table 14.1 Leadership Revolution Agenda *(continued)*

For Graduate Programs	Introduce leadership training and development into all course work.
	Promote internships and other opportunities for students to gain cultural leadership and entrepreneurial skills, perhaps from outside the field.
	Collaborate with training programs across the nonprofit sector to share expertise and offer training opportunities.
	Create scholarship programs specifically for leadership development.
	Develop mid-career leadership opportunities in partnership with museums, museum professional associations, nonprofit consortia, and funders.
	Work with the field's professional associations to develop and deliver leadership training and development opportunities.
For Funders	Work with the field and individual institutions to support the development and implementation of museum leadership development and training opportunities as key elements to organizational capacity building.
	Focus on board and staff leadership development with special funding initiatives, such as sabbaticals and other opportunities for staff to immerse themselves in leadership development.
	Support equality in hiring, promotion, access to leadership opportunities, and compensation through collaboration with graduate programs, allied associations, collection and dissemination of research, and training.
	Insist upon competitive pay, institutional support of the emerging leader and lone professional, and the diversification of governing boards.

Table 14.1 Leadership Revolution Agenda *(continued)*

Bibliography

Alexander, Edward P. *Museum Masters: Their Museums and Their Influence.* Nashville, TN: American Association for State and Local History, 1983.

American Association (Alliance) of Museums. *2012 National Comparative Museum Salary Study.* 2012. http://www.aam-us.org/resources/research/museum-salary-study (accessed August 4, 2013).

American Association (Alliance) of Museums. "Museums and the American Economy in 2011." April 2012. http://www.aam-us.org/docs/research/acme12-final.pdf?sfvrsn=0 (accessed December 18, 2012).

Americans for the Arts. *National Arts Index 2012.* http://www.artsindexusa.org/national-arts-index (accessed October 2, 2012).

Anderson, Gail. *Reinventing the Museum: Historical and Contemporary Perspectives on the Paradigm Shift.* Lanham, MD: AltaMira Press, 2004.

Anderson, Gail. *Reinventing the Museum: The Evolving Conversation on the Paradigm Shift.* Lanham, MD: AltaMira Press, 2012.

Anderson, Lisa A., Jody A. Crago, and Peter H. Webb. "A New Day for Local History: No Longer an Island." *History News* 66, no. 4 (Autumn 2011): 20.

Arroyo, Leah. "What They Really Want to Do Is Direct." *Museum News* 86, no. 5 (September/October 2007): 46–53.

Baldwin, Joan H. "Who's Next? Questioning the Future of Museum Leadership in New York State." Museum Association of New York, 2006. http://manyonline.org/wp-content/uploads/2010/09/MANY-WhosNext.pdf (accessed October 5, 2012).

Baldwin, Joan H. "Report to the Field: The Status of Succession Planning in New York State Museums." Museum Association of New York, 2008. http://manyonline.org/wp-content/uploads/2010/06/NYSMuseumsSuccessionPlanningStatus.pdf (accessed January 18, 2013).

Bonner, Barbara. "Museum Directorship—A Changing Profession: Perspectives of 28 Current and Former Museum Directors in New York City." MA thesis, Teacher's College, Columbia University, 1988.

Bridgespan Group. "The Challenge of Developing Future Leaders: Survey Results Say . . ." 2012. http://www.bridgespan.org/getattachment/6d0a44b3-a794-444e-b6a4-7594b825f659/The-Challenge-of-Developing-Future-Leaders-Survey.aspx (accessed March 12, 2013).

Bryant, Adam. "The Six Steps of Leadership (Plus Courage)." *New York Times*, January 5, 2013. http://www.nytimes.com/2013/01/06/business/california-pizza-kitchens-chief-on-6-steps-to-leadership.html (accessed January 7, 2013).

Carding, Janet. "What Can Museums Learn from Nonprofit Leadership?" *museum geek* Blog, August 2, 2012. http://museumgeek.wordpress.com/2012/08/02/guest-post-what-can-museums-learn-from-nonprofit-leadership/ (accessed August 9, 2012).

Center for the Future of Museums. "Voices of the Future: Phil Nowlen." TEDTalks, 2009. https://www.youtube.com/watch?feature=player_embedded&v=VzG1Iua_j7k (accessed May 3, 2013).

Center for the Future of Museums. "Voices of the Future: Robert Janes." TEDTalks, 2009. https://www.youtube.com/watch?NR=1&v=OSdvEtOxavs&feature=endscreen (accessed May 3, 2013).

Coleman, Christy. Interview that aired on WTVR, CBS 6, Richmond, December 10, 2012. http://wtvr.com/2012/12/10/virginia-this-morning-christy-coleman/ (accessed April 5, 2013).

Cooperstown Graduate Program, Grant Application to Institute for Museum and Library Services [IMLS], 2008.

Drexel Now, "New Drexel University Graduate Program Will Prepare Students for Museum Leadership." March 5, 2013. http://drexel.edu/now/news-media/releases/archive/2013/March/Museum-Leadership/ (accessed March 11, 2013).

Durel, John, and Anita Nowery Durel. "A Golden Age for Historic Properties." *History News* (Summer 2007): 8.

Friedman, Stewart D. *Total Leadership: Be a Better Leader, Have a Richer Life*. Watertown, MA: Harvard Business School Press, 2008.

Garber, Nathan. "Governance Models: What's Right for Your Board." 1997. http://garberconsulting.com/governance%20models%20what's%20right.htm (accessed January 10, 2013).

Genoways, Hugh H., and Lynne M. Ireland. *Museum Administration: An Introduction*. Lanham, MD: AltaMira Press, 2003.

Gilmore, Audrey, and Ruth Rentschler. "Changes in Museum Management: A Custodial or Marketing Emphasis?" *Journal of Management Development* 21, no. 10 (2002): 745–60.

Gladwell, Malcolm. *Outliers: The Story of Success*. New York: Little, Brown and Company, 2008.

Godfrey, Marian, and Barbara Silberman. "What to Do with These Old Houses." The Pew Charitable Trusts. April 30, 2008. http://www.pewtrusts.org/our_work_report_detail.aspx?id=38618 (accessed November 11, 2012).

Goldsmith, Marshall, Beverly Kaye, and Ken Shelton. *Learn Like a Leader: Today's Top Leaders Share Their Leadership Journeys*. Boston, MA: Nicholas Brealey Publishing, 2010.

Greenleaf, Robert. "The Servant as Leader." Westfield, IN: Robert K. Greenleaf Center, 1982.

Griffin, Des. "Five Issues for Museums." 2003. http://desgriffin.com/effective/five-issues/ (accessed May 3, 2013).

Heath, Chip, and Dan Heath. *Switch: How to Change Things When Change Is Hard*. New York: Crown Business, 2013.

Helgesen, Sally. "A Journey to Authentic Leadership." In *Learn Like a Leader: Today's Top Leaders Share Their Learning Journeys*, edited by Marshall Goldsmith et al. Boston: Nicholas Brealey Publishing, 2010.

Hesselbein, Frances, Marshall Goldsmith, and Richard Beckhard. *The Leader of the Future*. San Francisco: Jossey-Bass, 1996.

Hirzy, Ellen C., ed. *Excellence and Equity: Education and the Public Dimension of Museums* (Washington, DC: American Association (Alliance) of Museums Press, 1992).

Hudson, Samuel. "Re-Imagineering." *Fort Worth Weekly*, July 12, 2006. http://archive.fwweekly.com/content.asp?article=4056 (accessed February 7, 2013).

Hurst, Aaron. "Is the Tide Turning for the Nonprofit Board Model?" *Taproot Foundation Blog*, December 7, 2012. http://www.taprootfoundation.org/about-probono/blog/tide-turning-nonprofit-board-model (accessed April 28, 2013).

Hymel, Andrée Marie. "Museum Directorship: A Digest of Contemporary Opinion." MA thesis, Teachers College, Columbia University, 2000.

Institute of Museum and Library Services. *Museums, Libraries, and 21st Century Skills*. Washington, DC: Institute of Museum and Library Services, 2009.

Janes, Robert R. *Museums and the Paradox of Change: A Case Study in Urgent Adaptation*. Calgary, Canada: University of Calgary Press, 1997.

Janes, Robert R. *Museums in a Troubled World: Renewal, Irrelevance or Collapse?* New York: Routledge, 2009.

Janes, Robert R. "The Mindful Museum." *Curator: The Museum Journal* 53, no. 3 (July 2010): 325–28.

Johnson, Julie I. "Museums, Leadership, and Transfer: An Inquiry into Organizational Supports for Learning Leadership." PhD dissertation, Antioch University, 2012.

Kail, Colonel Eric. "Leadership Character: The Role of Courage." April 4, 2011. www.washingtonpost.com blogs/guest-insights/post/leadership-character-the-role-of-courage/2011/04/04/AGvfAohH_blog.html (accessed March 19, 2013).

Katz, Phil. "Some Notes on the Future of History Museums." *Center for the Future of Museums.* May 17, 2012. http://futureofmuseums.blogspot.com/2012/05/some-notes-on-future-of-history-museums.html (accessed January 15, 2013).

Katz, Phil. "By the Numbers." *Museum* (May–June 2013).

LitLamp Communications Group. "13 Things Breaking Through in 2013." Patricia Martin Consulting Services. http://patricia-martin.com/13ThingsBreakingThrough.htm (accessed January 10, 2013).

Male, Richard. "Nonprofit Weaknesses Start with Too Few Leaders and Too Many Managers." *Chronicle of Philanthropy,* February 10, 2013. http://philanthropy.com/article/Nonprofit-Weaknesses-Start/137189/ (accessed February 19, 2013).

Matelic, Candace Tangorra. "Organizational Change in History Museums." PhD dissertation, submitted to the University at Albany, SUNY, 2007.

McBean, Bill. "The 5 Characteristics of Great Leaders." *Fast Company,* January 23, 2013. http://www.fastcompany.com/3004914/5-characteristics-great-leaders (accessed January 25, 2013).

McCarthy, Dan. "A CEO's Guide to Leadership Development." *SmartBlog on Leadership,* February 28, 2013. http://smartblogs.com/leadership/2013/02/28/a-ceos-guide-to-leadership-development/ (accessed March 10, 2013).

McGuire, John B., Charles J. Palus, William Pasmore, and Gary B. Rhodes. "Transforming Your Organization." Center for Creative Leadership. www.ccl.org/leadership/pdf/solutions/TYO.pdf (accessed November 15, 2012).

McGuire, John B., Gary Rhodes, and Charles J. Palus. "Inside Out: Transforming Your Leadership Culture." Center for Creative Leadership, January–February 2008. www.ccl.org/leadership/pdf/publications/lia/lia27_6Inside.pdf (accessed November 15, 2012).

Miller, Barbara, and Jeanne Bergman. "Developing Leadership on Boards of Directors." *Journal for Nonprofit Management* 12, no. 1 (2008).

Monge, Matt. "Are You Encouraging the Change Leaders?" October 24, 2012. http://themojocompany.com/2012/10/are-you-encouraging-change-leaders/ (accessed January 18, 2013).

Morino, Mario. *Leap of Reason: Managing to Outcomes in an Era of Scarcity.* Washington, DC: Venture Philanthropy Partners, 2011.

Morris, Martha. "A More Perfect Union: Museums Merge, Grow Stronger." *Museum* (July–August 2012). http://onlinedigeditions.com/display_article.php?id=1093046 (accessed November 3, 2012).

Myatt, Mike. "10 Things Every Leader Should Challenge." Forbes.com, March 7, 2013. http://www.forbes.com/sites/mikemyatt/2013/03/07/10-things-every-leader-should-challenge/ (accessed March 24, 2013).

National Center for Education Statistics. "The Nation's Report Card: U.S. History 2010." Institute of Education Sciences, U.S. Department of Education. http://nces.ed.gov/nationsreportcard/pubs/main2010/2011468.asp (accessed April 3, 2013).

National Committee on Pay Equity. http://www.pay-equity.org/ (accessed April 26, 2013).

Nye, Joseph S. "Nature and Nurture in Leadership." *The Harvard Crimson,* June 2, 2009. http://www.thecrimson.com/article/2009/6/2/nature-and-nurture-in-leadership-as/ (accessed March 12, 2013).

Otten, Laura. "It's a Man's World." *The Nonprofit Center Blog.* April 26, 2013. http://www.lasallenonprofitcenter.org/its-a-mans-world/ (accessed April 26, 2013).

Perry, Georgia. "Innovator Drives Museum's Success." SantaCruz.com, March 19, 2013. http://www.santacruz.com/news/2013/03/19/innovator_drives_museums_success (accessed March 20, 2013).

Powell, William. "No Sacrifice. No Leadership." The Leadership Advisor.com. June 2, 2011. http://www.theleadershipadvisor.com/2011/06/02/no-sacrifice-no-leadership/ (accessed May 2, 2013).

Riven, Stephanie. "The State of the Arts: The Arts Are in a State." *Artsblog*. August 15, 2012. http://blog.artsusa.org/2012/08/15/the-state-of-the-arts-the-arts-are-in-a-state/ ?utm_source=rss&utm_medium=rss&utm_campaign=the-state-of-the-arts-the-arts-are-ina-state (accessed October 2, 2012).

Robinson, Tynesia Boyea. "Managing to Outcomes: Mission Possible." In *Leap of Reason: Managing to Outcomes in an Era of Scarcity*, edited by Mario Morino. Washington, DC: Venture Philanthropy Partners, 2011.

Roeger, Katie L., Amy S. Blackwood, and Sarah L. Pettijohn. *Nonprofit Almanac 2012*. Baltimore, MD: Urban Institute Press, 2012. http://www.urban.org/books/nonprofit-almanac-2012/ (accessed October 15, 2012).

Rutland, Ginger. "In the Spotlight: Sandra Day O'Connor: Retired but Hardly at Rest." *Sacramento Bee*, March 3, 2013, 3E. http://www.sacbee.com/2013/03/03/5229761/retiredbut-hardly-at-rest.html#dsq-form-area (accessed April 3, 2013).

Schwartz, Robert, James Weinberg, Dana Hagenbuch, and Allison Scott. "The Voice of Nonprofit Talent: Perceptions of Diversity in the Workplace." Commongood Careers and the Level Playing Field Institute, 2011. http://www.commongoodcareers.org/diversityreport.pdf (accessed January 4, 2013).

Senge, Peter. *The Fifth Discipline: The Art & Practice of The Learning Organization*. New York: Doubleday, 1990.

Simon, Nina. "On White Privilege and Museums." *Museum 2.0.*, March 6, 2013. http://museumtwo.blogspot.com/2013/03/on-white-privilege-and-museums.html (accessed April 10, 2013).

Skramstad, Harold. "An Agenda for American Museums in the Twenty-First Century." *Daedalus* 128, no. 3 (Summer 1999): 109–28.

Sorin, Gretchen Sullivan, and Dr. Martin Sorin. "Museums, Professional Training and the Challenge of Leadership for the Future." *History News* 59, no. 4 (Autumn 2004): 17–20.

Stoner, Jesse Lyn. "8 Things Collaborative Leaders Know." *Jesse Lyn Stoner—My Blog*, November 16, 2012. www.seapointcenter.com/what-collaborative-leader-know (accessed November 16, 2012).

Sturgeon, Keni. "A Guide to Museum Studies Programs in the US and Canada." *American Association of Museums*, June 2008. http://perceval.bio.nau.edu/downloads/acumg/museumstudiesprograms.pdf (accessed September 3, 2012).

Suchy, Sherene. "Grooming New Millennium Museum Directors." *Museum International* 52, no. 2 (April 2000): 59–64.

Suchy, Sherene. *Leading with Passion: Change Management in the 21st Century Museum*. New York: AltaMira Press, 2004.

Sundem, Garth. "Everything You Thought You Knew about Learning Is Wrong." *Wired*, January 29, 2012. http://www.wired.com/geekdad/2012/01/everything-about-learning/ (accessed February 1, 2013).

Tisdale, Rainey. "Widespread Mergers. Could It Work in the US?" *CityStories*, May 4, 2012. http://raineytisdale.wordpress.com/museum-mergers (accessed December 18, 2012).

Tolles, Bryant F. Jr., ed. *Leadership for the Future: Collected Essays*. New York: AltaMira Press, 1991.

Torgovnick, Kate. "A New Way to Judge Nonprofits: Dan Pallotta at TED2013." *TED Blog*. March 1, 2013. http://blog.ted.com/2013/03/01/a-new-way-to-judge-nonprofits-dan-pallotta-at-ted2013/ (accessed March 17, 2013).

Ulrich, Dave, and Norm Smallwood. *Leadership Sustainability: Seven Disciplines to Achieve the Changes Great Leaders Know They Must Make*. New York: McGraw Hill, 2013.

Watson, Michael. "Foreword." In *The Voice of Nonprofit Talent: Perceptions of Diversity in the Workplace*. Commongood Careers and the Level Playing Field Institute, 2011, 3. http://www.commongoodcareers.org/diversityreport.pdf.

Weil, Stephen E. "Beyond Management: Making Museums Matter." Keynote Address at the 1st International Conference on Museum Management and Leadership—Achieving Excellence: Museum Leadership in the 21st Century. INTERCOM/CMA conference held in Ottawa, Canada, September 6–9, 2000, 8–9. http://www.intercom.museum/conferences/2000/weil.pdf (accessed June 1, 2013).

Weil, Stephen E. *Making Museums Matter.* Washington, DC: Smithsonian Books, 2002.

Wilson, Denis. "Why Year-End Reviews Are a Big Fat Waste of Time," *Fast Company,* December 20, 2012. http://www.fastcompany.com/3004111/why-year-end-reviews-are-big-fat-waste-time?utm_source=dlvr.it&utm_medium=linkedin (accessed January 8, 2013).

Wisconsin Society of Association Executives. "Innovation for Associations." http://cdn0.pathable.com/attachments/797028403/1295640503___Innovation_for_Associations_White_Paper.pdf (accessed December 20, 2012).

Index

advice, for aspiring museum leaders, xvi, 170, 179, 183–186
agility, xvi, 42, 43, 179, 182, 187, 195
Alexander, Edward P., 11–12, 15
Alswang, Hope, xi, 126–129, 146, 169, 171, 172, 182, 183
American Alliance of Museums (AAM), 20, 32, 111, 113, 127, 136, 155; *2012 National Comparative Museum Salary Study*, 19, 25n20; Accreditation Program, 12; Center for the Future of Museums, 14; Education and the Public Dimension of Museums, 12, 74; *Excellence and Equity*, 12, 18, 23, 196; *Museums and the American Economy in 2011*, 21; Museums for the New Century, 12
American Association for State and Local History (AASLH), 32, 70, 82, 113, 127; Seminar for Historical Administration, 31, 47, 76, 77, 80, 83, 114, 168, 184; Standards and Excellence Program (StEPS), 197
Anderson, Gail, 14
Association of Midwest Museums, 32
authentic leader, 4, 8, 17, 44, 45, 57, 67, 87–122, 139, 150, 152, 167, 171, 172, 173, 185, 187, 188, 189, 190, 198; as map makers, 121; lessons learned, 121–122

authenticity, xvi, 45, 139, 150, 167, 187, 198; based on true life, 87, 88; values based, 88

Bailey, Dina, xi, 41, 88–91, 180, 182, 184
Bank Street College of Education, 30
Beatty, Bob, xi
Beemon, Trevor, xi, 129–131, 146, 172, 182, 185
Bjork, Robert, 170
boards of directors/trustees, 187–193; board-director fit, 52, 81, 113, 126, 160; culture, 8, 15, 176, 188; diversity in the boardroom, 18, 20; division of responsibilities, 71, 72, 97, 128, 187; doing and knowing, 188; facilitating change, 199; forward-leaning, 90, 179; hiring the chief executive, 161, 190–191; investing in leadership, 176, 177, 192, 198, 199; leadership succession, 191, 199; need for new governance model, 189–190; self-aware and authentic, 188–190; sharing authority, 34, 196; training, 28, 31, 45, 188, 193, 197, 199
Bonner, Barbara, 13
Bosket, Jamie, xi, 40, 91–93, 170, 183, 184
Bosley, Edward R., xi, 49–51, 84, 85, 169, 171, 185
Bridgespan Group, 33
Bryk, Nancy Villa, xii

About the Authors

ANNE W. ACKERSON

Little did Anne know when she began her first museum job that she would discover a passion that would fuel her work for a lifetime. Anne served as director of several historic house museums and historical societies in central and eastern New York before becoming the director of the Museum Association of New York. She currently serves the Council of State Archivists as its executive director and is an independent consultant focusing on the organizational development issues of the smaller cultural institution. Anne writes regularly about management and leadership issues for cultural institutions in her blog, *Leading by Design* (http://leadingbydesign.blogspot.com). Her article about the status of heritage organizations in New York State, "The History Museum in New York State: A Growing Sector Built on Scarcity Thinking," was published in the Summer 2011 issue of the journal *Public Historian*. A short essay, "Local Historical Societies and Core Purpose," appears in the *Encyclopedia of Local History*, published by AltaMira Press and the American Association for State and Local History (AASLH) in 2013.

JOAN H. BALDWIN

A Maryland native, Joan Baldwin served as director for several house museums, a staffer for the Museum Program at the New York State Council on the Arts, and as the director of education and interpretation at Hancock Shaker Village. She met Anne Ackerson while working as a consultant, a friendship that led to a decade-long collaboration during Anne's tenure at the

Museum Association of New York (MANY). While writing for MANY, Baldwin authored three monographs (on mission, hiring and developing staff and volunteers, and responsible relationship building for corporate philanthropy); three white papers (two on next-generation leadership and succession planning in New York State's museums); and a variety of shorter field reports. Her articles, "Who's Next? Research Predicts Museum Leadership Gap," was published in the journal *Museum Management and Curatorship* (MMC) in 2006, and "Who's Next: Museum Succession Planning in New York," was published in *History News* in Autumn 2007. Baldwin is currently the curator of special collections at The Hotchkiss School.